PHP

DEVELOPER'S COOKBOOK

201 West 103rd Street, Indianapolis, Indiana 46290

PHP Developer's Cookbook
Second Edition

International Standard Book Number: 0-672-32325-7

Library of Congress Catalog Card Number: 2001096690

Printed in the United States of America

First Printing: December 2001

04 03 02 01   4 3 2 1

Trademarks

Warning and Disclaimer

Acquisitions Editors
Shelley Johnston
Jeff Schultz

Development Editor
Scott D. Meyers

Managing Editor
Charlotte Clapp

Project Editor
Elizabeth Finney

Indexer
Becky Hornyak

Proofreader
Chip Gardner

Team Coordinator
Amy Patton

Interior Designer
Gary Adair

Cover Designer
Alan Clements

Page Layout
Ayanna Lacey

Contents at a Glance

Foreword xv

Introduction 1

Part I   Language Constructs and Techniques   9

1   Manipulating Strings 11

2   Working with Numbers, Dates, and Times 33

3   Using Arrays 69

4   PHP's Built-in Arrays and Constants 91

5   Matching Data with Regular Expressions 101

6   File Access 127

7   Working with Files in Directories 159

8   Functions 177

9   Classes 189

10   Maintaining Sessions with PHP 205

11   Interacting with Web Pages and Servers 231

Part II   Databases   253

12   Creating a Database-Independent API with PHP 255

Part III   Going Outside PHP   281

13   Interfacing with Other Programs and Languages 283

14   Communicating with Sockets 295

15   Handling E-mail 311

16   Working with SNMP Objects 325

17   LDAP 329

Part IV   Generating Other Languages   337

18   Creating and Managing Images 339

19   HTML 361

20   XML 369

Part V	**The Zend API**	**397**
21	Zend API	399
A	PHP Installation	437
B	Troubleshooting with PHP	445
C	PHP Online Resources	451
D	Migrating to PHP 4	455
	Index	459

Table of Contents

Foreword..xv
Introduction...1

Part I   Language Constructs and Techniques   9

1   Manipulating Strings   11

1.0   Introduction..11
1.1   Dissecting Strings...11
1.2   Using the Ternary Operator...15
1.3   Swapping Variables..16
1.4   Converting ASII Codes into Characters.....................................17
1.5   Splitting a String by Characters..18
1.6   Reversing Parts of a String...20
1.7   Converting the Case of a String..21
1.8   Removing Whitespace from a String...23
1.9   Escaping Special Characters in a String...................................23
1.10   Reading a Comma-Delimited Text File......................................25
1.11   Parsing a URL..26
1.12   Fuzzy Matching...27
1.13   Creating a Unique Identifier..28
1.14   Encrypting a String..29
1.15   Converting Between Cyrillic Character Sets..............................31

2   Working with Numbers, Dates, and Times   33

2.0   Introduction...33
2.1   Checking Whether a Variable Is a Valid Number......................34
2.2   Working on a Series of Numbers...35
2.3   Working with Numbers That Are Not Float or Integer...............36
2.4   Rounding Arbitrary-Precision Numbers.....................................38
2.5   Converting Numbers Between Different Bases..........................40
2.6   Finding the Log of a Number...41
2.7   Finding the Binary Representation of a Number........................41
2.8   Converting Between Arabic and Roman Numerals....................42
2.9   Validating Credit Card Numbers..43
2.10   Formatting Numbers..45
2.11   Converting Between Radians and Degrees...............................46

2.12 Calculating Cosines, Sines, and Tangents 47

2.13 Generating Random Numbers 48

2.14 Generating Unique Random Numbers 49

2.15 Weighting Random Numbers 52

2.16 Loading Today's Date into an Array 53

2.17 Checking the Validity of a Date 54

2.18 Determining Date Intervals 56

2.19 Finding the Date and Time for Different Locales 57

2.20 Formatting Timestamps 58

2.21 Parsing Dates and Times from Strings 61

2.22 Performing Benchmarks 63

2.23 Halting Program Execution 67

3   Using Arrays   69

3.0   Introduction 69

3.1   Declaring an Array 70

3.2   Printing Out an Array 71

3.3   Eliminating Duplicate Elements 72

3.4   Enlarging or Shrinking an Array 73

3.5   Merging Arrays 75

3.6   Iteratively Processing Elements in an Array 76

3.7   Accessing the Current Element in an Array 79

3.8   Accessing Different Areas of an Array 80

3.9   Searching an Array 82

3.10 Searching for the Different Elements in Two Arrays 83

3.11 Randomizing the Elements of an Array 84

3.12 Determining the Union, Intersection, or Difference Between
      Two Arrays 85

3.13 Sorting an Array 87

3.14 Sorting Sensibly 88

3.15 Reversing Order 89

3.16 Perl-Based Array Manipulation Features 90

4   PHP's Built-in Arrays and Constants   91

4.1   Working with File Constants 92

4.2   PHP's OS and Version Constants 93

4.3   Setting Breakpoints by Using PHP's Error Constants 94

4.4   Defining Your Own PHP Constants 95

4.5   Working with PHP Globals 96

4.6   Accessing Data Through PHP's Built-in Arrays 98

5   Matching Data with Regular Expressions   101

5.0   Introduction 101
5.1   Assigning the Results of a Pattern Replacement 109
5.2   Using Perl-Compatible Regular Expressions in PHP 110
5.3   Incompatibilities Between the PCRE Library and Perl Regular
       Expressions 112
5.4   Matching over Multiple Lines 114
5.5   Finding a Specific Occurrence of a Match 115
5.6   Working with Delimited Records 117
5.7   Extracting Specific Lines 118
5.8   Checking Characters 120
5.9   Validating Web Data 121
5.10   Validating an Email Address 122
5.11   Checking the Syntax of a Regular Expression 123
5.12   Checking for Duplicate Words 123
5.13   Abbreviating Input 125

6   File Access   127

6.0   Introduction 127
6.1   Checking Whether a File Exists 129
6.2   Checking File Permissions 130
6.3   Creating a Temporary File 131
6.4   Storing a File into Your Program 132
6.5   Opening a File 133
6.6   Handling Binary Data Safely 135
6.7   Flushing the Cache 136
6.8   Locking Files 137
6.9   Getting the Free Space Available on a Specified Drive 139
6.10   Displaying a Textfile to the User 140
6.11   Manipulating Standard I/O Streams 141
6.12   Reading a File Line by Line 142
6.13   Working with a File Word-by-Word 143
6.14   Processing a File in Reverse 145
6.15   Parsing a File with Pattern Separators 145
6.16   Changing a Specific Record 147
6.17   Accessing Fixed-Length Records 148
6.18   Extracting a Single Line from a File 149
6.19   Truncating a File 150
6.20   Counting the Number of Lines in a File 151

6.21 Extracting a Random Line from a File 152
6.22 Randomizing Lines and Words 153
6.23 Creating Configuration Files 156

7   Working with Files in Directories   159

7.0 Introduction 159
7.1 Working with Timestamps 160
7.2 Removing a File 161
7.3 Copying or Moving a File 162
7.4 Keeping Track of Filenames 162
7.5 Parsing the Parts of a Filename 164
7.6 Loading All Files in a Directory into an Array 164
7.7 Searching a Filesystem 165
7.8 Processing a Directory File-by-File 166
7.9 Recursively Deleting a Directory 167
7.10 Creating a Search Engine 169

8   Functions   177

8.0 Introduction 177
8.1 Passing a Default Value to a Function 178
8.2 Accessing Variables Outside a Function 180
8.3 Returning Values from a Function 181
8.4 Passing Arguments by Reference 182
8.5 Retaining a Variable's Value Between Function Calls 183
8.6 Returning More Than One Value from a Function 184
8.7 Declaring Functions Dynamically 184
8.8 Dynamically Creating Anonymous Functions 185
8.9 Calling Functions Indirectly 186
8.10 Fetching an Arbitrary Number of Parameters 187

9   Classes   189

9.0 Introduction 189
9.1 Creating a Class 190
9.2 Accessing Variables from Within a Class 191
9.3 Inheritance 193
9.4 Making Variables or Functions Public and Private 194
9.5 Creating a Constructor 195
9.6 Returning a Different Object from a Constructor 196
9.7 Creating a Class Destructor 197

21.4   Returning Arrays and Objects from Functions 407

21.5   Adding a Function to PHP 408

21.6   Creating Resource Identifiers 410

21.7   Fetching Resource Identifiers 411

21.8   Looping Through Arrays 412

21.9   Creating a PHP Module 414

21.10   Adding Your File to the PHP Installation 434

A   PHP Installation   437

B   Troubleshooting with PHP   445

Common Errors and What They Mean 445

    0 is not a * Result index 445

    Call to undefined function: * 446

    PHP Timed out! 446

    Premature End of script headers 447

    Headers already sent 447

Techniques to Cut Down on Errors and Bugs 447

C   PHP Online Resources   451

The Official PHP Web Site 451

The Zend Web Site 452

PHPBuilder 452

PHPWizard.net 452

The PHP Class Repository 453

Weberdev 453

DevShed 453

D   Migrating to PHP 4   455

Static Variable and Default Argument Initializers Accept Only

  Scalar Values 455

    Valid in PHP 3 455

    Valid in PHP 4 456

The Scopes of break and continue Are Local to That of an

  Included File, or an eval'd String 456

    Valid in PHP 3 456

    Valid in PHP 4 456

A return Statement from a required File Does Not Work 457

    Valid in PHP 3 457

    Valid in PHP 4 457

Unset Is Now a Statement, Not a Function 457

    Valid in PHP 3 457

    Valid in PHP 4 457

"{$" Is Not Supported in Strings 458

    Valid in PHP 3 458

    Valid in PHP 4 458

Index   **459**

Foreword

Think back to the late '80s and early '90s. The world was moving from dialup BBS systems to this new Internet thing. It was mostly limited to technical college students and eager hobbyists. Cool programs such as Gopher, Veronica, Archie, and IRC gave us a hint of what was to come.

In April of 1993, Mosaic started to pull things together, and when Netscape 1.0 was released in December of 1994, we were in high gear. Web servers were available from CERN and NCSA, and the recently released Perl 5 quickly emerged as the scripting language of choice for developing dynamic Web sites. The Internet—through the sugarcoated pill of the World Wide Web—was ready for the masses.

Writing Web applications in 1994 was an adventure. You either had to brave this weird Perl thing that was geared at system administrators who needed to manipulate large log files, or you had to write C programs that manipulated a lot of text and generated HTML output. Because Web programming involved parsing text input and generating text output, Perl was a much closer fit than C for most people.

For example, let's say we wanted to create a simple form that asked the user for her name and age and displayed it back to us when the submit button was clicked. Here is what you would need to do if you wanted to write this in C:

```c
#include <stdio.h>
#include <stdlib.h>
#include <ctype.h>
#include <string.h>

#define ishex(x) (((x) >= '0' && (x) <= '9') || ((x) >= 'a' && (x) <= 'f') || \
                  ((x) >= 'A' && (x) <= 'F'))

int htoi(char *s) {
    int     value;
    char    c;

    c = s[0];
    if(isupper(c)) c = tolower(c);
    value=(c >= '0' && c <= '9' ? c - '0' : c - 'a' + 10) * 16;

    c = s[1];
    if(isupper(c)) c = tolower(c);
    value += c >= '0' && c <= '9' ? c - '0' : c - 'a' + 10;
```

```
        return(value);
    }

    void main(int argc, char *argv[]) {
        char *params, *data, *dest, *s, *tmp;
        char *name, *age;

        puts("Content-type: text/html\r\n");
        puts("<html><header><title>Form Example</title></header>");
        puts("<body><h1>My Example Form</h1>");
        puts("<form action=\"form.cgi\" method=\"POST\">");
        puts("Name: <input type=\"text\" name=\"name\"><p>");
        puts("Age: <input type=\"text\" name=\"age\"><p>");
        puts("<input type=\"submit\">");
        puts("</form>");

        data = getenv("QUERY_STRING");
        params = data; dest = data;
        while(*data) {
            if(*data=='+') *dest=' ';
            else if(*data == '%' && ishex(*(data+1)) && ishex(*(data+2))) {
                *dest = (char) htoi(data + 1);
                data+=2;
            } else *dest = *data;
            data++;
            dest++;
        }
        *dest = '\0';
        s = strtok(params,"&");
        do {
            tmp = strchr(s,'=');
            if(tmp) {
                *tmp = '\0';
                if(!strcmp(s,"name")) name = tmp+1;
                else if(!strcmp(s,"age")) age = tmp+1;
            }
        } while(s=strtok(NULL,"&"));

        printf("Hi %s, you are %s years old\n",name,age);
        puts("</body></html>");
    }
```

For a coder, this wasn't actually so bad, except when a simple change to the HTML was needed. In that case, you had to recompile the CGI program. This is why Perl caught on: Not only is it much easier to write the code to deal with our simple form, but you don't need to compile Perl scripts. The same form in Perl using CGI.pm is

```
use CGI qw(:standard);
print header;
print start_html('Form Example'),
    h1('My Example Form'),
    start_form,
    "Name: ", textfield('name'),
    p,
    "Age: ", textfield('age'),
    p,
    submit,
    end_form;
if(param()) {
    print "Hi ",em(param('name')),
        "You are ",em(param('age')),
        " years old";
}
print end_html;
```

This is infinitely easier both to write and to read. But again, I am talking from a coder's perspective. As the Web caught on, the number of non-coders creating Web content grew exponentially. In the beginning, they cared only about static content and spent all their time learning the intricacies of HTML. But soon they were asked to add dynamic content to their sites. Writing CGI programs in C was out of the question for most of them. The brave ones dove into Perl and mastered the art of CGI.pm and the various other helper modules available for Perl.

This is where PHP found its niche. I would love to say today that I saw everything this clearly and thought up PHP to fit perfectly into this role. That wasn't quite the case. I found the overhead of launching a Perl interpreter for every request much too large. I also found writing CGI programs in C much too tedious. But I had written all sorts of CGI programs in C, and found that I was writing the same code over and over. What I needed was a simple wrapper that would enable me to separate the HTML portion of my CGI scripts from my C code so that I could change the HTML without needing to recompile the C code. This concept became PHP, and the previous C and Perl examples ended up looking like this in PHP:

```
<html><header><title>Form Example</title></header>
<body><h1>My Example Form</h1>
```

```
<form action="form.phtml" method="POST">
Name: <input type="text" name="name">
Age: <input type="text" name="age">
</form>
<?if($name):>
Hi <?echo $name?>, you are <?echo $age?> years old
<?endif?>
</body></html>
```

Compared to the C and Perl versions of the example, this is very HTML-centric. This was, and still is, what attracted many people to PHP. They didn't want to learn how to program, they just wanted to make their HTML pages more dynamic.

PHP has grown as a language over the years, and it is now very much a real programming language. But it has not lost its capability to enable people to get simple things done extremely quickly. It is still very friendly to non-programmers. In a way, PHP is a sneaky programming language in that it enables people to get things done without any programming experience, but as they work with it, they slowly teach themselves to program without realizing it.

PHP is very easy to use, and you should be able to get far by yourself. But it is sometimes interesting to see how other people have solved both simple and complex problems. There are times when you won't be able to come up with the one slick way of solving a problem. That is where this book comes in. Sterling and Andrei have put together a cookbook of solutions that shows you how to solve specific problems and at the same time provides you with the fundamentals required to solve almost any problem.

Sterling joined the PHP development team in early 2000 and he has contributed the Curl, SWF, and Sablotron extensions. Andrei has been a driving force behind the development of PHP since early 1999. His direct contributions have been mainly in the areas of Perl-style regular expressions, XML-based features such as WDDX, session support, and general-purpose array manipulation functions.

If you enjoy this book and you enjoy working with PHP, consider becoming involved with the development of PHP just as Sterling and Andrei did. It is fun and very rewarding to contribute to a popular Open Source project. The work you do is used by hundreds of thousands of people and the respect you earn from your peers in the industry is priceless. Most importantly, you can help make sure that free and open software continues to advance. New people and new ideas are the driving forces behind projects such as PHP.

- Rasmus Lerdorf (rasmus@php.net)

About the Authors

Sterling Hughes is a freelance software developer with over seven years experience developing high-end Web applications. He has written articles for Webreference, Devshed, Zend, and Webtechniques, and he speaks frequently about PHP at conferences around the world. He can be contacted by sending e-mail to `sterling@php.net`.

Andrei Zmievski is the lead development engineer and open source researcher at ispi, where he works on various e-commerce and Web publishing projects. He is a member of the PHP core development group and has contributed to several other open source projects. His other interests include piano and computer graphics. He can be reached at `andrei@php.net`.

Dedication

To my mother, for her unconditional love and support.

—Sterling

Acknowledgments

It is a common misconception that a book is written solely by the author. In reality, a book is a collaboration of many different people.

First of all, I want to thank all the folks at Sams Publishing for their support and guidance of a first-time author. Elizabeth Finney, my project editor, was a huge help in working to coordinate both the author review process and the technical revisions. Amy Patton, the team coordinator, for organizing many things behind the scenes that greatly improved the quality of this book (and might have saved my sanity). Thanks to Jeff Schultz, for giving me the opportunity to write this book. Shelley Johnston, my acquisitions editor, for her enthusiasm and support. Scott Meyers, my development editor, for helping me develop the concept of the book and then overseeing the whole process. Mike Henry, my copy editor; thank you for transforming my writing into coherent English (no small task). Mark Taber, the associate publisher, who extended the publication deadline in order to have an additional technical edit process. Katie Robinson, the formatter, had the daunting task of converting my messy files to Sams' formatting system.

This book had six technical editors who helped shield you from errors. They all worked quite hard, testing every piece of code in the book to make sure that it was of the highest quality possible. Patrick Lambert reviewed the entire manuscript and gave many valuable comments. Chris Newman, Kenneth J. Kloeppel, Mark Maslakowski, Brian Schaffner, and Ken Jenks all performed technical edits on different portions of the manuscript. Both Chris Newman and Kenneth J. Kloeppel went far beyond the call of duty.

In addition to the technical editors, this book had five technical reviewers who read the book over for accuracy and style. Zak Greant, Florian Lanthaler, and Sebastian Bergmann all reviewed the entire manuscript and gave me many valuable comments. Jannis Hermanns and Landon Bradshaw each reviewed different portions of the manuscript. Both Zak Greant and Florian Lanthaler deserve special mention: Their reviews were more detailed than I could have hoped for from a technical reviewer.

I'd especially like to thank Andrei Zmievski, for without his invaluable work, this book would not be what it is today. His expertise in PHP is truly unparalleled.

I would like to give special thanks to Rasmus Lerdorf, who not only created PHP in the first place, but also found time in his busy schedule to write the foreword for this book.

Thank you to all the people who have dedicated their time to the improvement of PHP. The PHP Group, Development team, Documentation team, Quality Assurance team, and everyone else who offers support for PHP either by writing books, authoring articles, teaching friends or spending way too much time on IRC. Without your many hours of hard work, this book could have never been.

Many thanks are also due to my teachers and my friends for their patience and understanding while I obsessed over this book.

My family is my center and my base. I could never have had the strength to author this book without them being a constant source of support. I love you all very much. A special thanks should go to my nanoo and grandpa, who have always stressed the importance of education and taught me to appreciate many of the finer things in life.

The last person I must thank is someone for whom I can't very well express my gratitude in words, my mother. Mom, you not only gave me life, but also kept my life running while I wrote this book. I love you.

—Sterling

I owe thanks to everyone who is involved in the PHP project, including the PHP core group, documentation team, Quality Assurance Team, and all the other developers who dedicate hours of their time to making PHP the best that it can be. Special thanks to Rasmus Lerdorf for getting me on this wild ride.

Additionally, Monte Ohrt, Eric Elliott, Luc Suryo, and David Hahn should be praised for making ispi a great place to work. Their comments and support proved invaluable.

I would also like to thank all the people at Sams Publishing who helped this book see the light of the day, especially Shelley Johnston and Amy Patton.

Most of all, thanks to my parents.

—Andrei

Tell Us What You Think!

As the reader of this book, *you* are our most important critic and commentator. We value your opinion and want to know what we're doing right, what we could do better, what areas you'd like to see us publish in, and any other words of wisdom you're willing to pass our way.

You can email or write me directly to let me know what you did or didn't like about this book—as well as what we can do to make our books stronger.

Please note that I cannot help you with technical problems related to the topic of this book, and that due to the high volume of mail I receive, I might not be able to reply to every message.

When you write, please be sure to include this book's title and author as well as your name and phone or fax number. I will carefully review your comments and share them with the author and editors who worked on the book.

Email: webdev@samspublishing.com

Mail: Mark Taber
             Associate Publisher
             Sams
             201 West 103rd Street
             Indianapolis, IN 46290 USA

INTRODUCTION

"A classic is something that everybody wants to have read and nobody wants to read."

Mark Twain

Purpose

I have an extensive library of books on the practice of programming—tomes of information in pristine condition sitting on my bookshelf. These books have influenced the way I program and the style of my programming. They are bibles; books around which programmers shape their whole philosophies.

However, I also have another set of books. These books sit on my desk, my bed, and my living room couch. They are tattered, bent out of shape, and thoroughly coffee-stained. And that is the greatest honor that I can bestow upon them because they are meant for practical use; they are references for problems that I encounter every single day.

This book is meant as such a text. It was crafted with the intention of helping you solve the everyday problems that you encounter as a programmer. The greatest honor you can do this book is to use it—find a way to make it useful to you, even if it means using the pages to wipe up the occasional coffee spill.

How to Use This Book

This book is in the unique position of being a combination of a reference manual and an instructional text. Although it is not a complete reference, it does cover previously undocumented material, and supplements the documentation for many functions. And even though it is not an instructional text, reading this book will make you a better programmer, and give you a more solid approach to problem solving.

This book should not be your only reference for PHP, but rather it should be a supplement. If you are looking for a printed reference, I highly recommend Leon Atkinson's *Core PHP*, published by Prentice Hall, and Rasmus Lerdorf's *PHP: Pocket Reference*, published by O'Reilly.

On the flip side, this book should not be your introduction to PHP. This book assumes a basic level of competence in and understanding of the PHP language. If you're looking for a good introduction to PHP, check out *PHP Fast & Easy Web Development* by Julie Meloni.

This book has no logical progression, so you can pick it up at any recipe and it will make as much sense as if you had started at the beginning. This is a cookbook, so when you need to know how do to something, you should just look up the appropriate recipe (either in the Table of Contents or the index) and turn to the appropriate page.

Chapter Summary

Every chapter aims to cover a set of common problems that developers face every day.

Chapter 1, "Manipulating Strings," is about working with strings. It covers such subjects as processing a string one character at a time and converting strings to different character sets.

Chapter 2, "Working with Numbers, Dates & Times," is all about numbers. It covers concepts such as working with arbitrary-precision numbers, generating biased random numbers, and PHP's built-in functions for manipulating and getting dates and times.

Chapter 3, "Using Arrays," covers topics ranging from merging two arrays to methods for naturally sorting arrays.

Chapter 4, "PHP's Built-in Arrays and Constants," explains items such as the `__FILE__` constant and the `$HTTP_POST_VARS` array.

Many New Extensions

PHP 4 comes with many new extensions that weren't available with PHP 3. These extensions include, but are not limited to, the swf, curl, exif, cybercash, sockets, and ingres_ii extensions.

PEAR

PEAR stands for PHP Extension and Application Repository. The concept of PEAR is akin to that of Perl's CPAN—it is a repository of PHP classes and supporting extensions to help you program. For example, the `File_Find` class is distributed through PEAR. This class enables you to map and search different directory trees. More information about PEAR is available at `http://pear.php.net/`.

PART I
Language Constructs and Techniques

CHAPTER

1   Manipulating Strings

2   Working with Numbers, Dates and Times

3   Using Arrays

4   PHP's Built-In Arrays and Constants

5   Matching Data with Regular Expressions

6   Handling Files

7   Working with Files in Directories

8   Functions

9   Classes

10   Maintaining Sessions with PHP

11   Interacting with Web Pages and Servers

And, finally, some examples

```php
<?php
$str = "Gumbi and PDOC are smelly";

$names = unpack ("A5name1/x5/A4name2", $str); // read 5, skip 5, read 4
// $names['name1'] is Gumbi and $names['name2'] is PDOC

$str2 = 'A box without hinges, key, or lid, Yet golden treasure inside is hid';
// J.R.R. Tolkien, The Hobbit

$results = unpack ("A1pronoun/x5/A7adjective/X11/A3noun", $str2);
// read 1, skip 5, read 7, go back 11, read 3
//(the answer is eggs)
?>
```

1.2 Using the Ternary Operator

You want to establish a default value for a variable, but change that value if the user submits some input.

Technique

Use the ?: conditional to test the value of the user input:

```php
<?php

// If the user has provided a first argument to the program use
// that, otherwise STDIN (php://stdin)
$filename = isset ($argv[1]) ? $argv[1] : "php://stdin";

$fp = @fopen ($filename, 'r')
    or die ("Cannot Open $filename for reading");

while (!@feof ($fp)) {
    $line = @fgets ($fp, 1024);
    print $line;
}

@fclose ($fp);
?>
```

Comments

The preceding code implementing the ternary operator is the equivalent of the following:

```php
<?php
if (isset ($argv[1])) {
    $filename = $argv[1];
} else {
    $filename = "php://stdin";
}
?>
```

However, PHP's ternary operator (?:) greatly reduces the time it takes for programmers to write these statements. Its syntax is as follows:

```
condition ? do_if_true : do_if_false;
```

The use of the ternary operator is what is known as "syntactical sugar"; that is, it is a construct that is not needed, but is a nice way of beautifying code. None the less, it can be used to replace ugly if .. else code blocks and improve the readability of your code.

You can also use PHP's or construct to establish a default value:

```php
<?php
$filename = $argv[1] or
            $filename = "php://stdin";
?>
```

1.3 Swapping Variables

You want to swap the values of two variables, but you don't want to use a temporary variable.

Technique

Use the list() and array() constructs to switch the variables:

```php
<?php
list ($var1, $var2) = array ($var2, $var1);
?>
```

Comments

In many other languages, you must use a temporary variable, like so:

```php
<?php
$temp = $var1;
$var1 = $var2;
$var2 = $temp;
?>
```

However, in PHP, the list() construct does this for you. The list() construct is used to assign a list of variables, and it is used for more than just swapping variables. You can also use it for processing arrays, as shown here:

```php
<?php
$items = array ("Linux",
                "Apache",
                "PHP",
                "A SQL Server",
                "Talented Administrator");

print "The essentials for operating your own webserver:\n";

reset ($items);
while (list (, $item) = each ($items)) {
    print "$item\n";
}
?>
```

> **Gotcha**
> Note that the actual syntax in the preceding example is list(, $item); the comma is there to denote that there is another element in the array (the numerical index of the item) we are processing. It is important to keep in mind that each() returns the item index as well as the item when dealing with numerically indexed arrays.

1.4 Converting ASII Codes into Characters

You want to convert ASCII codes into English or vice versa.

Technique

Use `chr()` and `ord()` or `sprintf()` to convert back and forth:

```php
<?php
$letter = chr (67); // Upper case C
$ascii_code = ord ($letter); // 67

$letter = sprintf ("%c", $ascii_code); // Upper case C
?>
```

Comments

On the surface, converting ASCII values seems to be a pretty useless task. When I was a beginning programmer (Perl at the time), I thought that it was pointless for people even to write these functions and explanations. However, there are many cases in which you do need to convert back and forth. For example, let's say that you have binary data stored in an ODBC database, and you want to extract it as a string, but (gasp) it is returned in ASCII codes instead of characters! If this happens, the `chr()` and `ord()` functions suddenly become incredibly useful. You can also try the `unpack()` function to help with the conversion.

The `chr()` function takes one ASCII code and converts it to a character. The `ord()` function does the same thing in reverse; it takes a character and converts it to an ASCII code. For the code to convert an ASCII string, look at recipe 1.5.

1.5 Splitting a String by Characters

You need to process a string one character at a time.

Technique

There are two basic ways to process strings character by character. The first way involves the familiar `for()` loop and the fact that strings are addressable using the `[]` operator:

```php
<?php
for ($i = 0; $i < strlen ($str); $i++) {
    $char = $str[$i];
    // manipulate $char here
    // …
}
?>
```

The second way involves the regular expression function `preg_split()`:

```php
<?php
$chars = preg_split ("//", $str);
// $chars is now an array of all the characters in $str
?>
```

Comments

PHP's regular expression functions are based on the POSIX standard (`http://www.delorie.com/gnu/docs/rx/rx_toc.html`). However, that standard does not easily support splitting a string by characters. Therefore, we must rely on PHP's support for Perl-based regular expressions (via the PCRE library). When the `preg_split()` function is used with the empty regexp `"//"`, it will split the string into an array of characters.

Let's take the knowledge we've gained from this recipe and recipe 1.4 and create a function that converts a string of characters to their corresponding ASCII codes:

```php
<?php
function str_ord ($str) {
    for ($i = 0; $i < strlen ($str); $i++) {
        $ascii_values[$i] = ord ($str[$i]);
    }
    return ($ascii_values);
}

$str = "Hello World";
$ascii_values = str_ord ($str);
print "The third letter of \$str, a $str[2],";
print " has an ASCII value of $ascii_values[2].";
?>
```

In the `str_ord` function, we process the string character-by-character using the method discussed in the beginning of this recipe. Then we use the `ord()` function to return the ASCII value for the current character in the string, which is added to the end of the `$ascii_values` array.

There is another way to convert a string to its ASCII values. You can get the ASCII values from a string by using `unpack()` function and the `C` format specifier:

```php
<?php
$ascii_values = unpack ("C*char", $str);
// $ascii_values is now an associative array with the first character
```

```
// having the index of "char1" and second character having an index
// of "char2", etc.
?>
```

The `unpack()` function returns an associative array. If you want your data in a numerically indexed array, use the `array_values()` function, which strips away the keys of the array returned by `unpack()`:

```php
<?php
$ascii_values = array_values (unpack ("C*char", $str));
?>
```

You can also convert the other way around (ASCII to string):

```
function ascii_value_to_char ($ascii_values) {
    foreach ($ascii_values as $value) {
        $str .= chr ($value);
    }
    return ($str);
}
?>
```

Here we simply loop through the user-passed array of ASCII values, convert each value back to a character, and append it to the return value (`$str`).

1.6 Reversing Parts of a String

You want to reverse all the words or characters in a given string.

Technique

To reverse all the words in a string, use a combination of the `preg_split()` function and the `array_reverse()` function:

```php
<?php

function word_reverse ($str) {
    return implode ("", array_reverse (preg_split ("/\s+/", $str)));
}

$str = "A rose by any other name";
$str_reversed = word_reverse ($str);
print $str_reversed;
```

```
// Outputs: name other any by rose A
?>
```

To reverse all the characters in a string, you can use PHP's `strrev()` function:

```php
<?php

$str = "A rose by any other name";
$chars_reversed = strrev ($str);
print $chars_reversed;
// Outputs: eman rehto yna yb esor A
?>
```

Comments

The `word_reverse()` function uses the `array_reverse()` function, which is available only with PHP 4. If you're still using PHP 3, you can use the following version:

```php
<?php

function word_reverse ($str) {
    $tmp_array = preg_split ("/\s+/", $str);
    for ($i = count ($tmp_array) - 1; $i > 0; $i--) {
        $new_str .= $tmp_array[$i] . " ";
    }
    return chop ($new_str);
}
?>
```

1.7 Converting the Case of a String

You need to convert the case of a string.

Technique

Use `strtoupper()`, `strtolower()`, `ucfirst()`, and `ucwords()`:

```php
<?php
setlocale (LC_CTYPE, "");

$str = "mary had a little lamb";

$str = strtoupper ($str);
```

PART I   Language Constructs and Techniques

```
// MARY HAD A LITTLE LAMB

$str = strtolower ($str);
// mary had a little lamb

$str = ucfirst ($str);
// Mary had a little lamb

$str = ucwords ($str);
// Mary Had A Little Lamb
?>
```

Comments

The natural instinct for many people is to use a regular expression search and replace to change the case of a character (or characters) in a string. Instead, you should consider using the functions here, which are considerably faster than using a regular expression.

Another common mistake is to use a regular expression for case-insensitive string comparisons. Instead, consider the following method:

```
if (!strcasecmp ($str1, $str2)) {
    //.. case-insensitive match
}
```

Here we use the strcasecmp() function to perform a case-insensitive string comparison on $str1 and $str2. This is much faster than using the more complex eregi() and preg_match() functions—especially on larger strings.

Note
Note that all the functions do exactly what they say they do and nothing more. Consider the following:
```
<?php
$str = "wE WILL ROCK YOU";
$str = ucwords ($str);
// $str is now WE WILL ROCK YOU
?>
```

The ucwords() function converts the first letter of each word in your string to uppercase. It does not modify any other part of the string; for instance, it does not make everything else lowercase.

1.8 Removing Whitespace from a String

You want to trim blanks from the beginning or end of your string.

Technique

Use the `chop()` or `rtrim()` function to remove whitespace from the end of the string:

```php
<?php
$str = "red apple    ";
// Get rid of that trailing whitespace
$str = chop ($str); // analogous to rtrim ($str);
?>
```

You can use the `ltrim()` function to remove whitespace from the beginning of a string:

```php
<?php
$str = '   Knock, Knock?';
$str = ltrim ($str); // Get rid of leading whitespace
?>
```

Comments

Perl programmers should be careful: The PHP `chop()` function is a little different from Perl's chop function. PHP's `chop()` function is equivalent to Perl's `chomp()` function. That is, it removes whitespace only from the end of a string, instead of arbitrarily removing any character.

If you want to remove the whitespace from the beginning and end of a string, you could use a combination of `ltrim()` and `chop()`. However, more efficiently, you could just use the `trim()` function:

```php
<?php
$str = "   This is a story about dogs...    ";
$str = trim ($str);
// All whitespace from the beginning and end is removed
?>
```

1.9 Escaping Special Characters in a String

You need to escape certain characters in a string.

Technique

Use the `addslashes()` or `quotemeta()` function, depending on what you need:

```php
<?php
$str          = "Well now, how's it going Mike?";
$slashed_str = addslashes ($str);
// $str is now "Well now how\'s it going Mike?"

$str          = "The $ is mine, ain't it?";
$escaped_str = quotemeta ($str);
// $str is now "The \$ is mine, ain't it\?"
?>
```

Comments

When manipulating data in databases using SQL queries, it is often necessary to escape the ', ", and NULL characters because they are considered special by some database systems. PHP offers the `addslashes()` function, which will add slashes before these characters, thus escaping them.

The `quotemeta()` function should be used to escape data before you pass it to a regular expression. This ensures that when you put variable data into a regular expression, doing so won't screw up the results. (Use the `preg_quote()` function if you need to quote a string that is being used with the Perl-compatible regular expression functions.)

PHP also has support for encoding and decoding a URL through the `urldecode()` and `urlencode()` functions.

```php
<?php
$str = "Welcome to John's World";
$str = urlencode ($str);
/* $str is now "Welcome+to+John%27s+World" */

$str = urldecode ($str);
/* $str is now "Welcome to John's World" */
?>
```

Another thing you might want to do is escape HTML entities in a string. To achieve this, you can use PHP's built-in `htmlspecialchars()` function.

```php
<?php
$str = 'Shakespeares "Hamlet" is a wonderful work.';
print htmlspecialchars ($str);
?>
```

This will output `"Shakespeares &quot;Hamlet&quot; is a wonderful work."`, which can be safely displayed in a text area. Note that if you want to escape characters other than &, ", <, and >, you should use the `htmlentities()` function, which escapes all HTML entities (not just &, ", <, and >).

1.10 Reading a Comma-Delimited Text File

You have data stored in a comma-delimited text file and you want to parse it.

Technique

Use the `fgetcsv()` function instead of the `fgets()` function when looping through the file:

```php
<?php
$file_name = isset ($argv[0]) ? $argv[0] : "php://stdin";

$fp = @fopen ($file_name, "r")
  or die ("Cannot open $file_name for read access");

while (!@feof ($fp))
{
    $row = @fgetcsv ($fp, 1024, ',');
    if (!is_array ($row)) { continue; }

    $rows[] = $row;
}

@fclose ($fp);
?>
```

Comments

Parsing comma-separated data seems like an easy programming job—just use PHP's `explode()` function to split the line by a comma, right? Wrong. Parsing comma-separated value (CSV) data is much more complex because the data stored in the CSV file often contains commas and, therefore, a pretty complex escaping system must be considered.

The fastest way to parse CSV data is to not parse it yourself, but rather to let PHP parse it for you with the `fgetcsv()` function. This works in any case in which you need to read data from a CSV file, but what about when you need to parse the data itself, without reading it line-by-line from a file?

The best solution is to create a temporary file using the `tmpfile()` function, write the data to that file, and then use the `fgetcsv()` function to read the data back in:

```php
<?php
// $data contains the CSV data

$tmp = @tmpfile()
  or die ('Cannot create temporary file');
@fwrite ($tmp, $data);
@fseek ($tmp, 0, SEEK_SET);

while (!@feof ($tmp))_{
    $row = @fgetcsv ($tmp, 1024, ',');
    if (!is_array ($row)) { continue; }

    $rows[] = $row;
}

@fclose ($tmp);
// $tmp is automatically deleted when the file is closed
?>
```

This solution—although it looks like (and is) a hack—is much better than using a complex regular expression (which will also be a CPU hog) to parse the comma-separated data.

1.11 Parsing a URL

You want to take a raw URL and make sense out of it.

Technique
Use the `parse_url()` and `parse_str()` functions to parse the URL.

Comments
The goal in parsing a URL is getting the list of its constituent parts—such as scheme, domain, path, and so on. The `parse_url()` function will free you from having to write complicated regular expressions. Here's an example:

```php
$url = 'http://www.php.net/search.php?show=nosource&';
$url .= 'pattern=parse_url&sourceurl=http%3A%2F%2Fwww.php.net%2F';
$url_parts = parse_url ($url);
```

`$url_parts` now is an associative array containing entries for

- Scheme—`"http"`

- Host—`"www.php.net"`

- Path—`"/search.php"`

- Query—`"show=nosource&pattern=parse_url&sourceurl=`
  `http%3A%2F%2Fwww.php.net%2F"`

`parse_url()` can also return `"port"`, `"user"`, `"pass"`, and `"fragment"` entries, depending on what kind of URL is passed.

But what if you want to turn the variables in the `$url_parts["query"]` query string into PHP variables? For that you can use `parse_str()` function:

```
parse_str ($url_parts["query"]);
// The current scope now contains variables $show, $pattern, and $sourceurl
```

> **Gotcha**
> You do not need to use the `parse_str()` function on the query string of your script. PHP automatically converts a query string into PHP variables.

1.12 Fuzzy Matching

You need to find the soundex key of a string.

Technique
Use PHP's `soundex()` function to calculate the soundex index of a string.

```
$soundex_str = soundex ($str);
```

Comments
Calculating the soundex equivalent of a string is very helpful in fuzzy queries, or queries where you have to be a little forgiving of the user. The `soundex()` function returns a key for a certain word. For example, the key for Euler is E460. Words that sound similar, such as Ellery, also have the same key. Therefore, while doing queries, you could search for all words that have the same or a similar soundex key to the word that your user entered.

The particular soundex function used by PHP is one described by Donald Knuth in *The Art Of Computer Programming*, vol. 3: Sorting and Searching, Addison-Wesley (1973), pp. 391–392.

Finally, here are a few examples from the documentation:

```
soundex("Euler")       == soundex("Ellery")   == 'E460';
soundex("Gauss")       == soundex("Ghosh")    == 'G200';
soundex("Knuth")       == soundex("Kant")     == 'K530';
soundex("Lloyd")       == soundex("Ladd")     == 'L300';
soundex("Lukasiewicz") == soundex("Lissajous") == 'L222';
```

Sometimes you want to find out how similar two strings are. For that, PHP has the `similar_text()` function. It takes two strings and an optional variable that will be used to store the similarity percentage, and it returns the number of matching characters in both strings. Here are some examples of `similar_text()` usage:

```
$num_match = similar_text("Euler", "Ellery", $similarity);
/* num_match is 4, $similarity is 72.7% */
$num_match = similar_text("Gauss", "Ghosh", $similarity);
/* num_match is 2, $similarity is 40% */
$num_match = similar_text("conscience", "consciousness", $similarity);
/* num_match is 7, $similarity is 60.9% */
```

`similar_text()` can be slow on very long strings, so use it carefully.

1.13 Creating a Unique Identifier

You want to create a unique identifier; for example, for a session ID or a product ID in the database.

Technique

You can use `uniqid()`, `getmypid()`, `md5()`, and `microtime()` to generate a random ID:

```
<?php
$id =  md5(uniqid(microtime(), 1)) . getmypid();
?>
```

Comments

In this example, the `getmypid()` function is optional—it's there to make sure that IDs generated by different server processes are not the same. But because `md5()` here depends on `uniqid()`, which in turn depends on `microtime()`, there is a very, very slim chance of ever generating the same ID.

1.14   Encrypting a String

You want to encrypt or decrypt a string.

Technique

You can write your own encryption/decryption routine:

```php
<?php
function encrypt_data ($data, $passwd) {
    for ($i = 0, $j = 0; $i < strlen ($data); $i++, $j++) {
        $middle = ord(substr($data,$i,1)) +
                  ord(substr($passwd,$j,1));
        if ($j > strlen($passwd)) { $j=0; }
        $estr .= chr ($middle);
     }
    return ($estr);
}

function decrypt_data ($data, $passwd) {
    for ($i = 0, $j = 0; $i < strlen($data); $i++, $j++) {
        $middle = ord (substr ($data, $i, 1)) -
                      ord (substr ($passwd, $j, 1));
        if ( $j > strlen ($passwd) ) { $j=0; }
        $estr .= chr ($middle);
    }
    return ($estr);
}
?>
```

This is one of the simplest forms of encryption. It is almost as insecure as regular, unencrypted data. You are better off using PHP's built-in functions for encryption and decryption (this will work if you have mcrypt support compiled in). Here is an example using TripleDES encryption:

```php
<?php
$key = "Sterling Hughes";
$string = "Super Secretive, Super Classified Information";
```

```
$encrypted_data = mcrypt_ecb(MCRYPT_TripleDES, $key, $string, MCRYPT_ENCRYPT);
$decrypted_data = mcrypt_ecb(MCRYPT_TripleDES, $key, $string, MCRYPT_DECRYPT);
?>
```

Comments

These built-in encryption functions work with the mcrypt library that can be found at `ftp://argeas.cs-net.gr/pub/unix/mcrypt/`.

The ability to encrypt data is very useful, especially when you are running an e-commerce Web site and need to encrypt information such as credit card numbers and Social Security numbers. The same situation comes up with banks; banks are required by United States law to encrypt sensitive data such as bank IDs, Social Security numbers, and more.

If you are looking for one-way encryption (you can encrypt the data but you can't decrypt it), you can use PHP's standard crypt() function. Given the same data, crypt() will give you the same encrypted result, but you can't ever get back the original data.

```
<?php
// $data1 and $data2 are submitted

if (!strcmp ($data1, $data2)) {
    print "\$data1 and \$data2 are the same before encryption\n";
} else {
    print "\$data1 and \$data2 are different before encryption\n";
}

$data1 = crypt ($data1, substr ($data1, 0, 2));
$data2 = crypt ($data2, substr ($data2, 0, 2));

if (!strcmp ($data1, $data2)) {
    print "What dya know they're the same after encryption!";
} else {
    print "Still different after the encryption!";
}
?>
```

PHP also provides the md5() function, which has a stronger one-way hash algorithm than the crypt() function:

```
<?php
$data = "Thanks for this idea Zak!";
```

```
$hashed_data = md5($data);
print "The md5 hash of $data is $hashed_data";
?>
```

1.15 Converting Between Cyrillic Character Sets

You want to convert from one Cyrillic character set to another (for example, Windows to ISO).

Technique

Use the `convert_cyr_string()` to convert between Cyrillic character sets:

```
$str = convert_cyr_string ($str, 'w', 'i');
```

Comments

The brothers and orthodox Slavonic monks Cyril and Methodius invented the Glagolitic script in Macedonia in the year 863 as an encrypted Greek alphabet with extensions for special Slavic sounds. The scholar Clement of Ohrid later invented the Cyrillic script as a more readable transformed Glagolitic alphabet. Over the course of centuries, the Cyrillic script was spread and transformed and it was modernized into its current Romanized shape (Grazhdanka) under Tsar Peter the Great.

Today, the Cyrillic script is used by more than 70 languages ranging from Eastern Europe's Slavic languages Russian (ru), Ukrainian (uk), Belarussian (be), Bulgarian (bg), Serbian (sr), and Macedonian (mk), through Central Asia's Altaic languages such as Azerbaijani (az), Turkmen (tk), Kurdish (ku), Uzbek (uz), Kazakh(kk), and Kirghiz (ky), to others such as Tajik (tg) and Mongolian (mn). Your library might have the 1965 booklet, "Alfavity jazykov narodov SSSR," by Kenesbai Musaevich Musaev. With a small accent-free alphabet, Russian and Bulgarian seemed equally well suited for computer processing as English.

The `convert_cyr_string()` function takes different Cyrillic character sets and converts them. In the earlier example, we took the Windows Cyrillic character (see Figure 1.1) and converted it into the ISO8859-5 character set (see Figure 1.2). A full list of supported conversions is available on the PHP Web site (http://www.php.net).

PART I   Language Constructs and Techniques

80 Ђ	81 Ѓ	82 ‚	83 ѓ	84 „	85 …	86 †	87 ‡	88 €	89 ‰	8A Љ	8B ‹	8C Њ	8D Ќ	8E Ћ	8F Џ
90 ђ	91 '	92 '	93 "	94 "	95 •	96 –	97 —	98	99 ™	9A љ	9B ›	9C њ	9D ќ	9E ћ	9F џ
A0	A1 ў	A2 ў	A3 Ј	A4 ¤	A5 Ґ	A6 ¦	A7 §	A8 Ё	A9 ©	AA Є	AB «	AC ¬	AD	AE ®	AF Ї
B0 °	B1 ±	B2 І	B3 і	B4 ґ	B5 µ	B6 ¶	B7 ·	B8 ё	B9 №	BA є	BB »	BC ј	BD Ѕ	BE ѕ	BF ї
C0 А	C1 Б	C2 В	C3 Г	C4 Д	C5 Е	C6 Ж	C7 З	C8 И	C9 Й	CA К	CB Л	CC М	CD Н	CE О	CF П
D0 Р	D1 С	D2 Т	D3 У	D4 Ф	D5 Х	D6 Ц	D7 Ч	D8 Ш	D9 Щ	DA Ъ	DB Ы	DC Ь	DD Э	DE Ю	DF Я
E0 а	E1 б	E2 в	E3 г	E4 д	E5 е	E6 ж	E7 з	E8 и	E9 й	EA к	EB л	EC м	ED н	EE о	EF п
F0 р	F1 с	F2 т	F3 у	F4 ф	F5 х	F6 ц	F7 ч	F8 ш	F9 щ	FA ъ	FB ы	FC ь	FD э	FE ю	FF я

Figure 1.1

The Microsoft Cyrillic character set.

A0	A1 Ё	A2 Ђ	A3 Ѓ	A4 Є	A5 Ѕ	A6 І	A7 Ї	A8 Ј	A9 Љ	AA Њ	AB Ћ	AC Ќ	AD	AE Ў	AF Џ
B0 А	B1 Б	B2 В	B3 Г	B4 Д	B5 Е	B6 Ж	B7 З	B8 И	B9 Й	BA К	BB Л	BC М	BD Н	BE О	BF П
C0 Р	C1 С	C2 Т	C3 У	C4 Ф	C5 Х	C6 Ц	C7 Ч	C8 Ш	C9 Щ	CA Ъ	CB Ы	CC Ь	CD Э	CE Ю	CF Я
D0 а	D1 б	D2 в	D3 г	D4 д	D5 е	D6 ж	D7 з	D8 и	D9 й	DA к	DB л	DC м	DD н	DE о	DF п
E0 р	E1 с	E2 т	E3 у	E4 ф	E5 х	E6 ц	E7 ч	E8 ш	E9 щ	EA ъ	EB ы	EC ь	ED э	EE ю	EF я
F0 №	F1 ё	F2 ђ	F3 ѓ	F4 є	F5 ѕ	F6 і	F7 ї	F8 ј	F9 љ	FA њ	FB ћ	FC ќ	FD §	FE ў	FF џ

Figure 1.2

The ISO Cyrillic character set.

CHAPTER 2

Working with Numbers, Dates, and Times

"Politics is for the moment, an equation is for eternity."

Albert Einstein

2.0 Introduction

PHP is a loosely typed language. This means that a variable's type does not need to be declared at runtime and the variable's type can change if needed. This makes it much easier for you to do math with PHP than with a traditional language such as C, where you have to declare your variable's type at runtime, such as

```
int i;
```

This declaration would limit the value of i to an integer. So, if i was assigned 2.45, it would be truncated down to 2 and in addition, the compiler would issue a nasty warning.

In PHP, however, numbers are automatically converted for you. Let us take the earlier example: If we had a value of a variable $k equal to 2.45, then because the number 2.45 is a float, $k would be a float automatically! Or, if $k now equaled 15, the type of $k would be converted to an integer automatically!

Although PHP does automatic type conversions for you, you can optionally cast a value to a certain type for added control. Here is a quick example:

```
$k = (int)2.125;
```

Here we force $k to be of type integer by using the (*type*) notation. You can also use settype() function to achieve the same goal.

This chapter will go over many of the important concepts related to PHP and numbers, such as

- Working with arbitrary-precision numbers
- Generating random numbers (very useful)
- Working with trigonometry
- Validating credit card numbers

2.1 Checking Whether a Variable Is a Valid Number

You want to see whether a variable is a number.

Technique

Use the is_int() function along with the is_float() function:

```php
<?php
if (is_int ($var) || is_float ($var)) {
    // .. $var is a number
}
?>
```

Comments

The is_int() and is_float() functions take a variable and return true if the variable is the correct type (type integer for is_int; type float for is_float).

PHP 4 has a convenient function, is_numeric(), that enables you to check whether the variable passed to it is a number or a numeric string, such as "34" or "-12.3".

```php
<?php

$num1 = '23.32';

if (is_float ($num1) || is_int ($num1)) {
    print '$num1 is a number';
} elseif (is_numeric ($num1)) {
    print '$num1 may not be a number, but its contents are numeric';
```

```
} else {
    print '$num1 is neither a number or numeric';
}

?>
```

Finally, you can check whether your variable is a number by getting its type with the gettype() function:

```
<?php
if ((gettype ($var) == "integer") || (gettype ($var) == "float")) {
    // .. It is a number
}
?>
```

2.2 Working on a Series of Numbers

You want to do an operation on a series of numbers from $x to $y.

Technique

Use a for loop to traverse all the numbers:

```
<?php
$x = 10;
$y = 20;

for ($i = $x; $i <= $y; $x++) {
    // $i will be every integer between $x and $y
    print "$i\n";
}
?>
```

Comments

In the example, all numbers from $x to $y are processed iteratively. This is helpful when, for example, you want to operate on coterminous sections of an array. Here is a short example:

```
<?php
$teachers = array("Sadlon",
                  "Lane",
                  "Patterson",
```

```
                    "Perry",
                    "Sandler",
                    "Kelly",
                    "Zung");

for ($i = 2; $i <= 5; $i++) {
    print "$teachers[$i]\n";
}
?>
```

This example will print

```
Patterson
Perry
Sandler
Kelly
```

If you want to loop through the numbers with noninteger intervals, modify the last argument of the for loop:

```
<?php
for ($i = $x; $i < $y; $i += .5) {
    // Loops through at half integer intervals
}
?>
```

> **Note**
> Don't use a direct comparison operator (== or !=) to break out of the loop. Because of rounding errors, such a test might not succeed, and you'll be stuck in that loop forever.

2.3 Working with Numbers That Are Not Float or Integer

You want to work with arbitrary-precision numbers.

Technique

Use the bcmath functions that PHP provides to work with arbitrary-precision numbers:

```
<?php
$float1 = "234.5769";
$float2 = "478.34299";
```

```
$sum = bcadd ($float1, $float2, 10);
print $sum;
?>
```

Comments

The title and the subsequent content of this recipe might be a little misleading. The title implies that we will be dealing with numbers that are neither float nor integer. However, in the example, it is quite clear that the numbers would be classified as floats. But this is just for sanity—the numbers in the example could be well beyond the range of a float and the bcadd() function would still work.

When performing operations on arbitrary-precision numbers, the computer often messes up the results. Therefore, the bcmath functions help you in that they enable you to perform all the regular mathematical operations on floating-point figures.

Note that we assign the arbitrary-precision numbers as strings. If we assigned them as simple floating-point numbers, the PHP compiler would quickly truncate them down to the regular precision.

So what are the bcmath functions? Here are some uses of the different functions:

```
<?php
$num1 = "32.45";
$num2 = "33.94";

// If the scale argument (the third argument) is not
// given then all of the bcmath functions will use
// an accuracy of 10 decimal places
bcscale (10);

// $num1 + $num2 accurate to four decimal places
$sum = bcadd ($num1, $num2, 4);

// $num1 - $num2 accurate to 10 decimal places
// (from the default scale, set by bcscale()).
$difference = bcsub ($num1, $num2);

// $num1 * $num2 accurate to 6 decimal places
$multi = bcmul ($num1, $num2, 6);

// $num1 / $num2 accurate to 7 decimal places
$div = bcdiv ($num1, $num2, 7);
```

```php
// square root of $num1 accurate to 12 decimal places
$sqrt1 = bcsqrt ($num1, 12);

// $num1² accurate to 20 decimal places
// This only works when the power is a whole number
$exp = bcpow ($num1, 2, 20);

// modulus of $num1 and $num2 accurate to 20 decimal places
$mod = bcmod ($num1, $num2, 20);

// Compare $num1 and $num2 accurate to 4 decimal places
if (!bccomp ($num1, $num2, 4))
    print '$num1 == $num2';
else
    print '$num1 != $num2';
?>
```

2.4 Rounding Arbitrary-Precision Numbers

You want to round an arbitrary precision number to a certain decimal place (for example, the hundredths place).

Technique

Write your own function, bcround():

```php
<?php
$rounded = bcround($num,$decimalplaces);
?>
```

Or use sprintf() with the formatting options:

```php
<?php
$rounded = sprintf("%.6f", $num); // Rounds to 6 decimal places
?>
```

Comments

sprintf(), in my opinion, is by far the easiest method of rounding an arbitrary precision number. You just use %.*num*f where *num* is the number of places you want to round to, and sprintf() does the rest for you. However, sprintf() rounds only to normal floating-point precision. You can't use it if you want to round to the fiftieth decimal place.

> **Note**
> To perform arbitrary precision arithmetic you can also use the GMP (GNU MP) extension.

What is `sprintf()`? `sprintf()` is a function that takes a variable, processes it, and returns the data of that variable in the desired format. Just like its counterpart `printf()`, which enables you to print the value of a variable in a desired format, `sprintf()` offers special formatting codes to help you convert between. For more information, see the PHP manual: `http://www.php.net/function.sprintf.php`.

The `bcround()` function rounds an arbitrary precision number to a certain number of decimal places. That means you can round numbers above the domain of a floating-point number:

```php
<?php
$number = 34.697405454021;
$rounded = bc_round($number, 5); // $rounded is now 34.69741
?>
```

Here is the source code of the `bc_round()` function:

```php
function bc_round($num, $count) {
    // Split up the number
    list($whole_num, $decimal) = explode(".", strval($num));

    // Let's work with the decimal
    $decimal_string = substr($decimal, 0, $count);
    $determinant = substr($decimal, $count, 1);

    // Check for special cases
    if (substr($decimal, 0, 1) == "9") {
        $len = strlen($decimal_string);
        for ($i=0; $i<$len; $i++) {
            if (substr($decimal_string, $i, 1) == "9") {
                $true++;
            }
        }
        if ($true == $len) {
            $whole_num++;
            return $whole_num;
        }
    }

    // Round for non-special cases
    if ($determinant >= 5)
        $decimal_string++;
```

```
// Put It Back together
$denom = pow(10, strlen($decimal_string));
$decimal_corrected = $decimal_string / $denom;
return("$whole_num.$decimal_corrected");
}
```

2.5 Converting Numbers Between Different Bases

You want to convert a number from one base to another—for example, from an octal or hexadecimal number to a decimal number.

Technique

Use the `octdec()` and `hexdec()` functions to convert between octals and hexadecimals to decimals:

```
<?php
$num = octdec ($octadecimal_num);
$num = hexdec ($hexadecimal_num);
?>
```

For other conversions use PHP's `base_convert()` function. For example, there is no `binoct()` function to convert a binary number to octal, so instead you can write your own:

```
<?php
function binoct($number) {
    return base_convert($number, 2, 8);
}
?>
```

Comments

The `octdec()` and `hexdec()` functions will convert octal and hexadecimal numbers to decimal numbers. If you want to convert your numbers back to octal and hexadecimal, use the `decoct()` and `dechex()` functions.

Usually, these will take care of most of your needs, but sometimes it's necessary to convert between weird bases, so `base_convert()` comes to the rescue. `base_convert()` takes a string representing the number, the base you're converting from, and the base you're converting to. Both bases have to be between 2 and 36. The reason is that digits in the numbers of base higher than 10 are represented with letters a through z, where a means 10, b means 11, and z means 36. In some cases, base_convert() could even be used as a primitive encryption function.

2.6 Finding the Log of a Number

You want to take the natural log of a number.

Technique

To take the natural log of a number, use PHP's log() function:

```
<?php
$elog = log (10);
?>
```

Comments

I'm betting that right now you're thinking, "Big deal. I want to find the log of a number with a base of five, not a base of e!" Well, it looks like you forgot your calculus. Remember that

$$\log_n x = \log_e x / \log_e n$$

so writing this as an extensible function is

```
<?php
function log_n ($number, $base) {
    return log ($number)/log ($base);
}
?>
```

> **Note**
> For logs of base ten, it is quicker to use the log10() function, like so:
>
> ```
> $num = log10 ($foonum);
> ```

2.7 Finding the Binary Representation of a Number

You want to find the binary representation of a given number or the number that represents a binary string.

Technique

Use the `decbin()` and `bindec()` functions to convert back and forth:

```php
<?php
$num = 23;

$binary  = decbin ($num);
$decimal = bindec ($binary);
print "The number $decimal is equivalent to the binary $binary";
?>
```

Comments

The `decbin()` function converts a decimal number to its binary equivalent; in contrast, the `bindec()` function converts a binary number to its decimal equivalent. Another method is to use PHP's `base_convert()` function:

```php
<?php
$num = 23;

$binary  = base_convert ($num, 10, 2);
$decimal = base_convert ($binary, 2, 10);
print "The number $decimal is equivalent to the binary $binary";
?>
```

2.8 Converting Between Arabic and Roman Numerals

You need to switch between regular Arabic numerals and Roman numerals.

Technique

Use PEAR's `Numbers_Roman` class to convert back and forth:

```php
<?php

$number = 43;
$numeral = Numbers_Roman::toRoman ($number);
$number  = Numbers_Roman::toNumber ($numeral);

print "$number in Roman Numerals is $numeral";
?>
```

Comments

The Numbers_Roman module works only with Roman numerals greater than 0 up to and including 3,999 (0 < x <= 3,999). This is because Romans didn't deal with negative numbers and zero, and 5000 (which is needed to display 4,000) uses a symbol that is not in the ASCII character set.

The Numbers_Roman module also provides an isRoman() method, which will return true if the first argument is a valid Roman numeral, and will return false otherwise.

2.9 Validating Credit Card Numbers

You want to validate a user's credit card number.

Technique

For simple validation, use the Luhn-10 algorithm:

```php
<?php
$validated = validate_credit_card ($cred_card_num, $cc_type);


function validate_credit_card ($cc_num,  $cc_type='no clue') {
    $cc_type = strtolower ($cc_type);
    $cc_num = ereg_replace ('[-[:space:]]',  '', $cc_num);

    switch ($cc_type)
    {
        case 'mastercard':
            if (strlen ($cc_num) != 16 ||
                !ereg ('^5[1-5]', $cc_num)) {
                return false;
            }
            break;
        case 'visa':
            if (strlen ($cc_num) != 13 &&
                (strlen ($cc_num)  != 16 ||
                 $cc_num[0] != '4')) {
                return false;
            }
            break;
        case 'amex':
            if (strlen ($cc_num) != 15 ||
```

```php
                !ereg ('^3[47]', $cc_num)) {
                return false;
            }
            break;
        case 'discover':
            if (strlen ($cc_num) != 16 ||
                substr ($cc_num, 0, 4) != '6011') {
                return false;
            }
            break;
        default:
            if ($cc_type != 'no clue') return -1;
            break;
    }

    $digits   =  preg_split("//", $cc_num);
    $num_digits = count ($digits);

    for  ($i = ($num_digits-2), $j = 0;
          $i >= 0;
          $i -= 2, $j++) {
        $double_digits[$j]   =  $digits[$i]  *  2;
    }

    $validate=0;
    for  ($i = 0; $i < $num_digits; $i++) {
        $tmp_add = preg_split("//", $double_digits[$i]);
        for  ($j = 0; $j < count ($tmp_add); $j++) {
            $validate += $tmp_add[$j];
        }
        unset($tmp_add);
    }

    for  ($i = ($number_digits-1);  $i >= 0;  $i -= 2) {
        $validate += $digits[$i];
    }

    if  (substr ($validate,  -1,  1)  ==  '0') { return true; }
    else { return false; }
}
?>
```

Comments

The `validate_credit_card()` function validates the credit card number based on the Luhn-10 algorithm. However, please note that any experienced hacker can easily spoof this routine, and it is more of a basic check to find user typos than a security system.

If `$cc_type` is `visa`, `mastercard`, `discover`, or `amex`, a little more than the normal validation will be done on the credit card. The function returns 1 if valid, 0 if not valid, and -1 if the `$cc_type` is given but is not any of the aforementioned.

> **Note**
> For more sophisticated credit card validation, you can use one of PHP's many payment processing systems which allow you to interface with various Internet services to accept payments in realtime.

2.10 Formatting Numbers

You want to output a number with commas in the correct places.

Technique

Use PHP's built-in `number_format()` function:

```php
<?php
$num = 12500000.8356;
$num = number_format ($num, 2);
?>
```

Comments

The `number_format()` function is another place where PHP makes your life easier. In other languages (C, Perl, and so on) you would have to write your own. Although it's not that hard to create a number formatting function, in PHP, we do it for you.

The `number_format()` function takes either one, two, or four (not three) arguments. If one argument is specified, the number has commas inserted in the proper places. If two arguments are provided, something like this

```php
$num = number_format ($num, $decimal_places);
```

then `number_format()` rounds to the number of specified decimal places. (The number `$num` in all cases must be a float.) If four arguments are specified, like so

```php
$num = number_format($num,
                     $decimal_places,
                     $decimal_identifier,
                     $thousands_separator);
```

then the number is rounded to `$decimal_places`, `$thousands_separator` is inserted in the place of commas between every group of thousands, and `$decimal_identifier` is placed before the decimals instead of a period.

This function is extremely useful because most of the time your users want to see data in human terms not in computer terms. The `number_format()` function enables you to clean up your data.

2.11 Converting Between Radians and Degrees

You want to do your trigonometry functions in degrees not radians.

Technique

Convert between degrees and radians:

```php
<?php
$num1 = 90;
$num2 = 3.14;

$rad = deg2rad ($num1);
$deg = rad2deg ($num2);

print "The value of $num1 degrees in radians is $rad\n";
print "and the value of $num2 radians is $deg degrees";
?>
```

Comments

The `deg2rad()` and `rad2deg()` functions can be used to convert a number from degrees to radians and back again. This can be very useful if you want to find the cosine of a number that is in degrees. You can use the `deg2rad()` function to convert the number and then use the `cos()` function on the result:

```php
<?php
$cos_60 = cos (deg2rad (60));
?>
```

2.12 Calculating Cosines, Sines, and Tangents

You want more trigonometry functions than are available in other languages such as C and Perl.

Technique

PHP has a plethora of trigonometry functions, including `acos()`, `asin()`, `atan()`, `atan2()`, `cos()`, `sin()`, and `tan()`:

```php
<?php
// $num will be the arc cosine of .5
// (the angle that yields a cos of .5)
$num = acos (.5);

// $num will be the arc sine of .5
// (the angle that yields a sine of .5)
$num = asin (.5);

// $num will be the arc tangent of .5
// (the angle that yields a tan of .5)
$num = atan (.5);

// $num is the arc tangent of .5 and .67
$num = atan2 (.5, .67);

// $num is the sin of ∏
$num = sin (M_PI);

// $num is the cosine of ∏
$num = cos (M_PI);

// $num is the tangent of ∏
$num = tan (M_PI);
?>
```

Comments

The `atan2()` function is the same as `atan((.5)/(.67))`, except that the quadrant of the result is accurate (and, therefore, so is the sign).

2.13 Generating Random Numbers

You want to generate a random number. This can be used for countless programs, including a random password generator, random quote displayer, and a Session ID creation tool.

Technique

Use PHP's `mt_rand()` function to generate a random number:

```php
<?php
$rand_num = mt_rand();
?>
```

Comments

The previous code would generate a random number with between 0 and an upper boundary that depends on the algorithm. The upper boundary can be retrieved with the `mt_getrandmax()` function. If you want, however, you can specify minimum and maximum values.

```php
<?php
// Random number between 12 & 29 (inclusive)
$rand_num = mt_rand (12, 29);
?>
```

This is helpful if you are accessing items in an array randomly. Just generate a random number within the range of the array:

```php
<?php
$rand_num = mt_rand (0, count ($ar) - 1);
?>
```

$rand_num would then be an element in the array between $0...n-1$, where n is the number of elements in the array. (We subtract 1 from the number of elements because arrays are indexed starting with 0.)

If the `mt_rand()` function is not generating different random numbers, make sure to seed the random number generator before you generate the random number:

```php
<?php
mt_srand ((double)microtime() * 1000000);

$num1 = mt_rand();
$num2 = mt_rand();
?>
```

Computers, unlike humans, cannot generate a truly random number—it is against the nature of the computer's engineering. Computers generate a pseudorandom number that is evenly distributed between a specified range of values. The number is generated using a complex mathematical formula, meaning that if the formula is given the same starting point (seed), it consistently generates the same number.

The `mt_srand()` function sets a new seed based on the number that we give it. Therefore, we give it a constantly changing and large number (`microtime() * 1000000`), typecast to a double.

Note
In PHP 4.1 the seeding of the random number generator is already done for you. Only use the `[mt_]srand` functions if you need to seed the generator with a specific seed.

Gotcha
Calling the `mt_srand()` function over and over is useless; it does not make your program generate a more random number.

2.14 Generating Unique Random Numbers

You want to ensure that the same random number does not appear twice.

Technique

Keep a database of numbers already stored and query that database:

```php
<?php
require_once 'DB.php';

class Unique_Random
{
    var $dbh;

    // Constructor, sets initial variables
    // $connstring is the database connection string
    function Unique_Random ($connstring)
    {
        $this->dbh = new DB($connstring);
        if (DB::isError ($dbh))
            die (sprintf ('Error [%d]: %s',
                            $dbh->getCode(), $dbh->getMessage()));
```

```php
    mt_srand ((double)microtime() * 1000000);
}

// Private function to check and see whether $number is
// in the database
// $number is the number to check for.
function _check ($number)
{
    $stmt = "SELECT num FROM num_table WHERE num='$number'";
    $sth = $this->dbh->query ($stmt);
    if (DB::isError ($sth))
        die (sprintf ('Error [%d]: %s',
                       $sth->getCode(), $sth->getMessage()));
    return ($sth->numRows);
}

// Private function to add a number to the database
// $number is the number to add
function _add ($number)
{
    $stmt = "INSERT INTO num_table (num) VALUES ('$num')";
    $sth  = $this->dbh->query ($stmt);
    if (DB::isError ($sth))
        die (sprintf ('Error [%d]: %s',
                       $sth->getCode(), $sth->getMessage()));
}

// Private function to generate the random number
function _generateNumber ()
{
    return md5 (uniqid (mt_rand(), 1)) + getmypid();
}

// {{{ random_number()

/**
 * Generates a random number that is not present within
 * the num field of the num_table table of your database.
 *
 * @return double the generated random number
 */
function random_number ()
{
    $number = $this->_generate_number();
```

```php
        while (!$this->_check ($number))
            $number = $this->_generate_number ();

        $this->_add ($number);
        return ($number);
    }


    // }}}
}

$connstring = "odbc://sterling:secret@localhost/numbers";
$generator = new Unique_Random($connstring);
$number = $generator->random_number();

print "\$number is $number, it has never been generated before";
?>
```

Comments

In the `Unique_Random` class, we use DB (a PHP 4 module, distributed through PEAR), which enables us to access the database without making database-specific function calls. For more information about DB, consult the PEAR documentation or Chapter 16, "Creating a Database-Independent API with PHP."

The concept behind the `Unique_Random` class is quite simple: We generate a random number and then check whether that number is stored in the database. If the number is not stored in the database, it is unique, so we add it to the database and return it. Otherwise we generate another random number and perform the same check.

Although we use a relational database to store the numbers to see whether the number was generated, we could just have easily done this with file access and the `serialize()` function. (For brevity, I'll omit the cleaner OO syntax and show a less advanced example.)

```php
<?php
mt_srand ((double)microtime() * 1000000);

$data = implode ("", file ('random_numbers.txt'));
$random_numbers = $data ? unserialize ($data) : array ();

$random = mt_rand();
while (in_array ($random_numbers, $random))
    $random = mt_rand();

array_push ($random_numbers, $random);

$data = serialize ($random_numbers);
```

PART I   Language Constructs and Techniques

```php
$fp = @fopen ("random_numbers.txt", 'w');
if (!$fp) {
    die ("Cannot open random_numbers.txt");
}

@fwrite ($fp, $data);
@fclose ($fp);

print "$random has not been generated before";
?>
```

2.15 Weighting Random Numbers

You want to generate biased random numbers; an example might be an ad rotation system in which different users will not get the same number of page views.

Technique

PHP does not have built-in support for this, so we'll just have to roll our own:

```php
<?php
//
// Company -> Weight
//
$ads = array("Spacely Sprockets" => 1,
             "The Rock Quarry" => 1,
             "Springfield Power Plant" => 3,
             "Microsoft"  => 10,
             "Phillip Morris" => 5);

$j = 0;
foreach ($ads as $company => $weight) {
    for ($i=0; $i < $weight; $i++) {
        $dist[$j++] = $company;
}

srand((double)microtime()*1000000);
$rand_num = mt_rand(0, $j - 1);
shuffle($dist); // randomize the array, see chapter 4 for more details

$company = $dist[$rand_num];
print "The Selected company was: $company";
?>
```

Comments

The previous script takes an array of companies and their respective weights, or how often they should be displayed in relation to each other. For example, Microsoft has a weight of 10, which means that it will be displayed more often than Springfield Power Plant that has a weight of 3.

We then initialize a foreach loop and loop through the $ads array. For each element of the $ads array, we put it into a new array for the amount of times specified by weight. For example, Microsoft has ten entries in the $dist array.

Finally, we seed the random number generator, pick out a random number that is the bounds of the array, and use that random number ($rand_num) as the index for the $dist array.

The example is only one method of generating a biased random number; for different methods, you should take a look at your statistics textbook.

2.16 Loading Today's Date into an Array

You want to load today's date and time into an array for further manipulation.

Technique

Use PHP's getdate() function, which returns an associative array of seconds, minutes, hours, mday (day of the month), wday (day of the week), mon (current month number), year (number), yday (day of the year as a number), weekday (day of the week in text form), and month (month of the year in text form):

```
<?php
$date_ar = getdate();
?>
```

Comments

This is very useful in many ways. It enables us to do things such as format the current date in MM/DD/YYYY format:

```
<?php
$da = getdate();
$datestamp = "$da[mday]/$da[mon]/$da[year]";
?>
```

In this case, you can also use the date() function, which returns a formatted string according to the arguments that you provide:

```php
<?php
$datestamp = date ("j/n/Y");
?>
```

If you are looking for C/Perl compatibility, you can use PHP's localtime() function, which returns a numerically indexed array with the current time or an associative array with the current time. The indexes have the same names as the corresponding C structure elements.

```php
<?php

$date1 = localtime();
$date2 = localtime (time(), 1);

print "$date1[5] is the same as $date2[tm_year]";
?>
```

2.17 Checking the Validity of a Date

You want to see whether the user has submitted a valid date.

Technique

Use the checkdate() function, which validates a date in the format MM/DD/YYYY:

```php
<?php
list ($month, $day, $year) = explode ('/', $date);

if (checkdate ($month, $day, $year)) {
    print "Valid Date!";
} else {
    print "Not Valid!";
}
?>
```

Comments

checkdate() checks the validity of a date according to the following criteria:

- year is between 0 and 32767, inclusive.

- month is between 1 and 12, inclusive.

- day is within the allowed number of days for the given month. Leap years are taken into consideration.

This solution can also be easily implemented in PHP. Here is an example of how it might be done:

```php
<?php

function is_leap_year ($year)
{
    return ((($year%4) == 0 && ($year%100)!=0) || ($year%400)==0);
}

function is_valid_date ($date)
{
    /* Split the date into component parts. */
    list($month, $day, $year) = explode('/', $date);
    $month_days = array(31, 28, 31, 30, 31, 30, 31, 31, 30, 31, 30, 31);

    if ($month < 1 || $month > 12)
        return false;

     /* Year has to consist of 4 digits. */
    if ((strlen($year) != 4) || eregi("[^0-9]", $year))
        return false;

    /* If it's a leap year, February will have 29 days. */
    if (is_leap_year($year))
        $month_days[1] = 29;

    if ($day < 1 || $day > $month_days[$month - 1])
        return false;

    return true;
}
?>
```

The previous example first splits the date by "/" and assigns the returned array to $month, $day, and $year. Then it simply tests whether each date part is within the specified range. This function also uses a little trick; $day is a string, but when it's compared against numbers, it is automatically converted to a number. So, if $day is not a numerical string, the result of the conversion will be 0, which is outside the specified range.

2.18 Determining Date Intervals

You want to find the time that has elapsed between two dates.

Technique

Convert each date to a timestamp, find their difference, and then convert the difference to human-readable output.

Comments

For this problem, we need to use the mktime() function, which returns the number of seconds since the UNIX epoch began (January 1, 1970). This is how this problem can be solved with mktime():

```php
<?php
$date1 = "11/15/1999";
$date2 = "12/10/2000";

list ($month1, $day1, $year1) = explode ("/", $date1);
list ($month2, $day2, $year2) = explode ("/", $date2);

$timestamp1 = mktime (0, 0, 0, $month1, $day1, $year1);
$timestamp2 = mktime (0, 0, 0, $month2, $day2, $year2);

$diff = ($timestamp1 > $timestamp2) ?
          ($timestamp1 - $timestamp2) :
          ($timestamp2 - $timestamp1);

print "The difference between the dates is ";
print date ("Y", $diff) - 1970;
print " year(s), " . (date ("m", $diff) - 1);
print " month(s) and " . (date ("d", $diff) - 1);
print " day(s).";
?>
```

Here we split each date into component parts and then create a timestamp for each date. Depending on which timestamp is later, we calculate the difference and then use the date() function to print out the nicely formatted output.

2.19 Finding the Date and Time for Different Locales

You want to find the date and time in Finland, but your servers are in Texas.

Technique

Write your own universaltime() function utilizing mktime(), gmdate(), and getdate():

```php
<?php
function universaltime ($offset)
{
    $day      = gmdate("d");
    $month    = gmdate("m");
    $hour     = gmdate("g");
    $year     = gmdate("Y");
    $minutes  = gmdate("i");
    $seconds  = gmdate("s");
    $hour     = gmdate("H") + $offset;

    $tm_ar = getdate (mktime ($hour,
                              $minutes,
                              $seconds,
                              $month,
                              $day,
                              $year));
    return ($tm_ar);
}

$currdate = universaltime ($offset);
?>
```

Comments

First, we find the GMT, or Greenwich mean time, the standard to which all time zones are compared. This is accomplished using the gmdate() function, which takes the same arguments as the date() function that was discussed partially in the last recipe and will be discussed fully in the next recipe.

Then we increment the hour by the hour offset from Greenwich mean time (the offset is passed to the function). Some of you might be wondering what happens if the change in hour affects the change in day, month, or year. No problem, the `mktime()` function automatically corrects for these differences.

We then use the `getdate()` function, which takes an optional UNIX timestamp created by the `mktime()` function. It returns an associative array with the following contents: seconds, minutes, hours, mday (day of the month), wday (day of the week, numeric), year, yday (day of the year), weekday (day of week, textual), and month (month, textual).

So, when we go back to the original problem to find the date and time in Finland, it is a cinch. All that we need to know is the GMT offset (which is 2) and then call our `universaltime()` function like so

```php
<?php
$finland_date = universaltime(2);
?>
```

2.20 Formatting Timestamps

You want to format a timestamp in string format, such as the MM/DD/YYYY format discussed earlier in this chapter.

Technique

The most efficient way of formatting a UNIX timestamp is to use the `date()` function or the `strftime()` function, both of which take an optional timestamp:

```php
<?php
// The day I was born
$date = date ("l F j", 404107200);

// Same thing, sensitive to locale settings
$date1 = strftime ("%A %B %d", 404107200);
?>
```

Comments

This recipe is a complete discussion of two functions with which you are already familiar. These functions are probably all that you need for printing out dates and timestamps in the format you choose.

First, let us talk about the date() function. As its first argument, the date() function takes a bunch of formatting codes interspersed with text. Here is a list of formatting codes for the date() function:

- a—"am" or "pm"

- A—"AM" or "PM"

- d—Day of the month, two digits with leading zeros; that is, "01" to "31"

- D—Day of the week, textual, three letters; for instance, "Fri"

- F—Month, textual, long; for instance, "January"

- h—Hour, 12-hour format; that is, "01" to "12"

- H—Hour, 24-hour format; that is, "00" to "23"

- g—Hour, 12-hour format without leading zeros; that is, "1" to "12"

- G—Hour, 24-hour format without leading zeros; that is, "0" to "23"

- i—Minutes; that is, "00" to "59"

- j—Day of the month without leading zeros; that is, "1" to "31"

- l (lowercase L)—Day of the week, textual, long; for instance, "Friday"

- L—Boolean for whether it is a leap year; "0" or "1"

- m—Month; that is, "01" to "12"

- n—Month without leading zeros; that is, "1" to "12"

- M—Month, textual, 3 letters; for instance, "Jan"

- s—Seconds; that is, "00" to "59"

- S—English ordinal suffix, textual, 2 characters; that is, "th" and "nd"

- t—Number of days in the given month; that is, "28" to "31"

- U—Seconds since the UNIX epoch, January 1, 1970

- w—Day of the week, numeric; that is, "0" (Sunday) to "6" (Saturday)

- Y—Year, 4 digits; for example, "1999"

- y—Year, 2 digits; for example, "99"

- z—Day of the year; that is, "1" to "366"

- Z—Time zone offset in seconds; that is, "-43200" to "43200"

You can put these codes into the date() function along with regular characters:

```php
<?php
print date ("n/j/Y");
?>
```

This would print out the date in *Month/Day/Year* format where *Month* is the current month, *Day* is the current day, and *Year* is the current year.

The date() function also takes an additional timestamp which is, as mentioned in the previous recipe, the seconds since the UNIX epoch began (January 1, 1970). "What?? I have to count the seconds since January 1, 1970?" No! Most UNIX timestamps are already in that format, so you just read them into the date() function. However, if you would have a need to count the seconds from January 1, 1970, just use the mktime() function to do it for you. Here is the format of the mktime() function:

```
int mktime(int hour, int minute, int second, int month,
 int day, int year [, int is_dst]);
```

Most of the parameters are self-explanatory. The optional parameter [*is_dst*] specifies whether mktime() should account for daylight saving time.

The strftime() function is a lot like the date() function. The only differences are _the formatting codes are different and the strftime() function is sensitive to locale settings that are set by setlocale(). So, you can have the string formatted for, Germany, if you have set the locale to German (de). Here is a list of the different formatting codes passed to strftime():

- %a—Abbreviated weekday name according to the current locale
- %A—Full weekday name according to the current locale
- %b—Abbreviated month name according to the current locale
- %B—Full month name according to the current locale
- %c—Preferred date and time representation for the current locale
- %d—Day of the month as a decimal number (range 01 to 31)
- %H—Hour as a decimal number using a 24-hour clock (range 00 to 23)
- %I—Hour as a decimal number using a 12-hour clock (range 01 to 12)
- %j—Day of the year as a decimal number (range 01 to 366)
- %m—Month as a decimal number (range 1 to 12)

- %M—Minute as a decimal number

- %p—Either 'am' or 'pm' according to the given time value, or the corresponding strings for the current locale

- %S—Second as a decimal number

- %U—Week number of the current year as a decimal number, starting with the first Sunday as the first day of the first week

- %W—Week number of the current year as a decimal number, starting with the first Monday as the first day of the first week

- %w—Day of the week as a decimal, Sunday being 0

- %x—Preferred date representation for the current locale without the time

- %X—Preferred time representation for the current locale without the date

- %y—Year as a decimal number without a century (range 00 to 99)

- %Y—Year as a decimal number including the century

- %Z—Time zone or name or abbreviation

- %%—A literal '%' character

2.21 Parsing Dates and Times from Strings

You want to extract the date and time from a string such as 10-24-2000 and convert it into a usable form (such as seconds since the UNIX epoch began).

Technique

Use the explode() function along with the mktime() function:

```php
<?php
list ($month, $day, $year) = explode ("-", $date);
$epoch = mktime (0, 0, 0, $month, $day, $year);
?>
```

Comments

You're probably saying (as I once did) that finding the number of seconds since the UNIX epoch began on January 1, 1970 is not really that helpful. However, I contend that it helps you in a great many things. For example, in recipe 2.19, we used it to have a universal time function. In recipe 2.18, we used it to add dates and times, and just last recipe (recipe 2.20) we found out that UNIX timestamps are in epoch seconds. So, finding the epoch seconds from a user-submitted string is extremely useful when doing any type of conversions with time.

In the solution code, we use the `list` statement along with `explode()` to first split the array by the "`-`" delimiter and then assign each element to $month, $day, and $year. Then we call the `mktime()` function, which returns the number of seconds since January 1, 1970, and our conversions are complete.

You can parse the date and time out of strings such as "`Mary bought her lamb on 6/15/99`" by using the following method:

```php
<?php
preg_match ("#(\d+)/(\d+)/(\d+)#", $string, $date);
?>
```

Then $date[0] would contain the entire date, $date[1] would contain 6, $date[2] would contain 15, and $date[3] would contain 99.

As an easter egg, PHP also has a built-in function, `strtotime()`, that will try to figure out the format of the date in the input string and return a timestamp for it. It recognizes most common date formats, such as "`05/02/2000`", "`May 2, 2000 20:00`", and so on. You can omit parts of the date, such as "`May 2`" and `strtotime()` will use the current date and time for the remainder. Here is an example:

```php
<?php
$birth_time = "November 2, 1976 01:50am";
$birth_timestamp = strtotime ($birth_time);
print "You are ";
print number_format (time() - $birth_timestamp);
print " seconds old!";
?>
```

`strtotime()` is also very handy for calculating timestamps for relative offsets. You can use it, for example, to find out what the date will be 40 days from some starting date:

```php
<?php
$start_date = mktime (0, 0, 0, 06, 07, 2000);
$target_date = strtotime ("+40 days", $start_date);
?>
```

The relative offset can be positive or negative and can be seconds, minutes, hours, days, months, and years. You can even combine it, like so:

```php
<?php
$start_date = mktime(0, 0, 0, 06, 07, 2000);
$target_date = strtotime("+4 months +5 days", $start_date);
?>
```

2.22 Performing Benchmarks

You want to perform a benchmark on a snippet of code to see how fast it runs.

Technique

Use the `microtime()` function to find the time in seconds and microseconds before and after your snippet is run:

```php
<?php

function get_microtime()
{
    $mtime = microtime();
    $mtime = explode(" ",$mtime);
    $mtime = doubleval($mtime[1]) + doubleval($mtime[0]);
    return ($mtime);
}

$time1 = get_microtime();

for ($i=0; $i<99999; $i++) {
    $ar[] = $i;
}

$time2 = get_microtime();

$diff = abs ($time2-$time1);

print "<br> For Loop: $diff seconds.\n";

$i = 0;
unset ($ar);
$time1 = get_microtime();
while ($i<99999) {
    $ar[] = $i;
    $i++;
}
```

```php
$time2 = get_microtime();

$diff = abs ($time2-$time1);
print "<br>While Loop: $diff seconds.\n";
?>
```

Comments

This code reports the time difference between using a `while` loop and using a `for` loop (the `while` loop is the faster of the two). The solution (not the code for testing whether a `while` loop was faster than a `for` loop) could have been slimmed down to the following:

```php
<?php
$time1 = get_microtime()
//… do the things that you want to time here
$time2 = get_microtime() ;

$diff = abs ($time2 - $time1);
?>
```

We use the `get_microtime()` function (you can't use `microtime()` directly because it returns seconds and microseconds in a string, separated by a space) to return the number of seconds since the UNIX epoch began. (This is known as *epoch seconds*, and is equal to the number of seconds since January 1, 1970.) We assign this value to the first time, execute the code that we want to benchmark, and then calculate the microtime again. We take the absolute value of the difference between the two times by using the `abs()` function and assigning that value to `$diff`.

If you are timing two different code segments in one script, you should use the `unset()` function between the different timings (see the solution for an example of this). That way you don't have any extra memory set aside for those variables when you run the second portion of your script.

If you find yourself benchmarking your code execution often, you can make use of this handy function contributed by someone on the PHP mailing list (formatted slightly):

```php
<?php
/*===========================================================*\
    Function:    debug_timing
    Purpose:     Utility function for timing the script
    Input:       $label  - text label marking point in execution
                 if 'init' - initializes a new run
                 if 'print' - dumps timing information
```

```
\*===============================================================*/
function debug_timing ($label) {
    static $basetime,
           $totaltime,
           $rpttimes;

    if ($label == 'init') {
        $rpttimes = array();
        $basetime = microtime();
        $totaltime = 0;
        ereg ("^([^ ]+) (.+)", $basetime, $r);
        $basetime = doubleval ($r[2]) + doubleval ($r[1]);

        return;
    }

    if ($label == 'print') {
        // send to screen
        echo "<B>Timing results:</B><BR>\n";
        for ($i=0; $i < count ($rpttimes); $i++) {
            echo "  $rpttimes[$i]\n";
        }
        echo "total: $totaltime\n";

        return;
    }

    // record current elapsed time, accumulate
    $newtime = microtime();
    ereg ("^([^ ]+) (.+)", $newtime, $r);
    $newtime = doubleval ($r[2]) + doubleval ($r[1]);

    $diff = $newtime - $basetime;
    $rpttimes[] = sprintf ("%-20s %s", $label, $diff);
    $basetime = $newtime;
    $totaltime += $diff;
}

?>
```

You use it like this:

```php
<?php

debug_timing('init');
for ($i=1000; $i>0; $i--) {
    $ar[] = $i;
}
debug_timing('array_populated');
sort($ar);
debug_timing('array_sorted');
debug_timing('print');

?>
```

The output of this script will be something like this:

```
array_populated       0.047430038452148
array_sorted          0.019858956336975
total: 0.067288994789124
```

debug_timing() helps you measure intervals between execution points in your code.

As this book was being released two new classes came out at Pear. They were authored by Sebastian Bergmann of phpOpenTracker.de and called Benchmark_Timer and Benchmark_Iterate. The Benchmark_Timer class offers similar functionality to that described above. You can instantiate a new Benchmark_Timer class and then start and stop timing as well as setting timer flags.

```php
<?php
require_once("Benchmark/Timer.php");

$timer = new Benchmark_Timer;

// Start the timer
$timer->start();

$timer->set_marker("Begin For Loop");
for ($i = 0; $i < 10000; $i++) {
    print "$i\n";
}
$timer->set_marker("End For Loop");

$timer->set_marker("Begin While Loop");
$i = 0;
```

```php
while ($i < 10000) {
    print "$i\n";
    $i++;
}
$timer->set_marker("End While Loop");

$profiling = $timer->get_profiling();

for ($i = 0; $i < count($profiling); $i++) {
    print "Marker Name: {$profiling[$i][name]}\n";
    print "Time Index: {$profiling[$i][time]}\n";
    print "Difference: {$profiling[$i][diff]}\n";
    print "Total: {$profiling[$i][total]}\n";
}
?>
```

The `Benchmark_Iterate` class inherits from the `Benchmark_Timer` class and allows you to time a singular function over a period of $x iterations.

```php
<?php
require_once("Benchmark/Iterate.php");

function print_hello() {
    print "Hello World!!";
}

$bench = new Benchmark_Iterate;
$bench->run("print_hello", 200);

$result = $bench->get();

print "Iteration 6 took $result[6], whereas iteration ";
print "20 took $result[20]\n";

print "The mean execution time was $result[mean] over a";
print " total of $result[iterations] iterations...";
?>
```

2.23 Halting Program Execution

You want to stop program execution for a couple of seconds or microseconds.

Technique

Use PHP's `sleep()` and `usleep()` functions, depending on how long you want your program to stop execution:

```php
<?php
print "Hello World";
sleep(5); // Sleep 5 seconds
print "This was done 5 seconds later";
usleep(70); // Sleep 70 microseconds
print "This was done 5 seconds and 70 microseconds after the first Hello
      World";
?>
```

Comments

The `sleep()` and the `usleep()` functions both make system calls to the `sleep()` function. However, the `usleep()` function converts the sleep time, like so:

```php
sleep((int) (useconds / 1000));
```

Sleeping is sometimes useful if you are working with sockets, or you are writing a daemon (CGI version of PHP only) that performs operations at regular intervals of time. (This usually can and should be done with `cron`.)

CHAPTER 3

Using Arrays

"Art strives for form, and hopes for beauty."

George Bellows

3.0 Introduction

When I go to the grocery store, I go with a list of what I want to buy. A sample grocery list might be

-eggs
-milk
-turkey
-curry

In PHP, we would probably specify that grocery list as an array, or a list of scalars, with each element of the array containing an item on the grocery list:

```
$grocery_array = array ("eggs", "milk", "turkey", "curry");
```

Then if I wanted to print out an element of that array, I would reference it by its number in the array. For example, the following would print out turkey:

```
print $grocery_array[2];
```

Note

As with almost all programming languages, PHP arrays are indexed from 0 instead of 1. Therefore, an index of 2 refers to the third element of the array.

Arrays are one of the most powerful parts of the PHP language; they allow for the organization of related data, and quick access to that data. In this chapter and the next, we will discuss in depth how to efficiently manipulate arrays, as well as a few tricks of the trade.

3.1 Declaring an Array

You want to specify a list for your program instead of sequentially adding items to your array:

```php
<?php
$my_ar[] = "Hello";
$my_ar[] = "Mrs.";
$my_ar[] = "Robinson";
?>
```

Technique

You can graduate from this basic method of specifying lists to array constructs, which enables you to easily specify lists in your program:

```php
<?php
$my_ar = array("Hello", "Mrs.", "Robinson");
?>
```

Comments

Using the array() construct to specify an array instead of manually adding items to an array was one of Rasmus Lerdorf's (the creator of PHP) top-ten signs of an experienced PHP programmer. The array() construct makes it much easier for programmers to quickly specify lists.

If you have a large array, it is usually better to store your array in a file and retrieve the array when you load your program:

```php
<?php
function load_data ($name) {
    $data = implode ("", file ('${name}_var'));
    $var = unserialize ($data);
    return ($var);
}

function save_data ($name, $var) {
    $fp = @fopen ("${name}_var", "w")
      or die ("Cannot open ${name}_var for write access");

    fwrite ($fp, serialize ($var));

    @fclose ($fp);
}

$friends = load_data('friends');
$friends[] = 'Tim';
save_data ('friends', $friends);
?>
```

In the code, we use the `serialize()` function, which returns the string representation of a variable, and write that string to a file. In the `load_data()` function, we read the file containing the string representation of our variable into the `$data` variable by using a combination of `implode()` and `file()`. After we have this data, we use the `unserialize()` function to convert the data back into the original variable, which we return from the function.

3.2 Printing Out an Array

You want to print an entire array separated by commas.

Technique
Use PHP's `implode()` function to print out your list with commas as the separator:

```php
<?php
$list = array ("Emily", "Jesse", "Franklin", "Chris");
print substr (implode (', ', $list), 0, -2);
?>
```

Comments

The `implode()` function inserts a comma after every array element and returns a string with the inserted commas. We eliminate the last two characters of the string by using the `substr()` function because we do not need to print the trailing `, `. This is a very useful function for printing out entire arrays. In PHP, when you `print $list;` where `$list` is an array, PHP prints `"array"` instead of the elements of an array; therefore, `implode()` offers a shortcut for printing out an entire array.

If you want to print out an array without commas, you have two options. Here is the first and less-efficient way:

```php
<?php
while ($i < count ($list) ) {
    print $list[$i++];
}
?>
```

And here is the efficient way using `implode()`:

```php
<?php
print implode("", $list);
?>
```

The first way of printing out an array loops through the array with a `while` loop, prints out the current item, and then increments to the next element. The second method strings the array elements one after another, separating them with an empty string.

3.3 Eliminating Duplicate Elements

You want to extract unique items in an array, eliminating duplicate elements.

Technique

Use PHP's built-in `array_unique()` function:

```php
<?php
$unique = array_unique ($duplicates);
?>
```

Or, if you want to define uniqueness by an arbitrary criterion, loop through the array and see whether more than one element matches your criterion:

```php
<?php
$n_array = array();
foreach ($array as $element) {
    // Only three duplicate values are allowed
    // in the new array.
    if ($tstarray[$element] < 3) {
        array_push ($n_array, $element);
        $tstarray[$element]++;
    }
}
?>
```

Comments

The `array_unique()` function will, given an array, strip the array of all its duplicate items and return a new array. The `array_unique()` function works on both associative and numerically indexed arrays.

If you want to be a little more specific than just checking whether an entry exists, you can write your own routine to search an array for what you define as duplicates. The basic idea of this is shown in the second example in the solution—we search through `$array` and keep track of how many times each element of `$array` has been seen. If the element has been seen fewer than three times, we add it to our array; otherwise, we move to the next item.

3.4 Enlarging or Shrinking an Array

You want to make an array bigger or cut off items at the end of an array. You think that enlarging an array can be useful because it is more memory efficient to set aside space.

Technique

In PHP, it is unnecessary to preallocate your arrays to a certain length. You simply store the data in the array at the indices/keys that you want, and let PHP handle the grunge work of memory allocation internally:

```php
<?php
$list = array();
// $list will not be 51 elements long, it has only 1 entry
// an index 50
$list[50] = "orange";
?>
```

To shrink an array, use the `array_splice()` function (PHP 4 only):

```php
<?php
$list = array ("dog", "cat", "rabbit", "ant", "horse", "cow");
// trim the list to five elements
array_splice ($list, 5);
?>
```

Comments

The `array_splice()` function takes up to four arguments:

```
array array_splice(array init, int start, int length, array replacement);
```

The first argument of `array_splice()` is the initial array that you want to manipulate, followed by where you want to start your replacement or subtraction in the array; if left empty, the replacement or subtraction will start with the first element. `length` is how many array elements you want to replace; if left empty, `array_splice()` will replace all elements from the start. Finally, `array_splice()` takes a replacement array for the part of the array that is deleted. The `array_splice()` function returns the elements of the array that are taken out and the original array is modified (destructively). Please note that `array_splice()` was just added in PHP 4. The following is some PHP3 code that will remove all but the first five elements:

```php
<?php
reset ($ar);
$i = 0;
while ($i < 5 && list ($key, $val) = each ($ar)) {
    $new_ar[$key] = $ar[$val];
    $i++;
}
$ar = $new_ar;
?>
```

To enlarge an array to a certain number of elements, you have to give a value to each array element:

```php
<?php
for ($c = 0; $c < 100; $c++) {
    $ar[$c] = "";
}
?>
```

This can also be done with the `array_pad()` function:

```php
<?php
$some_ar = array();
$some_ar = array_pad ($some_ar, 100, "");
?>
```

3.5 Merging Arrays

You want to append one array onto another and the `array_push()` function doesn't do the job.

Technique

Use PHP 4's `array_merge()` function to append one or more arrays:

```php
<?php
$good_guys = array ("Gandalf", "Radagast", "Saruman");
$bad_guys  = array ("Nazgul", "Sauron", "Orcs");

$all_guys = array_merge ($good_guys, $bad_guys);
?>
```

As a bit of syntactic sugar, you can also use the + sign to merge two or more arrays:

```php
<?php
$places = array ("Lothlorien", "Orthanc", "Rivendell", "Hobbiton", "Bree");
$people = array ("Galadriel",  "Saruman", "Elrond",   "Frodo",    "Butterbee");

$both = $places + $people;
?>
```

If you don't want to lose elements that are the same in both arrays, you can use the `array_merge_recursive()` function:

```php
<?php
$good_guys = array ("Gandalf", "Radagast", "Saruman");
$bad_guys  = array ("Nazgul", "Sauron", "Orcs");
$fallen    = array ("Denethor", "Saruman");

$everybody = array_merge_recursive ($good_guys, $bad_guys, $fallen);
?>
```

Comments

In Perl, you would use the push() function to merge two arrays together. (Arrays in Perl are automatically flattened when used in list context; thankfully, this is not so in PHP.) However, in PHP, using the array_push() function will give you a two-dimensional array:

```php
<?php
$good_guys = array ("Gandalf","Radagast","Saruman");
$bad_guys  = array ("Nazgul","Sauron","Orcs");

$all_guys = array_push ($good_guys, $bad_guys);

print $all_guys[3][1];
// prints Sauron
?>
```

You can also merge two arrays using a loop (PHP 3 compatible):

```php
<?php
for ($i = 0; $i < count ($ar2); $i++ ) {
    $ar1[] = $ar2[$i];
}
?>
```

3.6 Iteratively Processing Elements in an Array

You want to perform an action on each element of an array.

Technique

Take a stroll through the array using array_walk():

```php
<?php
function ascii_codes (&$element) {
    $element = ord ($element);
}

$nice_line = "What Up everyone";
$chars = preg_split ("//", $nice_line);
array_walk ($chars, 'ascii_codes');
?>
```

Or use a for loop to loop through the array:

```php
<?php
function ascii_codes ($element) {
    $element = ord ($element);
}


$nice_line = "What Up everyone";
$chars = preg_split ("//", $nice_line);

for ($i = 0; $i < count ($chars); $i++) {
    $chars[$i] = ascii_codes ($chars[$i]);
}
?>
```

Comments

The array_walk() function invokes a user-defined function on each element of the passed array. The elements are passed as the first argument of the specified function; if the function requires more than one argument, a warning will be generated each time array_walk() calls the function. These warnings can be suppressed by prepending the '@' sign to the array_walk() call, or by using the error_reporting() function (setting it to E_ERROR). By default, the elements are passed to the user function by value. If you prepend & to the declaration, the elements will be passed by reference and you will be able to modify them inside the function.

For Perl programmers, it might be helpful to think of array_walk() as the map() function, where the following:

```
@in = map { $_ * $_ } @in;
```

translates to

```php
<?php
function square (&$array_element) {
    $array_element = $array_element * $array_element;
}


array_walk ($in, 'square');
?>
```

If you want to use array_walk() but don't want to predeclare a function every time you want to loop over an array, you can use PHP's create_function() function and loop over the array:

```php
<?php
$ar = array ("hello", "world");
array_walk ($ar, create_function ('&$word',
                                   '$word = strtolower($word);'));
?>
```

You can also pass an array by reference and then work with that array.

Unlike some other languages such as Perl and C, in PHP, references do not need to be dereferenced. Therefore, the following will work:

```php
<?php
// This function trims message board topics down to 40 characters
// and makes sure that … occurs after a word boundary
function trim_topics (&$topics)
{
    for ($c = 0; $c < count ($topics); $c++) {
        if (strlen ($topics[$c]) > 40) {
            $topics[$c] = preg_replace ("/\s+(\S+)?$/","...", substr
            ($topics[$c], 0, 40));
        }
    }
}


trim_topics ($msg_topics);
?>
```

References in PHP are simply symbol table aliases, nothing more. That means when you declare a reference to a variable, $var1, you are telling PHP that the reference points to the same data to which $var1 points. If it helps, you can think of references in PHP as similar to hardlinks on the UNIX filesystem.

If you want to modify the data inside a function and have it changed in the outer scope as well, in C you would pass the pointer to the data to the function. In PHP, you declare that the function accepts a reference and simply pass the data. In fact, it's good programming practice not to use reference passing at the call time; it's much cleaner to do it in function declaration.

You can create a reference to an existing PHP variable by sticking an & sign before the variable, like so:

```php
<?php

$algernon = "Relations are simply a tedious pack of people,
            who haven't got the remotest knowledge of how to live,
            nor the slightest instinct about when to die."
// Oscar Wilde, The Importance of Being Earnest

$bumblebury = &$algernon;
?>
```

$bumblebury and $algernon now point to the same data. Performing some sort of operation on either variable will change the value of the other one as well.

> **Gotcha**
> In general, when looking to optimize your PHP code, don't worry too much about references; it is most often faster simply to let Zend handle such matters. One area however where references can pay off is when using objects, where you should *always* pass references.

3.7 Accessing the Current Element in an Array

You want to return the current element of an array to which PHP's internal pointer is pointing.

Technique

Use PHP's current() function, which returns the element to which the internal PHP pointer is currently pointing:

```php
<?php
$current_element = current ($ar);
?>
```

Comments

The current() function takes the specified array and returns the current element to which the internal array pointer points. However, if you are looking for information on iteratively processing arrays, I suggest you stay away from the current() function and use a while loop and the each() function:

```php
<?php
while (list ($key, $element) = each ($ar)) {
    print "key: $key, value: $element";  // print out $array
}
?>
```

Or, you could use a `for` loop to process the array:

```php
<?php
for ($i = 0; $i < count ($ar); $i++) {
    print $ar[$i];
}
?>
```

However, a `for` loop is good only when the array has only contiguous numeric keys.

In PHP 4, you can use a `foreach` loop to process an array:

```php
<?php
foreach ($ar as $element) {
    print $element;
}
?>
```

or

```php
<?php
foreach ($array as $key => $value) {
    print "Key: $key, Value: $value";
}
?>
```

3.8 Accessing Different Areas of an Array

You want to process more than one element of an array at a time.

Technique

Use the `array_slice()` command creatively to have the desired effects:

```php
<?php
$mash_cast = array ("Hawkeye",
                    "Trapper",
                    "Honeycutt",
                    "Radar",
                    "Klinger",
                    "Colonel Blake",
                    "Colonel Potter",
                    "General Clayton",
                    "Frank Burns",
                    "Charles Winchester",
                    "Hotlips");
```

```
$side_kicks = array_slice ($mash_cast,1,2);
// Trapper, Honeycutt

$annoyances = array_slice ($mash_cast,-3,3);
// Frank Burns, Charles Winchester, Hotlips

$assistants = array_slice ($mash_cast,3,2);
// Radar, Klinger

$officials = array_slice ($mash_cast,5,3);
// Colonel Blake, Colonel Potter, General Clayton

$main_character = array_slice ($mash_cast,0,1);
// Hawkeye
?>
```

Comments

The syntax of the `array_slice()` function is similar to `array_splice()` (if you omit the replacement array parameter), which is covered in recipe 3.4. This recipe illustrates how to get information out of arrays. In these examples, we assigned the values returned from `array_slice()` to new arrays, but you can also assign them to variables:

```
<?php
list ($var1, $var2) = array_slice ($ar, 0, 2);
// grab the first two items of the array and assign them
// to $var1 and $var2.
?>
```

If you are still coding in PHP 3 (upgrade already) and therefore the `array_slice()` function is not available to you, you can use the following method to work with a range of elements:

```
<?php
$start = 2;
$end = 6;

for ($i = $start; $i <= $end; $i++) {
    $partial_array[] = $orig_array[$i];
}
?>
```

3.9 Searching an Array

You want to find the first array element that passes a predefined test.

Technique

Use a `while` loop in conjunction with PHP's `break` statement:

```php
<?php
while ($idx < count ($big_array)) {
    if (preg_match ("/\w/", $big_array[$idx])) {
        $first_element = $big_array[$idx];
        break;
    }
    $idx++;
}
print "The first matching element is $first_element";
?>
```

Comments

Looping through the array with a `while` loop to find the first element that meets a predefined criterion is one way to find the first relevant match. Another way is to use the `preg_grep()` function:

```php
<?php
$first_element = array_shift(preg_grep("/\w/", $big_array));
?>
```

The `preg_grep()` method is quicker in terms of programmer efficiency, but it is slower, especially when working on large arrays, and does not allow as much flexibility as the first method.

If you want to find all items—not just the first item—that match a certain criteria you can loop through the different values of the array and test each item or use `preg_grep()` for coding ease.

A `foreach` loop:

```php
<?php
foreach ($list as $element) {
    if ($element == $criteria) {
        $matches[] = $elementcriteria;
    }
}
?>
```

Using preg_grep():

```php
<?php
$matches = preg_grep("/regex/", $list);
?>
```

The first approach uses a foreach loop to loop through the array and if the item matches the criteria, it is added to the $matches array. The second method uses the preg_grep() function, which searches the array for you, returning an array of the items matching the regular expression. For example:

```php
<?php
$republicans = array ("Senator Orrin Hatch",
                      "Governor George W. Bush",
                      "Senator John McCain",
                      "Gary Bauer",
                      "Alan Keyes");

$senators = preg_grep ("/^senator/i", $republicans);
?>
```

More information on preg_grep() is available in Chapter 5, "Matching Data with Regular Expressions," where we discuss regular expressions in depth.

3.10 Searching for the Different Elements in Two Arrays

You want to see what items are in one array but not in another array.

Technique

Use PHP's built-in array_diff() function to find the difference between two arrays:

```php
<?php
$dwarves1 = array ("Ori","Nori","Oin");
$dwarves2 = array ("Oin", "Gloin", "Ori");

$diff = array_diff ($one_ar, $two_ar);
?>
```

Comments

The array_diff() function will return all elements that are present in the array given by the first argument, but that are not present in the array (or arrays) given by the subsequent arguments. You can provide more than one array for `array_diff()` to search:

```php
<?php
$elves1 = array ("Tinuviel", "Luthien", "Galadrial");
$elves2 = array ("Arwen", "Elrond", "Gildor");
$elves3 = array ("Feanor", "Mahadriel", "Tuor");
$elves_men = array ("Luthien", "Beren", "Arwen", "Aragorn");

$diff = array_diff ($elves1, $elves2, $elves3, $elves_and_men);
?>
```

Note that this still allows for duplicates in the `$diff` array; to eliminate these duplicates, use the `array_unique( )` function:

```php
<?php
$diff = array_unique ($diff);
?>
```

3.11 Randomizing the Elements of an Array

You want to randomize all elements in an array.

Technique

Use the `shuffle()` function, which changes the order of the array elements:

```php
<?php
srand ((double)microtime()*1000000);
$some_array = range(1, 52);
shuffle($some_array);
// $some_array now contains numbers from 1 to 52 in random order.
?>
```

Comments

The `shuffle()` function is extremely useful for randomizing arrays because it saves you the time of writing your own complex routine. This can be useful if, for example, you make an online poker game or dice game and want the results to be completely random.

3.12 Determining the Union, Intersection, or Difference Between Two Arrays

You want to find out the unions and differences of two arrays.

Technique

To find the intersection of two arrays, use the `array_intersect()` function:

```php
<?php
// Define the Arrays
$common      = array ("Marriages","were","made","in","heaven");
$oscar_wilde = array ("Divorces","were","made","in","heaven");

$intersection = array_intersect ($common, $oscar_wilde);
?>
```

Or, if you want to know how many different items and how many similarities exist:

```php
<?php
// Define the Arrays
$common      = array ("Marriages","were","made","in","heaven");
$oscar_wilde = array ("Divorces","were","made","in","heaven");

$difference   = array_diff ($common, $oscar_wilde);
$intersection = array_intersect ($common, $oscar_wilde);

$diff_num      = count ($difference);
$intersect_num = count ($intersection);
?>
```

If you want to calculate the union of two arrays, keep an index of what you've already seen in one array and then match it with the next array:

```php
<?php
$common      = array("Marriages", "were", "made", "in", "heaven");
$oscar_wilde = array("Divorces", "were", "made", "in", "heaven");

$union = array();

foreach ($common as $ele) { $seen[$ele] = 1; }

foreach ($oscar_wilde as $ele) {
    if ($seen[$ele] == 1) {
```

```php
        array_push ($union, $ele);
        $seen[$ele]++;
    }
}
?>
```

Finally, let us calculate the symmetric difference of the two arrays:

```php
<?php
// Define the Arrays
$common      = array ("Marriages","were","made","in","heaven");
$oscar_wilde = array ("Divorces","were","made","in","heaven");

$symdiff = array();

foreach ($common as $ele) {
    if (!in_array ($oscar_wilde, $ele)) {
        array_push ($symdiff, $ele);
    }
}

foreach ($oscar_wilde as $ele) {
    if (!in_array ($common, $ele)) {
        array_push ($symdiff, $ele);
    }
}

$symdiff = array_unique($symdiff);
?>
```

Comments

The first part of the recipe finds the intersection of the two arrays without any
duplicates. The $intersection array contains the array of items that are common to
both arrays. The second part of the recipe does the same thing as the first part, except
that now we count how many items are in the $intersection array and how many
items are in the $difference array. The third part of the recipe finds the union of two
arrays, which is all elements that are in both arrays. Finally, the last part of the recipe
is a script that not only does what the earlier one does, but also finds the symmetric
difference of the two arrays. The symmetric difference of two arrays is the items that
are not in both arrays, but are in one array or the other.

3.13 Sorting an Array

> You want to sort an entire array by your own function because PHP's functions do not fit your need.

Technique

Use the usort() function to specify a user-defined function for sorting the array:

```php
<?php
function cmp_debt($a, $b)
{
    if ($a[1]== $b[1]) return 0;
    return ($b[1] > $a[1]) ? 1 : -1;
}


// Suppose you have an array that you use to keep track of
// how much your buddies owe you after that game of poker.
// You want to sort the array from largest debt to lowest, but
// regular sorting functions in PHP can't help.
$buddy_debts = array(array("John",31),
                     array("Dave", 12),
                     array("Kris", 15),
                     array("Werner", 38),
                     array("Phil", 9));

usort($buddy_debts, 'cmp_debt');
foreach ($buddy_debts as $buddy_debt) {
    print $buddy_debt[0]." owes ".$buddy_debt[1];
    print "<br>";
}
?>
```

Comments

The usort() function takes an array and sorts it by a user-defined function; in this case, the function is called cmp_debt(). The function must return -1, 0, or 1. From the PHP manual: "The comparison function must return an integer less than, equal to, or greater than zero if the first argument is considered to be respectively less than, equal to, or greater than the second. If two members compare as equal, their order in the sorted array is undefined."

We have to resort to using `usort()` because of the way our `$buddy_debts` array is structured. PHP's regular sorting functions look only one level deep inside the array, and comparing arrays of arrays is not currently supported.

If you want to use the `usort()` function without the hassle of declaring an extra sort function, you can use it in conjunction with PHP's `create_function()` function:

```php
<?php
$buddy_debts = array(array("John",31),
                     array("Dave", 12),
                     array("Kris", 15),
                     array("Werner", 38),
                     array("Phil", 9));

usort($buddy_debts,
      create_function('$a, $b', 'if ($a[1] == $b[1]) return 0;
                      return ($b[1] > $a[1]) ? 1 : -1;'));
foreach ($buddy_debts as $buddy_debt) {
    print $buddy_debt[0]." owes ".$buddy_debt[1];
    print "<br>";
}
?>
```

3.14 Sorting Sensibly

You want to make your program sort a list like a human would, where the number 10 would come after the number 2.

Technique

Use the `natsort()` function:

```php
<?php
$files = array("file001.txt", "file002.txt", "file003.txt",
               "file010.txt", "file023.txt", "file004.txt");
natsort($files);
foreach ($files as $file) {
    print "$file\n";
}
?>
```

Comments

The `natsort()` function uses a sorting algorithm that is described by Martin Pool at `http://www.linuxcare.com.au/projects/natsort/`. A case-insensitive version of the `natsort()` function is also available, `natcasesort()`.

3.15 Reversing Order

You want to process an array in reverse order or permanently reverse the order of the array.

Technique

Use the `array_reverse()` function to reverse the array:

```php
<?php
$ar = array_reverse ($ar);
?>
```

Or use a `for` loop to process the array backward:

```php
<?php
for ($i = count ($my_array) - 1; $i >= 0; $i--) {
    // Loop backwards through the array
}
?>
```

Comments

The first example actually reverses the entire array; if you have an enormous array, this approach can be inefficient as far as speed is concerned. The second method loops backwards through the entire array, which is much faster on larger arrays because it saves a step.

If you are sorting an array, you should automatically reverse your sort in the array sort. This can be done by using either `arsort()` for processing associative arrays or `rsort()` for arrays.

```php
$fruits = array ("Oranges", "Apples", "Pears", "Bananas");
$fruits = rsort ($fruits);
// $fruits is now "Pears, Oranges, Bananas, Apples"
```

3.16 Perl-Based Array Manipulation Features

You're a "Perl monger" and you want to know what array features PHP has that are related to Perl.

Technique

Here is a list of all the Perl-related array manipulation features, as well as (in the "Discussion" section) a list of incompatibilities with their Perl counterparts.

Perl Function	PHP Function(s)
pop()	array_pop()
push()	array_push()
shift()	array_shift()
unshift()	array_unshift()
splice()	array_splice()
join()	join(), implode()
grep()	preg_grep()
keys()	array_keys()
each()	each()
values()	array_values()
reverse()	array_reverse()
sort()	usort() (to some extent)

Comments

There are some incompatibilities between certain functions; for example, between Perl's push() function and PHP's array_push() function. This is more of a general incompatibility. In Perl, arrays specified in list context are automatically flattened, so

```
push (@list1, @list2);
```

would combine the two arrays—the same thing that array_merge() would do in PHP. However, with array_push() this example would create a two-dimensional array because PHP does not automatically flatten its arrays.

CHAPTER 4

PHP's Built-in Arrays and Constants

"Constants aren't."

John Peers

PHP provides a number of built-in arrays and constants that make your job as a programmer much easier. For example: In Perl, you would have to read the buffer or parse the query string to collect data. But PHP not only immediately converts data that is sent to the script into variables, it also stores the variables in associative arrays (see recipe 4.6). So, the following Perl code:

```
#!/usr/bin/perl -w
use strict;
use vars qw(%variables);

if (lc $ENV{REQUEST_METHOD} eq 'post') {
    read STDIN, $_, filesize(STDIN);
} else {
    $_ = $ENV{QUERY_STRING};
}

foreach (split /\&/) {
    my ($key, $val) = split /\=/;
    $key =~ s/\+/ /g;
    $val =~ s/\+/ /g;
    $key =~ s/%([A-Fa-f0-9]{2})/pack("c", hex($1))/ge;
    $val =~ s/%([A-Fa-f0-9]{2})/pack("c", hex($1))/ge;
    $variables{$key} = $val;
}
```

becomes

```php
<?php
$variables = strtolower($REQUEST_METHOD) == 'get' ?
             $HTTP_GET_VARS : $HTTP_POST_VARS;
?>
```

in PHP. (This is covered fully in recipe 4.6.)

In this chapter, we explain PHP's basic constants and built-in arrays. In particular, we discuss how to use them to create more secure, less error-prone programs.

4.1 Working with File Constants

You need to create an error-reporting function that reports errors and gives both the name of the file where the error occurred and the line of the file.

Technique

Use the __FILE__ and __LINE__ constants to obtain this information:

```php
<?php
require_once 'DB.php';

function ferror($file,
                $line,
                $message='General Error') {
    $errmsg = "There was an error in script $file, on $line: $message\n";
    error_log($errmsg);
    die('An error occurred, it has been logged in the system log');
}

$dbh = DB::connect("mysql://user:secret@localhost/dbname");
if (!$dbh) {
    $dbh = ferror(__FILE__,__LINE__, sprintf('[%d]: %s',
                  $dbh->getCode(), $dbh->getMessage()));
}
// Database connection stuff here
?>
```

Comments

The function itself should be pretty self-explanatory. It takes the arguments $file, $line, and $message from the user and prints them out with some formatting so that the error message is a little more readable. We also assign a default value for $message so that we may omit the $message argument when calling the function. For example, calling ferror() like so:

```
ferror(__FILE__,__LINE__)
```

is completely legal. The new code is when we actually call ferror() using the predefined __FILE__ and __LINE__ constants to give the current file and current line. The __FILE__ and __LINE__ constants are documented as such in the PHP manual:

> __FILE__
>
> The name of the script file presently being executed. If used within a file which has been included or required, then the name of the included file is given, and not the name of the parent file.

> __LINE__
>
> The number of the line within the current script file which is being executed. If used within a file which has been included or required, then the position within the included file is given.

4.2 PHP's OS and Version Constants

You want to find out information about PHP and the OS at runtime and make some determinations based on that information.

Technique

Use PHP's built-in constants PHP_OS and PHP_VERSION and make choices based on that information:

```php
<?php
switch (PHP_OS) {
    case "WIN32":
        win32_function();
        break;
    case "Linux":
        linux_function();
        break;
```

```
    case "OS/2":
        os2_function();
        break;
}
?>
```

Comments

The following will help you if you need to write different types of functions for different operating systems. This is especially useful if you are making a one-size-fits-all script, and you don't know the OS on which it will be run. However, note that some configurations of PHP do not support this constant, so you might want to use the following error checking:

```
if (!defined(PHP_OS)) {
    die("OS Detection cannot be done automatically");
}
// now use your funky OS detection code
?>
```

To detect the version of PHP being used, your code can be similar to the OS detection code, except you replace PHP_OS with PHP_VERSION and you will have different cases.

I must mention that this is not the best way to get information about your system and PHP in general. If you want complete information about PHP and your OS, use the phpinfo() function like so:

```
<?php phpinfo(); ?>
```

Just open this page in your browser and it will print out all information available about PHP, including extensions, your configuration options, environment, PHP variables, Apache environment, and HTTP header information.

4.3 Setting Breakpoints by Using PHP's Error Constants

You want to set different levels of error checking in a script.

Technique

Use PHP's error_reporting() function in conjunction with the predefined error constants:

```
<?
error_reporting(E_WARNING);
$line = "The\nQuick\nYoung\nProgrammer\nJumped\nOver\nThe\nLazy\nOld\
        nProgrammer";
$line = ereg_replace("(\n"," ",$line); // mis-matched parentheses
print $line;
?>
```

Comments

In this code, the regular expression in the first argument of `ereg_replace()` has a mismatched parenthesis (the correct syntax would be `ereg_replace("(\n)"," ", $line);`). Normally, PHP would not report this error, but because we told the PHP processor through the `error_reporting()` function that we want PHP to report regular expression errors, we now get the error reported to us. `E_WARNING` is just one of the different levels of error reporting. The following is a table of all the error constants.

Constant	Description
E_ALL	Enables all errors.
E_ERROR	Enables any error other than parsing from which recovery is not possible.
E_WARNING	Denotes a condition where PHP knows something is wrong, but will continue anyway; these can be caught by the script itself. An example is the invalid regexp in `ereg_replace()` shown earlier.
E_PARSE	The parser choked on invalid syntax in the script file. Recovery is not possible.
E_NOTICE	Something happened that might not be an error, and execution continues. Examples include using an unquoted string as an associative array index, or accessing a variable that has not been set.

Using these constants in conjunction with the `error_reporting()` function will help you better debug your scripts and find major flaws and quirks that PHP might not be reporting, but that are causing your program to act differently. The default error-reporting level is `E_ALL & ~E_NOTICE` (all errors except notices).

4.4 Defining Your Own PHP Constants

You want to define your own constants with PHP.

Technique

Use PHP's `define()` function:

```php
<?php
define("HI", "Hello World!");
print HI;
?>
```

Comments

This code defines HI as Hello World by using the `define()` function. Please note that these are constants, not C-style macros—only valid scalar data may be represented by a constant. For example, the following will not work:

```php
function four() {
    return 4;
}
define("HI","four()");
print HI;
```

This code would print `"four()"` instead of printing `"4"` (as `print four();` would do).

It is also possible to check whether a constant has already been defined. The `defined()` function will help you do so. The two functions in combination enable you to make sure that a library file is included only once (similar to C header file constructs).

```php
<?php
if (!defined("_MYLIB_INC_"))
    define("_MYLIB_INC_", 1);
else
    return;

// Library functions continue here
?>
```

4.5 Working with PHP Globals

You want to see all the different global variables existing in the script.

Technique

Print the entire `$GLOBALS` array using PHP's functions for processing associative arrays:

```php
<?php
reset($GLOBALS);
while (list($key, $var) = each($GLOBALS)) {
    print "$key => $var\n<br>\n";
}
?>
```

Comments

The example uses PHP's `list()` and `each()` functions to iteratively process the `$GLOBALS` array. It then prints the keys (names of the variables stored in the `$GLOBALS` array) and their corresponding values.

The `$GLOBALS` array contains all variables not defined within the scope of a function as well as PHP's built-in arrays and variables, which are discussed in the next recipe. Here is a quick example to better explain the `$GLOBALS` array:

```php
<?php
$foo = "fly";

function run() {
    $bar = "honey";
}
?>
```

In this example, `$foo` would be stored in the `$GLOBALS` array (because it is defined outside the scope of the function) and `$bar` would not be included in the `$GLOBALS` array (`$bar` is defined within the scope of function `run()`).

To access a variable that is not declared within the current function, you must do one of two things: either access it through the `$GLOBALS` array or declare the variable as the global variable. Still using the preceding example, if we want to access `$foo` in the function `set_bar()`, we have to do one of the following two things:

Example 1: Access `$foo` directly through the `$GLOBALS` array:

```php
<?php
$foo = "fly";

function run() {
    print $GLOBALS["foo"];
}
?>
```

Example 2: Tell the function that we are referring to the global $foo:

```php
<?php

$foo = "fly";

function run() {
    global $foo;
    print $foo;
}
?>
```

Both of these functions print the value of $foo—they are two different ways to do the same thing. There is, however, one difference: In example 2, $foo now refers to the global variable $foo throughout the function; in example 1, if you then accessed plain $foo, it would refer to the $foo that is local to the function. Another notable point is that in example 2, the variable $foo declared inside the function as global is actually a reference to the $GLOBALS['foo'] value.

Note also that you never need to declare the $GLOBALS array as global inside a function because it resides in the active symbol, not in the global symbol table. (However, it is a reference to the global symbol table, so it is present in the global symbol table.)

4.6 Accessing Data Through PHP's Built-in Arrays

You want direct access to the input sent by your users to the PHP script via the GET or POST method.

Technique

Use the $HTTP_POST_VARS and $HTTP_GET_VARS arrays:

```php
<?php
$submitted_vars = strtolower($REQUEST_METHOD) == 'get' ?
                  $HTTP_GET_VARS : $HTTP_POST_VARS;

$name = $submitted_vars['name'];
?>
```

Comments

PHP automatically registers the submitted data as global variables in your program. However, automatically registering global variables has some serious security ramifications. It is insecure because global variables are registered from the user, and PHP variables can be overwritten by submitted variables. That means if a malicious user sends an extra variable named dbh, and your PHP script has a variable named $dbh, the $dbh variable in your script will be overwritten. To avoid this potential security risk, you should set the register_globals directive in the php.ini file to off and rely instead on PHP's built-in "track" variables:

$HTTP_POST_VARS—An associative array of all variables sent to the user via the POST method

$HTTP_GET_VARS—An associative array of all variables sent to the user via the GET method

$HTTP_COOKIE_VARS—An associative array of all the cookies sent to the current script

$HTTP_POST_FILES—An associative array of information about all files sent using PHP's file upload feature

$HTTP_ENV_VARS—An associative array of all environment variables

$HTTP_SERVER_VARS—An associative array of all the variables that the server sends to PHP

$HTTP_SESSION_VARS—An associative array of all the current session variables

---

Note

As of PHP 4.1 shorter versions of the above variables are automagically available in all contexts (in function and global scopes). They are named respectively: $_POST, $_GET, $_COOKIE, $_ENV and $_SERVER. Additionally, a new array called $_REQUEST was added, which contains all $_GET, $_POST and $_COOKIE variables.

CHAPTER 5

Matching Data with Regular Expressions

"I believe that our Heavenly Father invented man because he was disappointed in the monkey."

Mark Twain

5.0 Introduction

What good is data if you can't interpret it? For data to be useful, we need it in a form that we can understand. For example, if we wanted to build a file crawler (see the program at the end of Chapter 7, "Working with Files in Directories"), the actual links we would parse look like this:

```
<a href="foo.htm">Foo Description</a>
```

However, this form is useless to us. If we wanted to get the link by itself, we would use a regular expression. The actual regular expression might look something like this:

```
<a.*href=\"(.+)\".*>.*<\/a>
```

But that is getting a little bit ahead of ourselves. First, let us go over some basic regular expressions.

Regular Expression Basics

In some languages, such as Perl, regular expressions are a part of the language core. That means, basically, that they are the same as using the or statement. Here is an example of how we might match this link in Perl:

```
my $url = "<a href=\"http://www.designmultimedia.com/\">DesignMultimedia</a>";
print "the link matches our stringent standards"
                            if $url =~ m{<a.*href=\"(.+)\".*>.*</a>}i;
```

However, in PHP, regular expressions are accessed through functions. The most basic of these functions are the `ereg()` and `eregi()` functions, which will do the same type of match that Perl does in the preceding code (with a different pattern matching syntax, of course). Here is the PHP equivalent of the Perl code:

```php
<?php
if (eregi('<a.*href=\"(.+)\".*>.*<\/a>', $url)) {
    print "the link matches our stringent standards";
}
?>
```

So, now we know that, in PHP, regular expressions are enclosed in functions—what do we do from here? Let's go over some basic syntax and problem-solving methods used with regular expressions.

Regular expressions, or *pattern matching* (as I will call it), work by applying the pattern you specify against a specified string, instead of comparing the string character-by-character to another string.

Matching Strings

Let's start with some basic regular expressions. Examine the following regular expression:

```
Lamb$
```

This matches any string that ends with the string `Lamb`. So, for example, it would match all the following:

```
Mary had a little Lamb
Donny stole Mary's Lamb
Donny got arrested for stealing Mary's little Lamb
```

To tell the previous regular expression to match any word at the *end* of the string, we use the `$` (dollar) sign. The `$` sign is a meta-character that tells PHP to match a pattern at the end of a string. Just as a dollar sign will match any occurrence of a pattern at the end of a string, the `^` (circumflex) sign will match any pattern at the beginning of a string:

```
^Donny
```

So, the previous expression would match all the following:

```
Donny noticed that Mary had a little lamb
Donny disliked Mary so he wanted to steal from her
Donny got in trouble with the law for being a bad boy
```

The ^ character matches the beginning of a string and the $ character matches the end of the string pattern. If we put these two meta-characters together, we can get a regular expression that will match only a string that contains a specific pattern, or a pattern that is at the beginning and the end of a string at the same time.

```
^Hello World$
```

This would match only Hello World, not Hello Beautiful World or Hello World I'm Sterling.

To search a string that to see whether it contains a certain pattern and nothing else, simply supply the pattern itself. This simple regular expression

```
http://www\.designmultimedia\.com
```

would match the following:

```
Mary went to http://www.designmultimedia.com
<a href="http://www.designmultimedia.com">DesignMultimedia</a>
http://www.designmultimedia.com - Creating order out of Chaos
```

Matching Escape Sequences

In PHP, you can also search for escape sequences (such as \n, \t, and so on). For example, the following will match certain two words separated by a line break (\n):

```
Mary\nLamb
```

Meaning that the following strings will match the criteria (Mary, linebreak (\n), Lamb):

```
I love Mary
Lamb am I

I hate Mary
Lamb be not I
```

Character Classes

Pattern matching is the process of applying a pattern to a string for the purpose of finding a match. So far, we have searched only for literal characters (such as D, o, n, n, and y) or escape sequences (such as \n). However, PHP also enables you to match a series of characters or escape sequences in what are known as *character classes*. Take the following pattern:

```
[a-z]
```

This will match any lowercase character from a to z, meaning that any of the following strings will be matched by the preceding pattern:

```
hedk fd
```

```
arpp
```

```
Here fido
```

```
BARKITY BaRK XYZ
```

The expression will match as long as the string contains one lowercase character from a-z (a to z). To denote a character, make sure that you place your character class within brackets (that is, [a-z] not a-z).

To negate your character class, you can use the ^ meta-character. When enclosed within brackets, the circumflex tells PHP to match any character except what is in the character class. (This works only if the circumflex is the very first character inside the brackets.) Therefore, the following will match any string that contains a non-lowercase letter:

```
[^a-z]
```

Some sample strings this pattern would match are

```
FACSIMILe
```

```
Rtdg
```

```
9034
```

```
3FH7*.
```

Finishing off this mini-section on matching character classes, here is a set of commonly used regular expressions:

```
[a-zA-Z] // Match any letter (e.g. W, w, t, Z, x)
[a-zA-Z0-9] // Match any letter or number (e.g. howdy, 9)
[ \f\r\t\n\v] // Match Any Whitespace character
[0-9\.\-] // Match any Number, minus sign or period
```

Matching More Than One Occurrence of a Character

To match more than one occurrence of a character (or character class) in a string, use the {} meta-characters. For example, the following will match a string that contains three lowercase letters in a row:

```
[a-z]{3}
```

The 3 inside the {} is what tells PHP to match a string that contains three lowercase letters in a row. If you want to match a range of character occurrences, separate the lower limit and the upper limit by a comma:

```
[a-zA-Z]{1,8}
```

This will match any occurrence of a set of letters between one and eight characters long, so the following would be valid:

```
W
```

```
WaREzkiD
```

```
ARMDe
```

```
.+
```

If you want to match zero or more, or one or more occurrences of a character, use the * and + quantifiers. The * quantifier will match zero or more occurrences of a character and the + quantifier will match one or more occurrences of a character. Consider the following:

```
[a-z]*
```

This will match zero or more occurrences of lowercase letters in a string, so the following would match:

```
ArfDoggy
67494304 // Remember **0** or more occurrences
Lepidus
WAR AND PEACE // Remember **0** or more occurrences
The Great Santini
```

Now you might be wondering whether there is a practical use for a regular expression that matches zero or more. Let us revisit the first example I gave you of a regular expression:

```
<a.*href=\"(.+)\".*>.*<\/a>
```

The previous regular expression matches '`<a`' followed by zero or more occurrences of anything (the '`.`' means anything). Then it matches '`href="`' plus one or more occurrences of anything (`.+`). Following that is a closing '`"`' and then it matches zero or more occurrences of anything before a > sign. It then matches another set of zero or more occurrences of anything before meeting a closing '`</a>`' sign. The * quantifier is useful if you're not sure whether anything is going to be there, but you want to account for it just in case.

Optional Matches Using ?

As shown previously, the * quantifier matches zero or more occurrences of an item. It basically makes that item optional to the regular expression. But what if you want to get more specific; for instance, what if you want to have an optional three-letter string? You would use the ? specifier, which basically says, "It is optional that this pattern exists." Here is an example to help illuminate this point:

```
[a-z]{3}?
```

This example would optionally match three occurrences of any lowercase character; therefore, each of the following would be valid:

```
34d3des
```

```
HDED
```

```
&(#LDJIIED
```

```
MR. KELLY
```

```
HI
```

In fact, pretty much anything at all would be valid because the match is optional. Why not just use `.*` to achieve the same effect? Read on...

PHP enables you not only to match certain types of text, it also enables you to save your matches in an array. To do this, you must enclose what you want to be saved in parentheses, like so:

```
([a-z]{4}?)[0-9]
```

If PHP found a four-character string with lowercase letters, it would be saved in either an array that you specify or the `\\1`, `\\2`, `\\3`, ... variables. (These are accessible only to `ereg_replace()`, `eregi_replace()`, and `preg_replace()`.) Examples of this will be shown in most of the recipes, so I am leaving out an explanation here.

The "or" of Regular Expressions

In PHP (and Perl), the pipe delimiter (`|`) enables you to say "This or that or this or that" (note that the keyword here is or). Here is an example to illustrate that concept:

```
(Bread|Milk|Eggs)
```

This example means that PHP will match either `Bread` or `Milk` or `Eggs`. Another place this is useful is in matching single characters, like so:

```
(a|b|c)
```

This would match either `a`, `b`, or `c`. Please note that matching single characters with an or statement is the same as

```
[abc]
```

except that using character classes whenever you can is a better programming practice because they execute much faster than the cases separated by `|`.

Well, that's it! You have now been sufficiently introduced to the concept of regular expressions and I've have just finished the first part of the introduction. Knowing the syntax of regular expressions is half the battle, but you also must have a method for problem solving to create regular expressions.

To start explaining this methodology, let us examine a sample scenario in the next section.

Mini-Problem

You want to write a regular expression that extracts information out of the `<meta>` tags (specifically the `description` and `keyword` tags).

Mini-Technique

First, let's write down two sample `meta` tags that we will match so we can see them in front of us as we build the regular expression. (This can more easily be done with the `get_meta_tags()` function, but the purpose of this exercise is to go through writing a regular expression.)

```
<meta name="description" content="This is a description of site xyz">
<meta name="keywords" content="keyword1, keyword2, keyword3">
```

Now, let's look at the first thing we want to match in each tag. In this case, it happens to be the content between two quotation marks after an equal sign. We know that the tag has to start with `<meta`, so we can draw the first part of our regular expression:

```
<meta.*name=[\'"]?(description|keywords)[\'"]?.*
```

The next item we want to match is the stuff after the = sign that comes after `content`. Our only concern is that it is something other than a single or double quotation mark, so here is the second and final part of the regular expression:

```
<meta.*name=[\'"]?(description|keywords)[\'"]?
.*content=[\'"]?([^\'"]*)[\'"]?.*>
```

Now that we have our regular expression, we need to find a function to put it in so that the regular expression can actually do its work. Because we want a case-insensitive match, we will choose the `eregi()` function:

```php
<?php
eregi('<meta.*name=[\'"]?(description|keywords)[\'"]?.*content=[\'"]?([^\'"]*)
    [\'"]?.*>', $line, $match);
?>
```

Subsequently, `$match[0]` will contain all the matching text, `$match[1]` will contain the name alone, and `$match[2]` will contain the content alone.

So, let's recap. When writing a regular expression, remember to

1. Assess the problem.

2. Write an example of the text you want to match.

3. Divide the problem into separate parts and solve those parts.

4. Put the problem back together for your final regular expression.

5. Find the right function for your needs.

6. Test and *retest*.

That's it. This is probably the longest introduction in the book, but I feel it was worth the space because regular expressions can be the most confusing and, at the same time, most powerful part of the language. The rest of this chapter is devoted to showing you different ways to solve common problems and some other neat features not covered in this introduction (for example, all the regular expression functions or look-ahead assertions). For a more advanced look at regular expressions, check out *Mastering Regular Expressions* by Jeffrey Friedl, published by O'Reilly.

5.1 Assigning the Results of a Pattern Replacement

You want to assign a new variable to the result of a pattern replacement without modifying the old one.

Technique

PHP's functions are nondestructive, which means the new string is assigned to whatever variable you choose:

```php
<?php
$str = "\t\tThis is not     …   a drill\n\n\n";
// compress multiple consecutive
// whitespace characters into one
$new_str = ereg_replace ("([\t\n ])+", "\\1", $str);
?>
```

Comments

The example is pretty trivial, but it points out a major problem that programmers encounter often. The regular expression functions in PHP do not actually affect the string on which they act, but rather return a new string based on the pattern and string that is given to them. Therefore, the following would be completely useless in a program:

```php
<?php
ereg_replace ("([\t\n ])+", "\\1", $str);
?>
```

The string itself is never modified by `ereg_replace()` and the return value is not given to anything (it just wastes processor time).

5.2 Using Perl-Compatible Regular Expressions in PHP

You want to use Perl-compatible regular expressions within PHP, either because you like them more or because you need their added functionality and speed. (I normally use them because I like their syntax so much more.)

Technique

PHP provides a set of functions for performing pattern matching using Perl-compatible regular expressions syntax via the Perl Compatible Regular Expressions Library (PCRE) included with PHP.

```php
<?php
// Non-Whitespace Character, Whitespace Character, Non-Whitespace Character
preg_match ('/(\S+)\s+(\S+)/', $line, $match);

// Match all occurrences of Non-Whitespace Character, Whitespace Character
// Non-Whitespace character, same as using the /g modifier in Perl
preg_match_all ('/(\S+)\s+(\S+)/', $file, $match);

// split $line into an array of characters
$chars = preg_split ('//', $line);

// Remove all whitespace elements of $chars
$chars = preg_grep ('/^\S+$/', $chars);

// Quote unquoted regular expression meta-characters
$input = preg_quote ($input);
?>
```

Comments

The Perl Compatible Regular Expressions Library was added in PHP version 3.0.9. When PCRE came out, it was like comfort food for me. (One of my favorite parts of Perl is its regular expression support; the other is the sort() function.) But the Perl-compatible regular expression library is not only a comfort food to converted Perl programmers, but it is also much faster and a more powerful regular expression library. (It still lacks some of the power that Perl contains, but that is discussed in the next chapter.)

Perl-compatible regular expressions are too large a topic for this book to cover. For a full discussion, I suggest O'Reilly's *Mastering Regular Expressions*. What we will do in this recipe is create an actual program in PHP using Perl-compatible regular expressions.

Mini-Problem

In the beginning, there was UNIX. UNIX begat the Internet, which begat the email system, which begat a program called uucp—an acronym for *UNIX-to-UNIX copy*. uucp used 7-bit characters, perfectly suited for its original purpose of email messages and Usenet news browsing, but woefully inadequate for handling binary files that used a full 8-bit character set. To work around this, resourceful programmers created UUencoding, which encoded 8-bit character sets to a 7-bit character set so that they could be sent over email. All modern UNIX systems come with the necessary encoding and decoding procedures. But what if you don't have UNIX decoding?

Mini-Technique

You can use PHP to convert the document back to its original format. This script combines imap8_bit with the PCRE to parse a uuencoded message provided by the user. (PHP must be installed in CGI format.)

```php
<?php
if (!isset ($argv[0])) {
    die ("You must specify an Infile");
}

$valid = false;

$fp = @fopen ($argv[0], "r") or
            die ("Cannot Open Uuencoded file");

while ($line = @fgets ($fp, 1024)) {
    if (preg_match ("/^begin\s+(\d+)\s+(.*?)/", $line, $match)) {
        $filemode  = $match[1];
        $writefile = $match[2];
        $valid = true;
        break;
    }
}

if (!$valid) {
    die ('Not a uuencoded file');
}

$fpw = @fopen ($writefile, 'w') or
            die ("Cannot Open $writefile");
```

```php
while ($line = @fgets ($fp, 1024)) {
    $decoded = imap_8bit ($line);
    if ($decoded == "\0") {
        die ("Invalid line");
    }
    fputs ($fpw, $decoded);
    if (preg_match ("/^end$/", $decoded)) {
        break;
    }
}

fclose($fpw);
fclose($fp);

chmod (oct ($filemode), $writefile);
?>
```

5.3 Incompatibilities Between the PCRE Library and Perl Regular Expressions

I'm using one of my Perl regular expressions in PHP, but it doesn't work as expected, or it generates an error.

Technique

The PCRE library is mostly compatible with Perl, but there are a few exceptions that I have listed in the discussion. If you have Perl installed on your system, you can do the following:

```php
<?php
exec("$perlscript $regex $variable", $line);
$line = implode ("\0",$line);
?>
```

Comments

The PCRE library, while extensive, has certain incompatibilities with Perl (a full list follows). So, what we can do is use a PHP workaround or make an exec call to a Perl script that we write to parse the data. (In fact, this is one of the areas in which Perl excels. When exec calls the Perl script, the first line of output is returned. However,

5.3 Incompatibilities Between the PCRE Library and Perl Regular Expressions

we discard it and all the output is stored in a user-specified array ($line). We then implode this line around the null character and get the actual array as a string.

Finally, to finish off my coverage of Perl-compatible regular expressions, here is a list of all the incompatibilities between Perl regular expressions (version 5.005) and the PCRE (from the PHP documentation):

1. As a default, a whitespace character is any character that the C function isspace() distinguishes, although it is possible to compile PCRE with alternative character type tables. Normally the isspace() matches space, formfeed, newline, carriage return, horizontal tab, and vertical tab. In Perl 5, the vertical tab is no longer included in its set of whitespace characters. The \v escape that was in the Perl documentation for a long time was never really recognized. However, the character itself was treated as whitespace at least up until 5.002. In 5.004 and 5.005, it does not match \s.

2. The PCRE does not allow repeat quantifiers on lookahead declarations. While Perl permits them, they might not mean what you might think they would mean. For example, (?!z){3} does not say that the next three characters are not "z". It just tells that the next character is not "z" three times.

3. Capturing subpatterns that occur inside of negative lookahead assertions are counted, but their entries in the offsets vector never become added. Perl sets its numerical variables from any patterns that are matched before the declaration fails to match something (subsequently succeeding), but only if the negative lookahead declaration has just one branch.

4. Though binary zero characters are supported in the subject string, they are not allowed in a pattern string because it is passed as a normal C string, terminated by zero. The escape sequence "\0" can be used in the pattern to represent a binary zero.

5. The following Perl escape sequences are not supported: \l, \u, \L, \U, \E, \Q. This is because they are a part of Perl's general string handling functions not a part of the regular expression library.

6. The Perl \G declaration is not supported at all.

7. Obviously the PCRE does not support the (?{code}) pattern set.

8. There are at the time of writing some oddities in Perl 5.005_02 concerned with the settings of captured strings when part of a pattern is repeated. For example, matching "aba" against the pattern /^(a(b)?)+$/ sets $2 to the value "b", but matching "aabbaa" against /^(aa(bb)?)+$/ leaves $2 unset. However, if the pattern is changed to /^(aa(b(b))?)+$/ then $2 (and $3) get set.

9. In Perl 5.004 $2 is set in both cases, and that is also true of PCRE. If in the future Perl changes to a consistent state that is different, PCRE may change to follow.

10. Another as yet unresolved discrepancy is that in Perl 5.005_02 the pattern /^(a)?(?(1)a|b)+$/ matches the string "a", whereas in PCRE it does not. However, in both Perl and PCRE /^(a)?a/ matched against "a" leaves $1 unset.

11. The PCRE adds unto the Perl Regular expression library in the following ways:

    (a) Although lookbehind declarations must match fixed length strings, each alternate branch of a lookbehind declaration can match a different length of string. Perl 5.005 requires them all to be of the same length.

    (b) If PCRE_DOLLAR_ENDONLY is set and PCRE_MULTILINE is not set, the $ matches only at the very end of the string.

    (c) If PCRE_EXTRA is set, a backslash without a special character class definition causes an error (i.e. \z would not be valid but \w ([a-zA-Z0-9_]) would be valid.)

    (d) If PCRE_UNGREEDY is set, the greediness of the repetition quantifiers is reversed, that is, by default they are greedy PCRE_UNGREEDY makes them by default ungreedy. (i.e. .*? is greedy when PCRE_UNGREEDY is set).

5.4 Matching over Multiple Lines

You need to write a regular expression that will match in a string containing more than one line, however, the special characters ".", "^", and "$" do not work.

Technique

With the basic POSIX standard regular expressions provided with PHP, matching over one line is pretty hard. But the PCRE library makes this simple. Just use the Perl regular expressions with the /m or /s modifier or use both in conjunction. The /m operator enables you to match "^" and "$" next to a newline (it does not normally allow this). For example, /Mary$/m will match all occurrences of Mary before a newline (not just before the end of the string).

The /s modifier will allow the "." to match newlines as well as any other character (besides the \0 character). The "." treats a newline just like a NULL character (\0) if the /s modifier is not set.

Comments

It might not be easy to match over multiple lines without PCRE installed, but it is possible. The following is a workaround:

```php
<?php
$lines = explode ("\n", $text);

foreach ($lines as $line) {
    if (ereg ('Mary$', $line)) {
        $matches[] = $line;
    }
}
?>
```

However, look at the same thing implementing the PCRE library:

```php
<?php
preg_match ("/Mary$/m", $text, $matches);
?>
```

It is obvious that the PCRE solution is not only much faster but also more elegant.

Let's take a small, practical example of matching over multiple lines. The following is a small program that, when given a file, opens it, and converts all lines that start with "Heading *X*" to <h*X*> tags:

```php
<?php

$fn = isset ($argv[0]) ? $argv[0] : 'php://stdin';
$text = @file ($fn);
$text = preg_replace ("/^Heading\s+([0-5])\s*:(.*?)/m", "<h\\1>\\2</h\\1>",
        $text);
print $text;
?>
```

As a side note: Inside of a regular expression that uses the /s modifier, the meaning of the . operator changes to [^\n] (any character but a newline).

5.5 Finding a Specific Occurrence of a Match

You want to find the *n*th occurrence of a certain match. For example, you want to locate the second occurrence of a word starting with the letter o in the phrase, "The quick brown fox jumped over the lazy old dog."

Technique

Use the `preg_match_all()` function to keep track:

```php
<?php
$str = "The quick brown fox jumped over the lazy old dog";

// Find all the matches of 'the', $matches[2][0] will contain
// the first match, and $matches[2][1] will contain the second match
preg_match_all ("/(^|\s+)(o\w+)($|\s+)/i", $str, $matches, PREG_PATTERN_ORDER);
?>
```

Comments

This is one of those places where PHP is incompatible with Perl as far as the regular expressions are concerned. In PHP, we use the `preg_match_all()` function to find the occurrence number we need. But in Perl 5, we use the `/g` modifier to specify a global match.

The `preg_match_all()` function returns a two-dimensional array. The structure of the array differs depending on the value of the last argument, which can be `PREG_PATTERN_ORDER` or `PREG_SET_ORDER`. (If you don't pass it, it defaults to `PREG_PATTERN_ORDER`.)

For `PREG_PATTERN_ORDER`, the results are ordered so that `$matches[0]` is an array of strings matched by the full pattern, `$matches[1]` is an array of strings matched by the first parenthesized subpattern, and so on. If you use `PREG_SET_ORDER`, however, the results are ordered so that `$matches[0]` is an array of the first set of matches (starting from full match and proceeding through subpattern matches), `$matches[1]` is an array of second set of matches, and so on.

The following code effectively illustrates the difference:

```php
<?php
preg_match_all ("|<[^>]+>(.*)</[^>]+>|U",
                "<i>Test: </i><div align=left>A Simple Experiment</div>",
                $matches,
                PREG_PATTERN_ORDER);

print "{$matches[0][0]}, {$matches[0][1]}\n";
print "{$matches[1][0]}, {$matches[1][1]}\n";
?>
```

which prints:

```
<i>Test: </i>, <div align=left>A Simple Experiment</div>
Test: , A Simple Experiment
```

The Second (PREG_SET_ORDER):

```
<?php
preg_match_all ("|<[^>]+>(.*)</[^>]+>|U",
                "<i>Test: </i><div align=left>A Simple Experiment</div>",
                $matches,
                PREG_SET_ORDER);

print "{$matches[0][0]}, {$matches[0][1]}\n";
print "{$matches[1][0]}, {$matches[1][1]}\n";
?>
```

Yields:

```
<i>Test: </i>, Test:
<div align=left>A Simple Experiment</div>, A Simple Experiment
```

5.6 Working with Delimited Records

You want to read values separated by a record separator that you define. This can be useful when parsing large complex files.

Technique

Use the explode() function to divide your string into an array from your specified record separator:

```
<?php
$line = explode (':', $line);
?>
```

Or, if you need more power, use the preg_split() function to tear apart your string:

```
<?php
// split HTML by tags
$text = preg_split ('/<[^>]+>/', $html);
?>
```

Comments

Separating records by text can be extremely useful if you have large text files and the normal line break just won't cut it as a separator. This is especially appropriate when handling binary file uploads with enormous sizes.

Use the `explode()` function whenever possible because it gives a great speed increase over the `preg_split()` function. However, if you need more power, the `preg_split()` function is about as powerful as you can get.

5.7 Extracting Specific Lines

You want to extract all lines from one starting pattern through an ending pattern, or something from a starting number to an ending number. For instance, you wanted to start operating on a newsgroup file only after all the headers had been stripped.

Technique

Use a Boolean value and some `if` statements:

```php
<?php
$in_range = false;
while ($line = @fgets ($fp, 1024)) {
    if (!$in_range && ereg ("beginpattern", $line)) {
        $in_range = true;
    } elseif (ereg ("endpattern", $line)) {
        break;
    }

    if ($in_range) {
        //..do if condition met
        // here's where we operate on $line
    }
}
?>
```

Comments

In the code, we simply match each line of the input against the beginning pattern, and once we find it, we set `$in_range` variable to `true`. Subsequently, the special code is executed on every line of the input until we match against the ending pattern. This could easily be modified so that it incremented through a range of line numbers:

```php
<?php
$start_line = 4;
$end_line   = 10;
$i  = 0;
while ($line = @fgets ($fp, 1024)) {
    if ($i >= $start_line && $i <= $end_line ) {
        // .. Do what you want to do here
    } elseif ($i > $end_line) {
        break;
    }
    $i++;
}
?>
```

One place this is useful is when parsing newsgroup messages. The following script will parse a newsgroup message and output the body to the browser:

```php
<html>
<head>
    <title> News-mess.txt body </title>
</head>
<body>
<?php

$fp = @fopen ("news-message.txt", "r") or
                die ("Cannot open news-message.txt");

$blanks = 0;
while ($line = fgets($fp, 1024)) // 1kb buffer
{
    if (ereg("^[[:space:]]*$", $line)){
        $blanks++;
    }

    if ($blanks >= 2) {
        print nl2br (htmlspecialchars ($line));
    }
}

@fclose($fp) or die("Cannot close news-message.txt");

?>
</body>
</html>
```

5.8 Checking Characters

You want to check whether a value contains only alphabetic characters.

Technique

Use eregi() in conjunction with character classes:

```php
<?php
if (eregi ("^[a-z]+$", $line)) {
    // .. do if true
} else {
    // .. do if false
}
?>
```

Or use the predefined character class along with ereg():

```php
<?php
if (ereg ("^[[:alpha:]]+$", $line)) {
    // .. do if true
} else {
    // .. do if false
}
?>
```

Comments

In the first solution, we use eregi(), which performs a case-insensitive query using a specified pattern (in this case, [a-z]). As discussed in the introduction, the regular expression [a-z] is a character class that will match any lowercase letter from a to z. Because we are using a case-insensitive search, [a-z] will match any character. We put a plus after the [a-z] character class to indicate that there must be one or more occurrences. The entire regular expression is enclosed within ^ and $, meaning that the entire string must match the pattern (this is also discussed in the introduction).

In the second solution, we simply substitute eregi() (case-insensitive) with ereg() (case-sensitive), and instead of [a-z] we use [[:alpha:]] which is a predefined character set that matches any alphabetic character. PHP provides several of these predefined character classes, listed in the following table.

Name	Description
[[:alnum:]]	All alphanumeric characters [a-zA-Z0-9]
[[:alpha:]]	All alphabetic characters [a-z]
[[:blank:]]	Tab and space [\t]
[[:cntrl:]]	All the control characters
[[:digit:]]	All decimal digits [0-9]
[[:graph:]]	All printable characters except space
[[:lower:]]	All lowercase letters [a-z]
[[:print:]]	All printable characters
[[:punct:]]	Punctuation marks [\.,;:-]
[[:space:]]	All whitespace characters
[[:upper:]]	All the uppercase letters [A-Z]
[[:xdigit:]]	The set of hexadecimal digits

These are just easy ways to access commonly used character classes. To negate reserved classes, make sure that you put the ^ inside the first bracket:

```
[^[:space:]] // Match anything that isn't a space
```

5.9 Validating Web Data

In this day and age, one would have to be insane to blindly accept data from users on the Web and do any operations on it. Therefore, we need a function for making sure that hackers cannot harm our system.

Technique

To make sure that the users do not do anything when we open a pipe or use any program execution functions, we need to use the escapeshellcmd() function shown here:

```php
<?php
exec (escapeshellcmd ($input), $output);
?>
```

You also might want to test whether a user has actually filled out his name. For this, we use the `empty()` function:

```php
<?php
if (!empty ($name)) {
    die ("You have to supply your name");
}
?>
```

Comments

The `escapeshellcmd()` functions escapes all shell meta-characters, rendering user input harmless to you and the security of your system. I recommend that you make it a habit to always run the `escapeshellcmd()` before putting user data into a program execution function (`system()`, `exec()`, `passthru()`, or `popen()`).

The `empty()` function tests whether the name field has been filled out, not whether the name field is valid. So, I could say that my name was "foo" and it wouldn't really matter to PHP as long as $name was filled out. That's about as precise as you can get with validating names. (Okay, you can check for alphabetical characters, but anybody with some intelligence can get around that.) More precision is available when checking things such as a user's email, but that will be addressed in later recipes.

5.10 Validating an E-mail Address

You want to do simple validation on an e-mail address.

Technique

Use the following regular expression. (The double escapes are for double quotation marks; use single escapes for single quotation marks.)

```
^([a-z0-9_]|\\-|\\.)+@(([a-z0-9_]|\\-)+\\.)+[a-z]{2,4}$
```

Comments

To call this code, you must use `eregi()`. (`ereg()` will not work because the search needs to be case-insensitive.) Here is how you might call this code in a Web page:

```php
<?php
if (!eregi ("^([a-z0-9_]|\\-|\\.)+@(([a-z0-9_]|\\-)+\\.)+[a-z]{2,4}$", $email))
    die ("Invalid E-mail");
?>
```

The previous regular expression is a PHP-compatible global e-mail-checking regular expression, but it is not the most secure way of checking an e-mail address. For example, somebody@something-foo.cde would be validated because it is in the correct format, but it is obviously not a valid e-mail address.

5.11 Checking the Syntax of a Regular Expression

You want to let users use their own patterns or you just need to check your own regular expressions.

Technique
Either set the error_reporting level in your php.ini file or use the error_reporting function to set an E_WARNING level of tolerance:

```
<?php
error_reporting(E_WARNING);

$line = "maray";
ereg("(marray", $line, $ar); // Invalid Regex
?>
```

Comments
The error_reporting() function is very useful for detecting blatant errors in your regular expressions such as the error here (a missing closing parenthesis). However, do note that error_reporting() is not a complete syntax checker, so your code is still subject to many mistakes and exploits.

The error_reporting() function should be used purely for debugging rather than for validating users' regular expressions. It does not check whether the regular expression makes sense, but rather whether the regular expression displays valid syntax. When you create programs, you should always set error_reporting() to the most stringent level possible (E_ALL). Then when the program is done with testing, you can lower the level of error_reporting().

5.12 Checking for Duplicate Words

You want to find duplicate words in a paragraph or in a string.

Technique

Use the array methods to check for duplicate words in a single string:

```php
<?php
$seen = array();
$paragraph = "The ugly lady chased the handsome man";

$paragraph = preg_split ("/\s+/", $paragraph);

foreach ($paragraph as $word) {
    $seen[strtolower ($word)]++;
}

print "There were $seen[the] occurrences of the word 'the'";
?>
```

Comments

This script would increment up to the number of case-insensitive occurrences of each word. To access the number of occurrences of a given word, just place the word as the string index of the array.

If you want to get the string position of each of the duplicates, you can use the following function:

```php
<?php

function get_dupes ($str) {
    $str = strtolower ($str);
    $words = preg_split ("/\s+/", $str);
    $seen = array();
    $start_pos = array();
    $i = 0;

    foreach ($words as $word) {  // loop through an array of words
        // 2-d associative array containing word positions
        $seen[$word][$i] = strpos ($str, $word, $start_pos[$word]);
        // assign the starting position to avoid repeats
        $start_pos[$word] = $seen[$word][$i] + strlen ($word);
        $i++;
    }

    return ($seen);
}
```

```
$str = "The The the Hello Truck Hello The the Jester Rye";
$duplicates = get_dupes ($str);
var_dump ($duplicates);


?>
```

5.13 Abbreviating Input

You have a bunch of commands, but you don't want to make the user type them in.
Therefore, you need to find a way to let the user abbreviate his input as much as
possible.

Technique

Create associative array mapping and then get the substring of the input, like so:

```php
<?php
function do_function ($option) {
    switch ($option) {
        case "Send":
            print "Sent";
            break;
        case "Delete":
            print "Deleted";
            break;
        case "Open Mail":
            print "Mail Opened";
            break;
        case "Read Message":
            print "Message Read";
            break;
        case "Reply-to Message":
            print "Reply-to Message";
            break;
    }
}

$mappings = array ("S" => "Send",
                   "D" => "Delete",
                   "O" => "Open Mail",
                   "R" => "Read Message",
                   "T" => "Reply-to Message");
```

```
do_function ($mappings[strtoupper (substr ($input, 0, 1))]);
?>
```

Comments

Allowing for abbreviations makes your function more forgiving of user input, and saves your user the time of having to type in exactly what he wants. This function creates an associative array in which the first letter the user enters is really all that matters.

CHAPTER 6

Handling Files

"These are the prerogatives of genius: to know without having learned; to draw just conclusions from unknown premises; to discern the soul of things."

Ambrose Bierce, Collected Works

6.0 Introduction

File access is unarguably an important feature in almost any language, but file access is especially important in Web applications programming. This is so because the Web is stateless—the program usually ends execution and HTML is returned to the user. (Applets are an exception; they end when the user exits the Web page.) Files (and databases, which are in essence structured files) enable us to remember the user's last visit or, in some cases, even her last action.

The purpose of this chapter is to show you how to access files and different ways of manipulating files and their contents. You access files in PHP much like you do in C: First, you open the file and assign the returned file pointer to a variable, and then you can read and write (depending on what mode you use) the file contents by accessing the file pointer. Here is an example of reading a file and then printing it out line-by-line:

```php
<?php

$fp = @fopen ("sample.txt", "r") or
  die("Cannot Open sample.txt");

while ($line = @fgets ($fp, 1024)) {
    print $line;
}
```

```
@fclose($fp) or die("Cannot Close sample.txt");
?>
```

Line 1: Start off the PHP document; I hope this is familiar to you.

Line 3–4: Open sample.txt with read permissions (`"r"`). The @ suppresses PHP's warning messages. We use or `die...` to print out a custom error message if the file opening fails.

Line 6: Start off a `while` loop to move through each line in the file. Now use the `fgets()` function, which has the following syntax:

```
string fgets (int filepointer, int length);
```

We then assign the string returned by `fgets()` to `$line` so that we can manipulate or print `$line`.

Line 7: Print the value of `$line`.

Line 8: Close the file with `fclose`. This is good practice even though the file is automatically closed when the script stops executing.

Line 9: Close the PHP document.

Perhaps it will help some of you who speak other languages to see the earlier script in a different language. So, for all you Perl programmers, here is the Perl equivalent of the previous script (the `while` loop can be simplified to `print while <FH>;`):

```
#!/usr/bin/perl -w
use strict;

print "Content-type: text/html\n\n";

open FH, "< sample.txt" or die "Cannot open sample.txt: $!";
while (<FH>) {
    print;
}
close FH or die "Cannot close sample.txt: $!";
```

Here is the Python equivalent:

```
fp = fopen("sample.txt", "r")

print "Content-type: text/html\n\n"
```

```
while 1:
    line = fp.readline()
    if not line: break
    print line
```

The rest of this chapter illuminates some of the tricks of accessing files in PHP.

6.1 Checking Whether a File Exists

You want to know whether a file exists before you try to perform any operations involving it.

Technique

Use the file_exists() function, which will return true (1) if the file exists and false (0) if the file does not exist:

```php
<?php
$fn = "/home/designmm/public_html/favorite_sites.info";

if (!file_exists($fn)) {
    die("File $fn does not exist");
}

$fp = @fopen ($fn, 'a')
  or die ("Cannot open $fn for append access");

// Add a favorite site to the list
fputs ($fp, "http://www.zend.com/\n");

@fclose ($fp);
?>
```

Comments

In this example, we simply use file_exists() to check whether the specified file exists. The file_exists() function is a slow function due to the fact that it must perform a stat() on the file in question. Therefore, the results are cached for the duration of the script's execution. The following is an example in which file_exists() will not work as expected:

```php
<?php

$fn = "/usr/local/files/somefile.txt";
```

```
if  (!file_exists ($fn)) {
    $fp = fopen($fn, "w");
}

if (file_exists ($fn)) {
    echo "The File exists";
}




?>
```

If you run this script, you will notice that no output is sent (if the file does not exist, and in this case it doesn't). The reason is that the results of the first `file_exists()` function call have already been cached into memory, so the second time `file_exists()` is called, nothing will change. It is the same as doing the following:

```
<?php

$fn = "/usr/local/somefiles/";
$exists = file_exists ($fn);

if (!$exists) {
    $fp = fopen ($fn, "w");
}

if ($exists) {
    print "The File Exists";
}
?>
```

6.2 Checking File Permissions

You want to get the file permissions on a file.

Technique

Use the `fileperms()` function to accurately get the number value of the permissions, or use the `is_*` (`is_dir()`, `is_executable()`, `is_file()`, `is_link()`, `is_readable()`, and `is_writable()`) functions to get human-usable results.

Using `fileperms()`:

```php
<?php
if ((fileperms ($fn) & 0777) != 0644) {
    chmod ($fn, 0644); // rw-r--r-
}
?>
```

Using the `is_*` functions:

```php
<?php
if (!is_readable ($fn)) {
    chmod ($fn, 0777); // rwxrwxrwx
}
?>
```

Comments

The `fileperms()` function returns the current permissions numerically (in octal form). This is a more advanced way of checking the file permissions. The bits making up the permissions returned by `fileperms()` are described in more detail in the man page for the `mknod()` function in UNIX. If you simply want to check whether the file is available for read access, write access, and so on, use the `is_*` functions.

Please be aware that these functions are costly on the system, and therefore they are cached. To make multiple calls on the same file, you need to use the `clearstatcache()` function. For more information see recipe 6.7.

6.3 Creating a Temporary File

You want to create a temporary file to store program data.

Technique

Use the `tempnam()` function, which generates a temporary filename in a specified directory:

```php
<?php
$tmp = tempnam ("/home/designmm/public_html", "foobar");
?>
```

Comments

The `tempnam()` function always creates a unique file in the directory specified (`/home/designmm/public_html`) and with the prefix specified (`foobar`). After the file is created, the name of the file is returned (in this case, we assign it to `$tmp_file_name`). After the script is done, make sure to delete the file using the `unlink()` function:

```php
<?php
$tmp = tempnam ("C:\\", "tmpFile");

$fp = @fopen ($tmp, "w");
if (!$fp) {
    die ("Cannot open $tmp");
}

fputs ($fp, "Hello World\n");
fputs ($fp, "Another Line in a Temporary File");

@fclose ($fp);

$fp = @fopen ($tmp, "r");
if (!$fp) {
    die ("Cannot open $tmp");
}

while ($line = @fgets ($fp, 1024)) {
    print $line;
}

@fclose ($fp);

@unlink ($tmp)
    or die ("Cannot delete $tmp");
?>
```

Note that if the file directory is not found, the file will be created in the computer's temporary directory (usually stored in the $TMP environment variable).

6.4 Storing a File into Your Program

You want to copy an entire file into memory all in one move.

Technique

If you want to load the file into a variable, use the `fread()` function in conjunction with the `filesize()` function:

```php
<?php
$fp = @fopen ("http://www.designmultimedia.com/", "r") or
  die ("Cannot open URL: designmultimedia.com");

$f_contents = fread ($fp, filesize ($fp));

@fclose ($fp);
?>
```

Or, if you want to read the file into an array of lines, use the `file()` function:

```php
$f_contents = file('http://www.designmultimedia.com/');
```

Finally, here's an alternative way (using `file()`) to load the contents into one big variable:

```php
$f_contents = implode ("", file ('http://www.designmultimedia.com/'));
```

Comments

In PHP, as shown here, there are multiple ways to do the same thing. If we wanted to copy a file into memory line-by-line, we could also do the following:

```php
<?php
$fp = @fopen( "ftp://ftp.designmultimedia.com", "r" ) or
          die("Cannot Open FTP Connection: ftp.designmultimedia.com");

while ($line = @fgets ($fp, 1024)) {
    $f_contents .= $line;
}

@fclose ($fp);
?>
```

6.5 Opening a File

You want to open a file. This can be useful in a plethora of ways, including saving form results, reading records, storing records, and printing files.

Technique

Use `fopen()` to open a file and assign the pointer to a variable:

```php
<?php
$fp = @fopen ("somefile.src", "r") or
  die("Could not open somefile.src for read access");
?>
```

Comments

The `fopen()`function opens a pointer to the file on the filesystem. You can then work with that pointer with the following functions: `fclose()`, `feof()`, `fgetc()`, `fgetcsv()`, `fgets()`, `fgetss()`, `flock()`, `fpassthru()`, `fputs()`, `fread()`, `fseek()`, `ftell()`, and `fwrite()`.

The first argument of `fopen()` is the file to be opened. It can be a local file, a Web address (must start with `http://` and trailing slashes must be provided), or an FTP server (must start with `ftp://`). The second argument of `fopen()` is the mode in which you want to open the file. In this case, we open the file for read access. The following is a table of the codes that you can use to open a file and their corresponding modes.

Code	Mode
`"r"`	Open with read access; file pointer is at the beginning of the file.
`"r+"`	Open with read and write access; file pointer is at the beginning of the file.
`"w"`	-Open with write access; file pointer at the beginning of the file. If the file exists, delete its contents. If the file does not exist, create it.
`"w+"`	-Open with read and write access; file pointer at the beginning of the file. If the file exists, delete its contents. If the file does not exist, create it.
`"a"`	-Open with write access; file pointer at the end of the file. If the file does not exist, create it.
`"a+"`	-Open with read and write access; file pointer at the end of file. If the file does not exist, create it.

> **Note**
> Appending a `"b"` to any of these codes will tell PHP that the file is binary. (This is useless on UNIX, but needed on systems such as Windows where there is a difference between binary and ASCII files.) Also, you cannot use any other mode besides the `"r"` mode when opening Web addresses or when connecting to FTP servers.

fopen() is just one way to open a file. You can also use the file() function to open a file and return an array of lines like the following, which prints out a file line-by-line:

```php
<?php
$f_contents = file('somefile.src');
foreach ($f_contents as $line) {
    print $line;
}
?>
```

6.6 Handling Binary Data Safely

You want to handle a binary file, but your data keeps getting mangled.

Technique

Although fopen() is binary-safe (using the b flag), you have to use fread() and fwrite() when accessing binary files instead of using functions such as fputs() and fgets().

Good:

```php
$fp = @fopen($fn, "ab+")
  or die ("Cannot open $fn in 'ab+' mode");
fwrite ($fp, "This is a binary safe file write");
fseek ($fp, 0);
$f_contents = fread ($fp, filesize($fp));
@fclose ($fp);
```

Bad:

```php
$fp = @fopen ($fn, "a");
fputs ($fp, "This is not Binary Safe");
fseek ($fp,0);
while ($line = @fgets($fp, 1024)) {
    print "reading line by line, not binary safe...\n";
}
@fclose ($fp);
```

Comments

If your systems don't distinguish between binary and text files (like UNIX), you don't have to worry about placing the "b" in the mode for fopen(). However, this syntax is important for systems such as Windows, which distinguish between binary and text files. Therefore, if you are writing for portability, use the "b" even if you will be using the script on a UNIX box.

fwrite() and fread() are both binary-safe, meaning that they don't mangle your binary data. However, functions such as fputs() and fgets() are not binary safe. Therefore, even if you open your file with the "b" flag, there is still a possibility that your binary data will be messed up in the translation.

When handling binary data in PHP, there are some functions that will support it and some functions that will mangle it. As a general rule, I suggest that you test and retest your script for all possible cases when you are handling binary data.

6.7 Flushing the Cache

You want to call the status functions (stat(), lstat(), file_exists(), is_writeable(), is_readable(), is_executable(), is_file(), is_dir(), is_link(), filectime(), fileatime(), filemtime(), fileinode(), filegroup(), fileowner(), filesize(), filetype(), and fileperms()), more than one time on the same file in your program, but they are cached by your server.

Technique

Use the clearstatcache() function before calling any of the previously listed status functions.

```php
<?php

if (fileperms ($fn) < 644) {
    chmod ($fn, 0644);
}

clearstatcache();

if (fileperms ($fn) < 644) {
    die('chmod failed');
}

?>
```

Comments

Because the status functions are so taxing on the system when called, the results of these functions are cached for faster access. Therefore, you must clear the stat cache with the `clearstatcache()` function.

Please note that results from the status functions are cached only for the lifetime of the program execution, meaning that if you call the function only once for a particular file, you do not need to clear the cache. In the following example, a `clearstatcache()` function call would be unnecessary.

```php
<?php
if (file_exists($fn)) {
    print "$fn exists";
}

if (is_readable ($fn)) {
    print "$fn is readable";
}

unlink ($fn);

if (file_exists ($new_file)) {
    print "$new_file exists";
}
?>
```

6.8 Locking Files

You want to make sure that, when you are accessing a file, no other programs or processes are accessing that same file.

Technique

Use PHP's `flock()` function:

Lockfile.inc

```php
<?php
function lock ($fp, $lock_level=LOCK_EX) {
    @flock ($fp, $lock_level)
        or die ("Cannot flock filepointer to $lock_level");
}
```

```php
function unlock ($fp) {
    @flock ($fp, LOCK_UN)
        or die ("Cannot Release the Lock");
}
?>
```

Then use these wrappers as follows:

```php
<?php
include("Lockfile.inc");

$filename = "/home/designmm/www/index.df";

$fp = @fopen($filename, "w")
        or die("Cannot Open $filename for write access");

// Always exclusively lock a file when you are writing to it
// this is the same as flock($fp, LOCK_EX);
lock ($fp);

fwrite ($fp, "Hello");

// Unlock the file, this is the same as flock($fp, LOCK_UN);
unlock ($fp);

@fclose ($fp);
?>
```

Comments

When accessing files concurrently (especially for write access), there is a very real possibility of your files becoming corrupt. The solution to this is flock(). flock() takes a file pointer and sets a certain access level for that file. PHP supports a portable way to lock complete files in an advisory way (which means that all accessing programs have to use the same way of locking or it will not work).

Let me further explain: The flock() function is sort of like a crossing guard. It tells the different cooperating processes when they can and cannot access the files in different modes (shared and exclusive). A file may have multiple concurrent shared locks, meaning that many processes may have a shared lock on the file at the same time. However, an exclusive lock (which should be used when you write to files), allows only one user at a time to have a lock on the file. That means other processes requesting shared locks or exclusive locks have to wait until the already existing exclusive lock is released before they can have access to the file.

However, this will affect only programs that implement portable file advisory locking. If another process does not respect or recognize the lock that `flock()` has put on your file, that process will simply ignore your existing lock. The bottom line is that for `flock()` to work, all programs modifying the file must respect `flock()`.

`flock()` uses three codes to specify lock operations: `LOCK_SH` to specify a shared lock, `LOCK_EX` to specify an exclusive lock, and `LOCK_UN` to release the lock. If you do not want `flock()` to block while it acquires a lock, add `LOCK_NB` to the code you are using. So, creating a shared lock would be `LOCK_SH + LOCK_NB`, creating an exclusive lock would be `LOCK_EX + LOCK_NB`, and releasing a lock would be `LOCK_UN + LOCK_NB`.

You must tell your program to `die` if `flock()` does not work, otherwise your program will hang until `flock()` locks. To accomplish this, you can do the following:

```php
<?php

$fp = @fopen ($fn, "r")
  or die("Cannot open $fn");
@flock ($fp, LOCK_SH + LOCK_NB)
  or die ("Cannot Get Shared lock");
@fclose($fp)
  or die ("Cannot close $fn");
?>
```

6.9 Getting the Free Space Available on a Specified Drive

You want to see how much free space is available in a directory or on a certain drive.

Technique

Use the `diskfreespace()` function, which returns the number of bytes available in a certain drive or directory:

```php
$free_space = diskfreespace("C:\\");
```

Comments

Finding out the amount of free space in a directory seems like a trivial thing, sort of like those background faders that they have for JavaScript, or "under construction" signs on a Web page. To an extent, this is the case, but the `diskfreespace()` function can be very helpful when debugging or when you need to find out how much free space you have to work with when writing extensible scripts.

A little bit about the internals of the `diskfreespace()` function call: On Windows NT|95|98|2000, the `diskfreespace()` function—if available—makes the `GetDiskFreeSpaceEx()` function call; otherwise, it uses the `GetDiskFreeSpace()` function call. On other operating systems, it uses the `statvfs` or `statfs` function calls.

6.10 Displaying a Textfile to the User

You want to print an entire textfile to the user, but do not want to have to loop through the file line-by-line.

Technique

If you want to work with part of a file and then pass through the rest of the file to the screen, use `fpassthru()`. The `fpassthru()` function takes a file pointer and "passes thru" the remaining contents of the file to standard output (`STDOUT`):

```php
<?php
$fp = @fopen("some_file.txt", "r")
  or die ("");
    $twenty_bytes = fread($fp, 20);
    fpassthru ($fp); // Print out the rest of the file
@fclose ($fp);
?>
```

If you just want to print the entire file, use the `readfile()` function:

```php
<?php
    readfile ("http://www.perl.com/");
?>
```

You can also use a combination of `file()` and `implode()` to print a complete file:

```php
<?php
    print implode ("\n", file ('http://www.webreference.com'));
?>
```

Comments

The last solution is sort of a hack. What we do is fetch the specified file as an array of lines, and then `implode` (join) that array around the newline (`\n`) character. Unless you are fetching the entire file into a variable, it is much better to use the `readfile()` function for these cases. The `readfile()` function is basically like `fpassthru()` without the fat: It opens a file and prints it to the browser.

6.11 Manipulating Standard I/O Streams

You want to read from or write to the standard streams.

Technique

PHP provides access to the standard I/O streams via the `php://` type of server. (It's weird, I know, but it makes it easier on the C side.)

```php
<?php
$fp = @fopen("php://stdin", "r") or
  die("Cannot access Standard In");
//... manipulate STDIN with the different file access functions
fclose($fp);
?>
```

Comments

`STDIN`, `STDOUT`, and `STDERR` are the common input, output, and error streams for most programming languages. However, PHP has traditionally been a Web-scripting language, so access to these streams is a fairly new feature with version 3.013. For the uninitiated, here is a description of each of the streams:

`STDIN`

This is standard input; this is either what you type in at the command prompt or data that is sent from a post request.

`STDOUT`

This is standard output; it is the stream for normal data output.

`STDERR`

This is standard error; this is where the error messages are usually output. You can use this if you want to log errors instead of printing them to the screen.

The following is an example of using STDERR to send errors to the standard error stream:

```php
<?php
include_once 'DB.php';

function log_error ($message = "error") {
    error_log ($message, "php://stderr", 3);
}

$dbh = DB::connect('mysql://sterling:secret@localhost/dbname');

if (DB::isError ($dbh)) {
    $errmsg = sprintf ('MySQL Error [%d]: %s',
                        $dbh->getCode(), $dbh->getMessage());
    log_error ($errmsg) && die ($errmsg);
}

$stmt = "SELECT * FROM tablename";

$sth = $dbh->query ($stmt);

if (DB::isError ($sth)) {
    $errmsg = sprintf ('MySQL Error [%d]: %s',
                        $dbh->getCode(), $dbh->getMessage());
    log_error ($errmsg) && die ($errmsg);
}

$sth->free();
$dbh->close();
?>
```

6.12 Reading a File Line-by-Line

You have a file that has long lines split over two or more lines, with backslashes indicating that a continuation line follows. You want to put those lines back together. Shells, scripts, makefiles, and many other scripting or configuration languages let you use backslashes to break a long line into several shorter ones.

Technique

Build up complete lines one at a time until you reach one without a backslash:

```php
<?php

$is_more =0;
while ($buf = @fgets($fp, 1024)) {
    trim($buf);
    if (substr($buf, -1) == _\\_){
        $line .= substr($buf, 0, -1);
        $is_more = 1;
        continue;
    } else {
        $line = $is_more ? $line . $buf : $buf;
        $is_more = 0;
    }
    //...Work with $line here
}
?>
```

Comments

Here is an example of a file that this program would parse:

```
Here is some text \
Next Line after the continuation character
```

What the code does to parse these files is as follows: First, read the file line-by-line in the `while` loop, and trim all whitespace on either end. If the line has a continuation character at the end, append $buf to $line, set $is_more to `true`, and move on to the next line in the file. Otherwise, assign the buffer to $line and set $is_more to 0. Then we process the full line and continue on to the next line.

6.13 Working with a File Word-by-Word

You want to perform a particular action separately on every word in a file.

Technique

Load the file into an array of lines, implode it into a single variable, and split the variable by spaces:

```php
<?php
$f_contents = preg_split ("/\s+/", implode ("", file ($fn)));
?>
```

Comments

Splitting up a file by words can be tricky because one person might consider "words" to mean everything but whitespace (as we did here), whereas another person will consider as words all the words in the English language (or Korean, or Latin, or French, and so on). To summarize, the term *words* is not at all clearly defined for programmers. So, the best way to work with a file word-by-word is to split a file by whitespace (no definition of *words* has whitespace in it), and then test the criterion for each individual non-whitespace character.

Here is an example that will test for duplicates of words in a file:

```php
<?php
$f_contents = preg_split ("/\s+/", implode ("", file ($fn)));

foreach ($f_contents as $word) {
    $ar[$word]++;
}
print "the following words have duplicates\n";
foreach ($ar as $word => $word_count) {
    if ($word_count > 1) {
        print "Word: $word\nNumber Of Occurrences: $word_count\n\n";
    }
}
?>
```

Note that even this simple script is not perfect. For example, Massachusetts Institute of Technology would not be equated with MIT. Whenever you have a system dealing with humans, you will not catch all the exceptions; you just have to test and retest until you catch all the common ones.

This solution requires more memory at a single point in time than if we had read the file line-by-line; therefore, when dealing with extremely large files:

```php
<?php
$fp = fopen ($fn, 'r') or die("Cannot open file $fn");
while ($line = fgets($fp,1024)) {
    $words = preg_split ('/\s+/', $line);
    //... manipulate all the words in line, see above techniques
}
```

```
fclose($fp) or die("Cannot open file $fn");
?>
```

6.14 Processing a File in Reverse

You want to process each line of a text file in reverse.

Technique

Read all the lines into an array and then reverse the array to loop through it (the code illuminates my meaning):

```
<?php
$f_contents = array_reverse (file ($fn));
foreach ($f_contents as $backwards_line) {
    print $backwards_line;
}
?>
```

Comments

There are certain limitations on accessing files, and not being inherently able to loop backward through files is one of those limitations. Therefore, the simplest way is simply to load the file into an array of lines, reverse the array, and then process the array. You can also loop backward through the file lines to avoid the expense of array_reverse():

```
<?php
$f_contents = file ($fn);
for ($n = count ($f_contents) - 1; $n >= 0; $n--)
    print $f_contents[$n];
?>
```

6.15 Parsing a File with Pattern Separators

You need to process files separated by some pattern separator, something like the following:

```
First Name -|- Last Name -|- E-mail -|-Address -|- City
➥-|- State -|- Zip -|- Date -|- Comments
```

Technique

Use `explode()` to split by the pattern separator (`-|-` in this case) and then use `list` to capture the returned values:

```php
<?php
while ($line = @fgets ($fp, 1024)) {
    list ($firstname,  $lastname,  $email,
          $address,    $city,      $state,
          $zip,        $date,      $comments) = explode ("-|-", $line);

          // ... do some stuff with the variables
}
?>
```

Comments

This is a pretty simple recipe. Basically, the file is read line-by-line, and each line is subsequently split up into smaller segments (separated by `-|-`). We then assign these segments to variables via the `list` statement. If you want to create variables from the values, you can use "variable" variables or "soft" references (as they are known in Perl), which create a variable from the value of another variable:

```php
<?php
while ($line = @fgets ($fp, 1024)) {
    list ($firstname,  $lastname,  $email,
          $address,    $city,      $state,
          $zip,        $date,      $comments) = explode ("-|-", $line);

//if first name is Sterling then this would
// assign the value of $email to $Sterling
    $$firstname = $email
}
?>
```

If you are reading fixed-length records, you can use the `unpack()` function to parse the file faster:

```php
<?php
while ($line = @fgets ($fp, 1024)) {
    list ($firstname,  $lastname,  $email,
          $address,    $city,      $state,
          $zip,        $date,      $comments) =
```

```
        array_values (unpack ("A20first/A20last/A40email/A10addr/A19city/
                              A2state/A5zip/A7date/A250comments", $line));

        # ... do some stuff with the variables
    }
?>
```

For a full discussion of unpack(), refer to recipe 1.1.

6.16 Changing a Specific Record

You need to read a particular record from a binary file containing fixed-length records, change the value of the record, and then write the record back.

Technique

Read the old record, pack the updated values, seek to the previous address, and then write the updated record back to the file:

```php
<?php
$address = $record_number * $record_size;
fseek ($fp, $address);
$f_contents = fread ($fp, $record_size);
$fields = array_values (unpack ($format_specifier, $f_contents));
// ... update the fields here
$f_contents = pack ($format_specifier, implode ("", $fields));
fseek ($fp, -$record_size);
fwrite ($fp, $f_contents);
@fclose ($fp);
?>
```

Comments

This recipe is pretty much what it appears to be. On the first line, we find the address where the record starts. On the second line, we seek to that address, and then read the contents into $f_contents (notice the binary-safe fread()). Then we unpack the values of the record; array_values() makes it a regular, not associative, array. Finally, we pack the record back into its original format. (Note that we implode the array around " " instead of "\0" because \0 is a binary end of line.) Then we write the record back to the file (again notice that fwrite() is binary-safe) and close the file.

This will work only for fixed-length records—any other type would cause the file to lose its integrity.

6.17 Accessing Fixed-Length Records

> You know the length of your records, but they don't have any special specifier. Therefore, you need to read a certain length at a time and assign it.

Technique

Although `substr()` will work, it is terribly inefficient and time-consuming; `unpack()` is a much better bet:

```php
<?php
while ($line = @fgets($fp, 1024)) {
    list (, $name, , $email, , $url) =
            unpack("A20name/x5/A50email/x5/A30url", $line);
    //... manipulate $name, $email and $url
}
?>
```

Comments

`unpack()` is an extremely fast and efficient way of parsing fixed-length records. In the script, we read 20 bytes and place it in `$name`. (Note the extra comma in the `list` construct; it is there because `unpack()` returns an associative array and we want only the array's values.) Then we skip five bytes, read 50 more bytes into `$email`, skip another five bytes, and read 30 bytes into `$url`.

Although `unpack()` is a much faster method of access fixed-length records, you can also use `substr()` to access fixed-length records, like so:

```php
<?
while ($line = @fgets ($fp, 1024)) {
    $name = substr ($line,0,20);
    $email = substr ($line, 25, 50);
    $url = substr ($line, 80, 30);
    // ... manipulate $name, $email and $url
}
?>
```

However, not only is `substr()` less efficient than `unpack()`, it is also not nearly as fast for parsing fixed-length records.

6.18 Extracting a Single Line from a File

You want to read a particular line in a file.

Technique

The quickest (as far as programming time is concerned) solution is to load the file into an array of lines and specify which line you want:

```php
<?php
$f_contents = file ($fn);
$your_line = $f_contents[$line_num];
?>
```

Or you can loop through the file until you reach the desired line number:

```php
<?
$line_cnt = 0;
while ($line = fgets($fp, 1024)) {
    if ($line_cnt == $line_num) {
        $right_line = $line;
        break;
    }
    $line_cnt++;
}
?>
```

Comments

The second solution is faster and more memory efficient; instead of reading the whole file into an array, we loop through the file until we reach the desired line number. With small files, you won't really see this speed increase, but as the files become larger, so does the speed increase.

The following program takes a filename and line number and returns the related line:

getline.php

```php
#!/usr/bin/php
<?php
// PHP must be installed as a cgi for this to work

list(, $file, $line_num) = array_values ($argv);
$fp = fopen($file, "r");
$line_cnt = 0;
```

```
while ($line = fgets($fp, 1024)) {
    if ($line_cnt == $line_num) {
        $what_we_want = $line;
        break;
    }
    $line_cnt++;
}

if (isset($what_we_want))
    print $what_we_want;
?>
```

Running this at the command prompt (UNIX)

```
% ./getline.php http://www.yahoo.com/ 59
```

or the DOS prompt

```
>php getline.php http://www.yahoo.com/ 59
```

would fetch the 60th line on Yahoo!

6.19   Truncating a File

You want to chop off the last line of a file.

Technique

Use the `ftruncate()` function along with the `ftell()` function:

```
<?php
$fp = @fopen ($fn, "r+")
  or die ("Cannot open $fn");
while (true) {
    $last_addr = $addr;
    $addr = ftell ($fp);
    if (!@fgets ($fp, 1024))
        break;
}
ftruncate ($fp, $last_addr);
fclose ($fp)
  or die ("Cannot close $fn");
?>
```

Comments

In this recipe we read the file line-by-line, remembering $addr (address of the current line) and $last_addr (address of the previous line). Finally, when we reach the end of the file, we use the ftruncate() function to remove the last line of the file.

Loading the file into an array, removing the last line of the file, and then writing the data back to your file can also obtain this effect (less effectively):

```
<?
$f_contents = file ($fn);
array_pop ($f_contents);
$fp = fopen ($fn, "w")
  or die("Cannot open file $fn");
fwrite ($fp, implode ('', $f_contents));
@fclose ($fp)
  or die("Cannot close file $fn");
?>
```

6.20 Counting the Number of Lines in a File

You want to find the number of lines in a file (with the first line indexed as 1).

Technique

Use count() in conjunction with file() for smaller projects:

```
<?
$line_count = count (file ($fn));
?>
```

Or, if you are on UNIX, use the wc program to count the number of lines for you:

```
<?
preg_match("/\s*(\d+)/", system("wc -l $fn"), $match);
$line_count = (int)$match[1];
?>
```

Comments

In the first solution (which is much slower), we return the file as any array of lines (via the file command) and then count the number of entries in the file. However, the second way uses the system program wc, which is optimized for counting lines, words, and characters. We use the -1 flag to specify that we want only the line count, and then we use preg_match() to parse the number out of the result.

6.21 Extracting a Random Line from a File

You want to take a random line from a file; an example of this might be those fortune-telling programs.

Technique

You can load a file into an array and then pick a random element of the array:

```php
<?php
$f_contents = file ($fn);
srand ((double)microtime()*1000000);
$random_line = $f_contents[ rand (0, (count ($f_contents) - 1)) ];
?>
```

Or you can use the built-in array_rand() function to return the key for a random array element:

```php
<?php
$f_contents = file ($fn);
srand ((double)microtime()*1000000);
$random_line = $f_contents[array_rand ($f_contents)];
?>
```

Comments

Both of these solutions use the same concept: reading a file into an array and picking a random element. array_rand() comes in handy when you want to pick several lines because you can call it with an extra argument that specifies how many random elements you want and array_rand() returns the keys for them in an array.

This solution is especially useful for programs such as the following fortune-telling program:

```html
<html>
<head>
    <title> Fortune Teller, Find out your fortune </title>
</head>
```

```
<body bgcolor="#ffffff" text="#000000" link="#0000FF" vlink="#FF00FF"
 Âalink="#FF0000">

<h1>YOUR FORTUNE IS:</h1>

<?php
srand ((double)microtime()*1000000);
$f_contents = file ("/usr/home/sterling/fortunes.txt");
$line = $f_contents[array_rand ($f_contents)];
print $line;
?>
<br><br>
<a href="<?php echo $PHP_SELF; ?>">Get your fortune again</a>

</body>
</html>
```

6.22 Randomizing Lines and Words

You want to randomize every line in a file.

Technique

Load the file into an array of lines, shuffle the array, and then write it back to the file:

```
<?
$fn = "/usr/home/sterling/random_file.txt";
$reg_array = file ($fn);

srand ((double)microtime()*1000000);
shuffle ($reg_array);

$fp = @fopen($fn, "w") or die("Cannot Open file $fn");
    fputs ($fp, implode ("", $reg_array));
@fclose ($fp) or die ("Cannot Close file $fn");
?>
```

Comments

First, we load the file into an array using the `file()` function. Now that we have an array of lines, we can randomize the array. Next, we seed the random number generator for `shuffle()`, and then pass the array to `shuffle()`. (Note that we do not need to assign the return value from `shuffle()` because it operates on the array directly.) Finally, we open the file again, truncate it to zero, and write the entire array to the file (with randomized lines).

Here is a neat program that randomizes all the words of a particular file and then prints them to the browser:

```php
<?php
$fn = 'somefile.txt';
srand ((double)microtime()*1000000);

foreach (file ($fn) as $line) {
    $words = preg_split("/\s+/", $line);
    shuffle ($words);
    $data .= implode(" ", $words) . "\n";
}

print $data;
?>
```

So, if this program were fed something like the following poem from Robert Frost:

```
Gathering Leaves

Spades take up leaves
No better than spoons,
And bags full of leaves
Are light as balloons.

I make a great noise
Of rustling all day
Like rabbit and deer
Running away.

But the mountains I raise
Elude my embrace
Flowing over my arms
And into my face.

I may load and unload
Again and again
Till I fill the whole shed,
And what have I then?
```

```
Next to nothing for weight;
And since they grew duller
From contact with earth
Next to nothing for color.

Next to nothing for use.
But a crop is a crop,
And who's to say where
The harvest shall stop?
```

It would output:

```
Leaves Gathering

take Spades leaves  up
than No better  spoons,
of And full bags leaves
light Are balloons. as

noise make I a great
rustling  Of all day
deer Like  rabbit and
 away. Running

raise I the But mountains
Elude my embrace
Flowing over arms my
my And face.  into

may I load and  unload
again and  Again
I the fill  shed, whole Till
 I have what And then?

Next weight; to nothing for
And grew duller since they
contact From with  earth
color. Next  to nothing for

to  Next for nothing use.
a crop is a crop,  But
And who's say where to
shall harvest The stop?
```

6.23 Creating Configuration Files

You are distributing files and you want to include a configuration file with which any user can work.

Technique

Use PHP's regular expression library to parse the file into an associative array:

```php
<?php
$config_file = "program.conf";

$fp = @fopen($config_file, "r");

while ($line = @fgets ($fp, 1024)) {
    $line = ereg_replace ("#.*$", "", $line);
    list ($name, $value) = explode ('=', $line);
    $name = trim ($name);
    $value = trim ($value);
    $config[$name] = $value;
}
?>
```

Comments

This script will parse a configuration file that looks like this:

```
Name = Sterling Hughes
Power = God #access to everything
Super User Privileges = Yes
```

where comments (a pound sign) are allowed. The file will then be loaded into an associative array in which the data on the left side of the equal sign is the key, and the data on the right side of the equal sign is the value. If you do not want to use an associative array, you can implement symbolic references, or "variable variables," like so:

```php
<?php
$config_file = "somefile.txt";

$fp = @fopen ($config_file, "r")
  or die("Cannot open file $fn");
```

```
while ($line = @fgets ($fp, 1024)) {
    $line = ereg_replace ("#.*$", "", $line);
    list ($name, $value) = explode ('=', $line);
    $name = trim ($name);
    $value = trim ($value);
    $$name = $value;
}
fclose($fp)
  or die("Cannot close file $fn");
?>
```

Now, instead of accessing variables through an associative array, you can simply call the variable names. That is, if you have the configuration variable `"ip_address"`, you can access it simply by typing `$ip_address`.

CHAPTER 7

Working with Files in Directories

"Man is the only animal that blushes. Or needs to."

Mark Twain, *Following the Equator*

7.0 Introduction

Directories allow for the organization of related data. Instead of having all programs and files in one area, directories enable you to categorize and subcategorize your data in a sane form. This strategy is the basis of both the Windows and the UNIX filesystems. PHP provides a standard set of features for manipulating and searching directories.

In fact, if you are a C programmer, you should feel right at home with PHP's support for directory access. Besides the basic differences between C and PHP, the functions and methods for accessing directory trees are fundamentally the same. Consider the following example:

```php
<?php
$dh = opendir ('/usr/home/designmm/public_html/');
while ($file = readdir ($dh)) {
    print "$file\n";
}
closedir ($dh);
?>
```

This would loop through all the files in the `html/` directory and print them out on a line. Seem familiar? It should, it is basically the same way you loop through a file using `fopen()`, `fgets()`, and `fclose()`, but now we use `opendir()`, `readdir()`, and `closedir()`.

This chapter covers both directories and how to modify their contents with PHP's filesystem functions.

7.1 Working with Timestamps

You need to get the date that a file was last modified or set the modification date of a file.

Technique

To get the timestamp of a file, use the `file*time()` functions:

```
print "$fn was last accessed on: " . fileatime ($fn);
print "$fn was last changed on: " . filectime ($fn);
print "$fn was last modified on: " . filemtime ($fn);
```

To change the modification time of a file, use the `touch()` function:

```php
<?php
if (touch ($fn, $date)) {
    print "Timestamp changed...";
} else {
    print "Modification Failed";
}
?>
```

Comments

On a UNIX system (where the `stat` functions will work), there are three different times associated with a particular file: the `atime`, the `ctime`, and the `mtime`. The `atime` (get with `fileatime()`) is the last time that the file was accessed. This is changed when the file is opened for read or write access. The `ctime` value is the time when the file's `inode` was last changed. Finally, the `mtime` is the time at which the file was last modified.

In PHP, the `touch()` function is the only way to change a file's timestamp information, and the only thing that `touch()` changes is the modification time of a file. Therefore, unless you go outside of PHP through `exec()` or `system()`, you cannot change anything but the `mtime` of a file.

7.2 Removing a File

You want to delete a file.

Technique

Use the `unlink()` function:

```php
<?php
unlink ($somefile)
  or die ("Cannot delete $somefile");
?>
```

Comments

`unlink()` returns `1` on success and `0` on failure. Therefore, you can test the return value with either an `or` (or) operator or an `if-else` block.

If you want to delete a list of files, you can use a `foreach` loop to loop through the array items and unlink each subsequent file:

```php
<?php
foreach ($files as $file) {
    unlink($file)
     or die("Cannot delete $file");
}
?>
```

If you are having trouble deleting a file, keep in mind that to delete a file under the UNIX operating system, you do not need write access to a file, but rather to the directory in which the file is held. The reason is that on a systems level, when you delete a file you are not modifying the file, but rather you are modifying the directory. This causes funny quirks when it comes to file permissions. Sometimes you can have write access to a file, but you won't be able to delete it because of directory permissions and vice versa.

7.3 Copying or Moving a File

You need to copy a file or move a file from one directory to another.

Technique

Use PHP's built-in `copy()` function:

```php
<?php
if (copy ($original, $new)) {
    print "$original copied to $new successfully";
} else {
    print "alas, thine wish cannot be the computers command";
}
?>
```

Or, if you need to move a file, use `rename()`:

```php
<?php
rename($original, $new)
  or die("Cannot Rename");
?>
```

Comments

The `copy()` function takes a source file and a destination file, and copies the source to the destination. If the destination file does not exist, PHP creates it. The `rename()` function makes a system call to the `rename` program.

7.4 Keeping Track of Filenames

You want to make sure that two filenames are not pointing to the same file (this can happen because of hard and soft links).

Technique

Use two associative arrays to keep track of the device and inode number of files that you have used:

```php
<?php
function remember_file ($file_name) {
    list($dev, $ino) = stat ($file_name);
    clearstatcache();
    return !($file_info[$dev . $ino]++) ? 1 : 0;
}
?>
```

Comments

For two files to be the same, they must have the same device and inode number. Knowing this enables us to create a unique ID using the device and inode number, and then check whether any other file has the same device or inode number. One way to implement this function is as follows:

```php
<?php
// $file_list contains a list of file to check
// for uniqueness, if they are unique
// we pass them off to the imaginary modify() function
foreach ($file_list as $file) {
    remember_file ($file) and modify ($file);
}
?>
```

Another use for this might be reporting which files are the same in a list of files. Consider the following:

```php
<?php
foreach ($file_list as $file_name) {
    list ($dev, $ino) = stat ($file_name);
    if ($file_info[$dev . $ino]++) {
        array_push ($similar_files, $file_name);
    }
    clearstatcache();
}
?>
```

7.5 Parsing the Parts of a Filename

You want to split up a file into its different parts, such as the directory path, the filename, and the file extension.

Technique

Use PHP's built-in `pathinfo()` function, which provides all the information you need.

```php
<?php
$pinfo = pathinfo("/home/sterling/monkey.php");
print "Directory name is: $pinfo[dirname]\n";
print "Filename is: $pinfo[basename]\n";
print "Ending is: $pinfo[extension]\n";
?>
```

Comments

PHP's `pathinfo()` function will give you all the information you need about the different elements of a filename (in a portable manner—i.e., it works with both Win32 and UNIX filenames). Note that the "extension" element of the array returned by `pathinfo()` is only present if the file has an extension, otherwise it is not present.

You can also access only individual elements of a path name via the pathinfo constants (`PATHINFO_DIRNAME`, `PATHINFO_BASENAME` and `PATHINFO_EXTENSION`):

```php
<?php
$path = "/home/sterling/monkey.php";

$dirname = pathinfo($path, PATHINFO_DIRNAME);
print "Directory name is: $dirname\n";
?>
```

7.6 Loading All Files in a Directory into an Array

You want to load all the files in a directory into an array for easy processing and manipulation.

Technique

Use the `maptree()` method in PEAR's `File_Find` class:

```php
<?php
include_once 'File/Find.php';

list ($directories, $files) = File_Find::maptree('/www/htdocs');
?>
```

Comments

To load an entire directory tree into an array, we use PEAR's `File_Find` class. The `File_Find` class provides many useful methods for loading and searching directory trees. The `maptree()` method will return an array containing two arrays: The first array is a list of all the directories in the specified directory, and the second is a list of all the files in all the directories.

If you want to load only the current directory, use the `mapdir()` method. It has the same syntax as the `maptree()` method, except that it returns an array of all the file and directory names in the specified directory:

```php
<?php
include_once 'File/Find.php';

$fsystem = File_Find::mapdir ('/www/htdocs');
foreach ($fsystem as $ent) {
    print "$ent\n";
}
?>
```

7.7 Searching a Filesystem

You want to make a list of filenames matching a singular pattern in a particular directory.

Technique

Use the `glob()` function in the File/Find.php file at PEAR:

```php
<?php
include_once 'File/Find.php';
$fsearcher = new File_Find;
$matching = $fsearcher->glob ('/\.php$/i',
    '/home/designmm/public_html','perl');
?>
```

Or, if you want to search an entire directory tree, use `File_Find`'s `search()` method:

```php
<?php
include_once 'File/Find.php';
$fsystem = new File_Find;
$matching = $fsearcher->search ('/\.php$/i',
    '/home/designmm/public_html','perl');
?>
```

Or, write our own routine and not depend at all on PEAR:

```php
<?php
$dh = dir('/home/designmm/public_html');
while ($entry = $dh->read()) {
    if (preg_match('/\.php$/i', $entry)) {
        $matching[] = $entry;
    }
}
$dh->close();
?>
```

Comments

The `File_Find` class from PEAR contains functions to aid you in searching the filesystem; one of those functions is the `glob()` function. The `glob()` function will search the current directory (but not subdirectories) for the specified regular expression. The syntax for `glob()` is as follows:

```php
array glob( string regular_expression, string directory
[, string type_of_regex]);
```

where `glob()` returns an array of matches via the regular expression in the specified directory. The optional *type_of_regex* argument enables you to specify (currently) whether you want to use PHP's regular expressions or PCRE library. If the option is left out, PHP's regular expressions are used by default. If you want to specify a case-insensitive search in your PHP regular expression (usually done via `eregi()`), you must add `'/i'` to the end of your PHP regular expression, just as you would do in Perl (see earlier examples).

7.8 Processing a Directory File-by-File

You want to process a directory file-by-file, the same way that you would process a file line-by-line with `fgets()`.

Technique

Either use the `dir()` function and manipulate the directory via a pseudo-object, or use the `opendir()`, `readdir()`, and `closedir()` functions to read the directory.

1. Using `dir()`

```
$dh = dir ($directory_name);
while ($entry = $dh->read()) {
    print $entry . "\n";
}
$dh->close();
```

2. Using `opendir()`, `readdir()`, and `closedir()`

```
$dh = opendir ($directory_name);
while ($entry = readdir ($dh)) {
    print $entry . "\n";
}
closedir ($dh);
```

Comments

Both solutions will work equally well; which one you choose is a matter of preference. The `dir()` function actually calls `opendir()` and creates an object that calls the corresponding functions in the second solution, so when you call `$dh->read()`, you are really calling `readdir($dh)`. As a matter of practice, I use the first solution just because I enjoy using the object interface.

You might have noticed that the functions PHP offers are much like the C functions for manipulating directories. In fact, `readdir()`, `rewinddir()`, `opendir()`, and `closedir()` are simply wrappers for the C functions.

7.9 Recursively Deleting a Directory

You want to remove a directory and its contents.

Technique

Use the `maptree` method from PEAR in the `File_Find` class (File/Find.php).

```
<?php
include_once 'File/Find.php';
$fsearcher = new File_Find;
list ($subdirs, $files) = $fsearcher->maptree ($your_directory);
```

```php
usort($subdirectories, 'sort_len');

foreach ($files as $file) {
    unlink ($file)
      or die ("Cannot remove $file");
}

foreach ($subdirectories as $directory) {
    rmdir ($directory)
      or die ("Cannot remove $directory");
}

function sort_len ($a, $b) {
    if (strlen ($a) == strlen ($b)) {
        return 0;
    }
    return (strlen ($a) > strlen ($b)) ? 1 : -1;
}
?>
```

Comments

The maptree()function in File_Find is useful not only in situations such as the following, but it is also the crux of most of the other methods (such as search) in File_Find. Therefore, we are including the source to maptree() and all relevant methods that it implements as a further illustration of directory and file access functions.

```php
<?php
var $_dirs;
var $files = array();
var $directories = array();

function &maptree ($directory)
{
    $this->_dirs = array ($directory);

    while (count ($this->_dirs))
    {
        $dir = array_pop ($this->_dirs);
        File_Find::_build ($dir);
        array_push ($this->directories, $dir);
    }
```

```php
        return array ($this->directories, $this->files);
    }


    // This is the File_Find::_build that was called above
    function _build ($directory)
    {
        $dh = @opendir ($directory);

        if (!$dh) {
            $pe = new FileFindException ("Cannot open directory");
            return ($pe);
        }

        while ($entry = @readdir ($dh))
        {

            if ($entry != '.' &&
                $entry != '..') {

                $entry = "$directory/$entry";

                if (is_dir ($entry))
                    array_push ($this->_dirs, $entry);
                else
                    array_push ($this->files, $entry);

            }

        }

        @closedir ($dh);
    }
?>
```

7.10 Creating a Search Engine

One of the most useful features to have on a site is a search engine, so I thought that to end our discussions of both files and directories, I would roll our own search engine. The search engine has two main parts: the indexer (octopus.php and finalize.php) and the search engine itself (voyager.php).

The indexer first searches the directory tree from the base directory (specified in the configuration file, config.txt) for all files with file endings that match those in specified in the filter option of the configuration file. We then index the meta tags of each file that is found in the search. Finally, we write those results to the browser and to a temporary file, giving the user a chance to delete the current index and re-index the site at a later time. If the user decides to go through with the index, we add the index to the SQL database—specifically, into the following table:

```
CREATE TABLE sites_table (
  id INT(4) PRIMARY KEY AUTO_INCREMENT,
  filename VARCHAR (70),
  keywords TEXT,
  description TEXT
);
```

After the results are added to the SQL database, the indexing portion of the site is done. We now move to the search portion of the script.

Most of the querying is done in SQL. We search the filename, description, and keywords for any occurrence of the search query. If we find a match, we print it out; otherwise, we tell the user that his search yielded zero results.

Now for the source code:

config.txt

```
; This is the configuration file for the search engine
; the semi-colon is a comment and a colon sets apart the
; name value pairs

dbtype: mysql        ; SQL Server type
Host: localhost      ; SQL server location
User: username       ; SQL username
Password: password ; SQL password
database_name: designmultimedia1 ; Name of database for searchengine
                                 ; information
filters: html,htm,php,php3,php4 ;Allowed File Endings for
                                ;indexing separated by a comma
saveresults: yes ; Save the results of each successful indexing
basedir: /home/designmm/www  ;Base directory where files are held
```

octopus.php

```php
<?php
include_once 'File/Find.php';
include_once 'LoadConfig.php';

$config = LoadConfig ('config.txt');

# Build Regex
$regex = "/$config[filters]/i";

$fs = new File_Find;
$files = $fs->search ($regex, trim ($config['basedir']), 'perl');

while ($file = array_pop ($files)) {
    $meta_tags = get_meta_tags ($file);
    $indexed .= "$file | " . $meta_tags[keywords] . ' | ';
    $indexed .= str_replace ("\n", ' ', $meta_tags[description]) . "\n";
}

if (strtolower ($config['saveresults']) == 'yes' or
    $config['saveresults'] == '1') {
    touch ('savefile'); # Create if doesn't exist
    $n = (int)join('', file ('savefile'));

    $fp = @fopen ('savefile','w') or die("Cannot Open savefile");
    fputs ($fp, ++$n);
    fclose($fp) or die("Cannot Close savefile");

    $filename = 'octopus_index' . $n . '.txt';
    $fp = @fopen ($filename, 'w') or die ("Cannot Open $filename");
    fwrite ($fp, $indexed);
    @fclose ($fp) or die("Cannot Close $filename");
    confirm ($indexed);
} else {
    $filename = 'octopus_index.txt';
    $fp = @fopen ($filename,'w') or die("Cannot Open $filename");
    fwrite($fp, $indexed);
    @fclose($fp) or die("Cannot Close $filename");
    confirm ($indexed);
}

function confirm() {
    global $filename, $indexed;
```

```php
?>
<html>
<head>
    <title> Files Indexed Successfully </title>
<body>
The Following files have been indexed:<br><br>
<?php
$indexed = explode ("\n", $indexed);

while(list (, $file) = each ($indexed)) {
    $file = str_replace ('|', '<br>', $file);
    print "$file\n<br><br>\n";
}

?>
<br><br>

<form action='finalize.php' method='get'>
<input type='hidden' name='filename' value='<?php echo $filename; ?>'>
<input type='radio' name='finalize' value='yes'> Finalize Index<br>
<input type='radio' name='finalize' value='no'> Redo Index<br>
<input type='submit' value='Make It So!'>
</form>
</body>
</html>
<?php
}
?>
```

finalize.php

```php
<?php
include_once 'DB.php';
include_once 'LoadConfig.php';

$config = LoadConfig ('config.txt');

if ($finalize == 'yes') {
    $dbconn = array ('phptype'  => $config[dbtype],
                     'username' => $config[User],
                     'password' => $config[Password],
                     'database' => $config[database_name],
                     'hostspec' => $config[Host]);
    $dbh = DB::connect($dbconn);
```

```php
    if (DB::isError ($dbh)) {
        die (sprintf ('Error [%d]: %s',
                    $dbh->getCode(), $dbh->getMessage()));
    }

    $fcontents = file ($filename);
    while (list ($line) = each($fcontents)) {
        list ($fname, $keywords, $desc) = explode ('|', $line);
        $fname = trim ($fname);
        $keywords = trim ($keywords);
        $desc = trim ($desc);
        $stmt = 'INSERT INTO sites_table filename, keywords, description';
        $stmt .= " VALUES ('$fname', '$keywords', '$desc')";
        $dbh->query ($stmt);
    }
    $dbh->close();
    print "Results Finalized";
} elseif ($finalize == 'no') {
    unlink($filename)
      or die("Cannot Delete $filename");
    if ($saveresults == 'yes' or $saveresults == '1') {
        $n = (int)join ('', file ('savefile'));
        $fp = @fopen ('savefile','w') or die ("Cannot Open savefile");
        fputs ($fp, --$n);
        @fclose ($fp) or die ("Cannot Close savefile");
    }
    print "Results Discarded";
} else {
    die ("Invalid Option for finalize");
}

?>
```

voyager.php

```php
<?php

include_once 'DB.php';
include_once 'LoadConfig.php';

$config = LoadConfig ('config.txt');
```

```php
// Submitted data is $query -- Users search term

$dbconn = array ('phptype'  => $config[dbtype],
                 'username' => $config[User],
                 'password' => $config[Password],
                 'database' => $config[database_name],
                 'hostspec' => $config[Host]);
$dbh = DB::connect($dbconn);

if (DB::isError ($dbh)) {
    die (sprintf ('Error [%d]: %s',
        $dbh->getCode(), $dbh->getMessage()));
}

$stmt = 'SELECT * FROM sites_table ';
$stmt .= "WHERE keywords LIKE '%$query%' OR description LIKE '%$query%'";
$stmt .= " OR filename LIKE '%$query%'";

$sth = $dbh->query ($stmt);

if (DB::isError ($dbh)) {
    die (sprintf ('Error [%d]: %s',
        $dbh->getCode(), $dbh->getMessage()));
}

$count = $sth->numRows();

$header = ($count > 0) ?
            "There were $count results to your query" :
            'There were no results for your query, please try again';

function result_set() {
    global $sth;
    while ($row = $sth->fetchRow()) {
    ?>
    <a href='<?php echo $row[filename]; ?>'> <?php echo $row[filename]; ?> </a>
    <br>
    <dir><?php echo $row[description]; ?></dir><br><br>
    <?php
}
}
```

```php
$dbh->close();
?>

<html>
<head>
    <title>
        <?php echo $header; ?>
    </title>
</head>
<body>

<h1> <?php echo $header; ?> </h1>

<br><br>
<?php
if ($count) {
    result_set();
} else {
    echo $header;
}
?>

<form action='<?php echo $PHP_SELF; ?>' method='GET'>
Search Terms: <input type='text' name='query'>
<input type='submit' value='Search!'>
</form>

</body>
</html>
```

LoadConfig.php

```php
<?php

function LoadConfig ($filename, $seperator=':', $comment=';')
{
    $regex = "/$comment.*/i";
    $fp = @fopen ($filename, 'r');
    if (!$fp) {
        die ("Cannot open $filename");
    }
```

```php
    while ($line = @fgets ($fp, 1024)) {
        $line = preg_replace ($regex, "", $line);
        list ($key, $val) = explode ($seperator, $line);

        $key = trim ($key);
        $val = trim ($val);

        $config[$key] = $value;
    }

    @fclose ($fp);
    return ($config);
}
?>
```

CHAPTER 8

Functions

"Duty, n. : That which sternly impels us in the direction of profit, along the line of desire."

Ambrose Bierce, *The Devil's Dictionary*

8.0 Introduction

In PHP, there are two types of functions: *built-in functions* and *user-defined functions*. The recipes and discussions in most of this book have to do with the former, but the focus of this chapter is on the latter. User-defined functions enable you to encapsulate and categorize your code, as much as arrays enable you to encapsulate and categorize your data. PHP provides more than adequate support for functions via the function declaration. Consider the following:

```
function hello_world ()
{
    print "Hello World";
}
```

This encapsulates the statement print "Hello World" into the function hello_world(). If you wanted to say "Hello World" at any other point in the script, you could simply call the hello_world() function:

```
print "I am about to say hello...\n";
hello_world();
print "\nThere you go, I said hello";
```

As you see in the example, PHP enables you to encapsulate blocks of code and then call them at any time. Another ability that you gain when using functions in PHP is passing arguments to a function. Examine the following:

```
function say_something ($something)
{
    print $something;
}
```

Putting the variable $something between the parentheses on the first line tells PHP that the variable $something will be set by the user within the scope of the function. Knowing this enables us to rewrite the code in the hello_world() example:

```
say_something("I am about to say hello... \n");
say_something("Hello World");
say_something("\nThere you go, I said hello");
```

We just created a *wrapper* for the print function (print statement, actually, but who's counting). That means whenever you call say_something($something), it is the same as calling print $something (note that there *must* be parentheses around the say_something() function call because it is a function, not a statement). This is just one of the many uses of functions in PHP.

As we said earlier, this chapter is about user-defined functions and the different ways that you can use them to create reusable, slim, PHP code. So, here is the first problem/solution pair, which teaches you about...

8.1 Passing a Default Value to a Function

You want to pass an argument to a function, but you want to make the argument optional by providing a default value.

Technique

Specify the default value in the function declaration, like so:

```
<?php
function log_message($message, $prefix="GENERAL")
{
    print "$prefix: $message\n";
}
```

```
log_message("Startup");
/* logs "GENERAL: Startup" */

log_message("Cannot open file", "ERROR");
/* logs "ERROR: Cannot open file" */
?>
```

Comments

As discussed in the introduction, you can pass arguments to a function simply by declaring them as variables within the parentheses. If you want to establish a default value for variables, you simply assign it the default value within the parentheses. If no argument is specified when the function is called, the default value for the argument will be used.

An argument without a default value is required to be present at call time. By setting a default value, you make the argument optional even if you set the default value to empty, like so:

```
function say_hello ($name='')
{
    print "hello";
    if (!empty($name)) {
        print ", $name";
    }
}
```

The function say_hello() can now be called as say_hello() or say_hello("Erin Keiser-Clark"), and it will behave accordingly.

The arguments with default values have to be declared at the end of the argument list. Therefore, the following declaration is illegal:

```
function log_message($prefix = "GENERAL", $message)
{
}
```

The expression used as a default value has to be constant—using a variable, an array of variables, or a function call is illegal.

Note that in PHP 4, it is possible to specify a NULL value as the default. The result would be as if the argument were not set at all—it will fail the isset() test. This can be useful in certain situations, such as where an empty string '' would actually be a valid value.

8.2 Accessing Variables Outside a Function

You want to access a global variable from inside the scope of a function.

Technique

Use the global declaration to say that the variable you are referring to is a global variable:

```
$foo = "noobar";
function foobar () {
    global $foo;
    print $foo; // prints noobar
}
```

Or access the variable directly via the $GLOBALS array:

```
$foo = "noobar";
function foobar() {
    $foo = 5; // The local foo
    print "The global variable is $GLOBALS[foo], ";
    print "The local variable is $foo";
}
```

Comments

In PHP, the $GLOBALS array contains all variables that are of global scope, or all variables not within the scope of a function or class. (For more information on the $GLOBALS array, see recipe 14.5.)

If you are working within a class, you might want to instead declare your global (not really, but it is global within the class) variable as a var. Then you can access it through the $this variable (for more on OOP, see Chapter 9, "Classes"); consider the following:

```
class foo {
    var $name = "noobar";
    function foobar () {
        print $this->name;
    }
}
```

8.3 Returning Values from a Function

You want to return a variable or an array or a Boolean value from a function.

Technique

Use the `return` statement to return values from a function, like so:

```php
<?php
function need_full_report()
{
    // For this example, we'll just check if it's the end of the week
    return (date("w") == 6); /* return true if it's Saturday */
}

if (need_full_report ()) {
    send_full_report();
} else {
    send_current_report();
}
?>
```

Comments

The `return` statement allows you to return only *one* value. (To return more than one value, see recipe 8.6.) This value can be of any PHP-supported type. In the example, we use the return value of the function to determine what kind of report to send.

PHP 4 supports returning values by reference. This is helpful when you want to return a large array or an object that was created in the function. The declaration of a function that returns a value by reference looks like this:

```php
<?php
function &get_product_list($department)
{
    $product_list = array();

    // Do database query and return the list of products which may be large
    // ....

    return $product_list;
}
$products = &get_product_list('rd');
?>
```

The result will be that instead of making a copy of `$product_list` and passing it back, the function will return a reference to `$product_list`, saving memory and execution time.

8.4 Passing Arguments by Reference

You want to force your users to have their arguments passed by reference.

Technique

If you declare that the variable will be passed by reference in the function definition, the variable will always be passed by reference, no matter whether the user passes a reference.

```php
<?php
$tree = new Tree;
$tree->depth = 3;
generate_tree($tree);

function generate_tree(&$tree)
{
    // Here we generate some data and fill in the tree
    // by calling methods on $tree.
}
?>
```

Comments

References in PHP are somewhat (again, *somewhat*) equivalent to the concept of pointers in C. Before I go into the details here, a little disclaimer to appease fellow C programmers: Although the references in PHP are loosely equivalent to pointers in C, there are a couple of major differences. One difference is that in PHP, you never have to dereference your variables as you do in C (via *). PHP references are more similar to references in C++.

For those unfamiliar with concepts of pointers and references, here is a brief explanation. (For more information, see recipe 4.5.) It all boils down to the fact that every variable has a memory address, sort of like every book in a library has a book number. A reference is the "book number" of the variable. So, instead of passing a copy of a variable to a function, you are really passing only a memory address, which, when dealing with large variables and arrays, is much more memory efficient. Also, passing references enables you to use what are known as *destructive* functions or functions that modify the variable that is passed to them (as in the example).

PHP 4 is more optimized with regard to value passing. Even if the value is not passed by reference, PHP is smart enough not to pass a copy of the value. Instead, it uses the value from the calling scope and makes a note that this value is being used in one more place. But changing the variable contents in the function will have no effect on the calling scope.

Please note that in the example, we require the arguments to be passed by reference. Although it is possible not to declare the reference in the function but rather pass the variables on a call-by-call basis, doing so constitutes bad programming practice. The person who calls the function should not control what is or is not passed by reference—that is the duty of the programmer who wrote the function. To that purpose, PHP 4 provides a php.ini directive (`allow_call_time_pass_reference`) that will disallow passing values by reference at call time.

8.5 Retaining a Variable's Value Between Function Calls

You want a variable to retain its value between function calls.

Technique

Use the `static` statement to have PHP remember the value of the variable from the last function call:

```
function sequence_get_next_value()
{
    static $x = 0;
    return $x++;
}

print sequence_get_next_value (); #prints 0
print sequence_get_next_value (); #prints 1
print sequence_get_next_value (); #prints 2
```

Comments

The `static` statement is an elegant way to avoid using global variables in your function. It remembers the value of $x from function call to function call for the amount of time that the PHP script executes. This means that after the script execution is complete, PHP forgets about the value of the static variable.

8.6 Returning More Than One Value from a Function

You need to return more than one value from a function, but PHP only allows you to return one value.

Technique

Use the `array()` and `list()` constructs to return more than one value from a function. These values can be of any PHP-supported type.

```
function get_current_date ()
{
    $plain_date = date("m/d/Y");
    $fancy_date = date("l, F d, Y");

    return array($plain_date, $fancy_date);
}

list($plain_date, $fancy_date) = get_current_date ();
if (user_prefs("fancy"))
    print $fancy_date;
else
    print $plain_date;
```

Comments

In PHP, as in C, you cannot legally return more than one value from a function. However, you can return an array of values. In the example, we return an array of values from the `get_current_date()` function. We then use the `list` statement to capture the returned values.

8.7 Declaring Functions Dynamically

You want to declare a function dynamically, depending on a certain condition.

Technique

PHP enables you to do so, although you probably will not use this feature much. It might come in handy if you expect the function to be called by some other user's code and want to restrict the call somehow.

```
if ($superuser) {
    function get_user_info($user_id, $verbosity_level = 5)
    {
        ...
    }
} else {
    function get_user_info($user_id)
    {
        $verbosity_level = 1;
        ...
    }
}
```

Comments

In the example, if the user calling get_user_info() is a superuser, she will be able to pass an additional $verbosity_level parameter. A non-superuser caller will get an error if she tries to pass that parameter.

8.8 Dynamically Creating Anonymous Functions

You want to create an anonymous (unnamed) function dynamically and then allow the user to access that function.

Technique

Use the create_function() function, which creates an anonymous function and returns its name:

```
<?php

function greet ($type)
{
    return create_function ('$greeting',
                            "print \"$type: \$greeting\";");
}

$greeting1 = greet("Casual");
$greeting2 = greet("Formal");

$greeting1("How's it going?");
$greeting1("What's up doc?");
```

```
$greeting2("Hello");
$greeting2("Hello, my name is Sterling, it is a pleasure to meet you");
?>
```

Comments

The `create_function()` function will dynamically create a PHP function with arguments given by the first parameter and the code given by the second argument. It will return the function's unique name so that you can then call that function. This primitive form of closure can be used for many things, including smart callbacks.

Another use of the `create_function()` function is for the custom sort functions. Examine recipe 4.15 for more information. For further information about dynamically calling functions using variables, see the next recipe.

8.9 Calling Functions Indirectly

You want to call function by its name, which is stored in a variable.

Technique

PHP enables you to use a variable value as the function name at call time. For example, you might have a classified-ad system that has several functions—called `process_camera()`, `process_computer()`, `process_car()`, and so on—that perform specific actions. You want to call the appropriate function depending on the type of the ad.

```
<?php
// Support ad type is stored in $ad_type.
// Then calling the function is as simple as: */
$process_function = "process_$ad_type";
$process_function($HTTP_POST_VARS);
?>
```

Comments

First, we create the full name of the function we want to call, and then we use that name instead of the static function name.

Of course, it's possible to have one function called `process_ad()` with a long "switch" statement inside that does appropriate processing. However, the indicated approach is more extensible and a bit cleaner. To support a new ad type, all you have to do is define a new function. (You could even define that function in a different source file and then "include" it.)

8.10 Fetching an Arbitrary Number of Parameters

You want to fetch an arbitrary number of parameters from 0...N–1, where N is the total number of parameters.

Technique

Use the `func_get_args()` function to return an array containing the arguments passed to the function:

```php
<?php
$input_record_seperator = " ";

function perl_print ()
{
    $args = func_get_args();
    foreach ($args as $arg) {
        print $arg . $input_record_seperator;
    }
}


perl_print("Hello World\n", "My Name is", "Sterling");
?>
```

Comments

PHP offers a set of handy functions for accepting an arbitrary amount of parameters. The `func_get_args()` function returns an array of all the function arguments passed to the script. As an alternative, you can also use the `func_get_arg()` and `func_num_args()` functions to loop through all the parameters sent to a function:

```php
<?php
$input_record_separator = " ";

function perl_print ()
{
    $argc = func_num_args();
    for ($idx = 0; $idx < $argc; $idx++) {
        $current_arg = func_get_arg($idx);
```

Part I   Language Constructs and Techniques

```
        print $current_arg . $input_record_separator;
    }
}
?>
```

CHAPTER 9

Classes

"To make oneself an object, to make oneself passive, is a very different thing from being a passive object."

Simone De Beauvoir

9.0 Introduction

The fundamental notion of both object-oriented design and object-oriented programming is that the program is a model of an aspect of reality. The classes in the program are a summary of the reality that is being modeled; they contain both the data and operations that can be performed on the data. The real-world objects of the implementation are represented by the objects of these classes. To quote a classic example, you might have a `Vehicle` class, which generically describes a transportation vehicle. It might have attributes such as `number of wheels`, `color`, `brand`, and so on. From this generic class, you might derive more specific classes, such as `Car`, `Bicycle`, and others. The derived classes will inherit their parent's attributes and will probably add some of their own. And, of course, the classes will most likely contain methods that operate on class data (or attributes).

The idea of grouping related ideas to create a larger entity under the umbrella of a class is often referred to as encapsulation, which is an example of information hiding. Information hiding reduces complexity because it enables programmers to focus on only the exposed methods of the class, instead of worrying about internal implementation.

Moving from the abstract idea of classes to the concrete, in PHP, classes can contain variables and functions. The variables are usually called class variables or member variables, and they hold data that is necessary for the functionality of the class, such as its attributes. The functions are called methods, and they operate on member variables or expose some other class functionality. So, if you have a class named `Session` that creates and saves session IDs of users, one method of the class might be a method that saves the user's session ID into a database. Another method might be a method that sets the user's cookie. Each method builds on another to achieve the reality that is sought; in the case of the `Session` class, each method builds on the other to create a session management system.

PHP, although not a true object-oriented language, provides most of the functionality that is needed to package data and functions into classes, thus implementing encapsulation.

9.1 Creating a Class

You know what classes are, and you want to create one in PHP.

Technique

Use the `class` declaration to create a class:

```php
<?php
class Car {
    //... The data of your class goes here.
}
?>
```

Comments

The declaration of a class in PHP is as simple as it gets. What you see in the preceding code is exactly what you do. After you declare the class, you can put all member methods and attributes inside the curly brackets and you have a class. Consider the following example:

```php
class Name {
    var $property1;
    var $property2;

    function print_name($first_name, $last_name) {
        print "Your first name is: $first_name, ";
```

```
        print "and your last name is: $last_name";
    }
}
```

You now have a class that contains both methods (print_name(), in this case) and attributes ($property1 and $property2). Note the var statement when declaring variables; this makes the variables attributes of the class, and therefore accessible by objects of the class. This concept leads us to the next subject of this recipe.

Instances, also referred to as objects, are specific implementations of a class. A good analogy is saying that an instance (object) is related to a class like a house is related to its blueprint.

Taking the Name class defined earlier in this recipe, you need to create an instance of the class in order to work with the class for individual cases. To do this, you need to use PHP's new statement, which automatically creates an object from the specified class. That means memory is set aside for the object, necessary initialization is performed, and the class attributes and methods are now accessible through the object by using the arrow notation:

```php
<?php
// Create new object
$obj = &new Name;
// Set $firstname in class Name equal to the string Oliver
$obj->firstname = 'Oliver';
// Set $lastname in class Name equal to the string Butin
$obj->lastname  = 'Butin';

// Call the print name method in Class name
$obj->print_name($obj->firstname, $obj->lastname);
?>
```

9.2 Accessing Variables from Within a Class

You want to access variables declared via the var statement, but you can't call them by name from within the class.

Technique

Use the built-in $this object to access variables in the class:

```php
<?php
class Name {
```

```php
    var $firstname;
    var $lastname;

    function print_names() {
        print 'Firstname: ' . $this->firstname;
        print "\nLastname: " . $this->lastname;
    }
}
?>
```

Comments

$this is a special variable that is created in an object. It refers to the object itself, meaning that through $this you can access class variables and methods in the current class. The $this object represents the same idea as manually creating an instance of the class within the class. Therefore, we can also change the values of the object's properties:

```php
<?php
class Name {
    var $firstname;
    var $lastname;

    function print_names() {
        print 'Firstname: ' . $this->firstname;
        print "\nLastname: ' . $this->lastname;
    }

    function change_name ($name) {
        $name = preg_split('/\s+/', $name);
        $this->firstname = $name[0];
        $this->lastname  = $name[1];
    }
}

$obj = &new Name;
$obj->change_name("Sterling Hughes");
$obj->print_name();
$obj->change_name("Andrei Zmievski");
$obj->print_name();
?>
```

The change_name() method will change the name of the person who is described in the Name object, and the print_name() method will reflect the change.

9.3 Inheritance

You need to create a new class that is derived from an existing class.

Technique

Java programmers will be familiar with the extends keyword, which enables you to declare a new class that inherits methods and variables from a parent class. PHP's syntax is the same:

```php
<?php
class Car extends Vehicle {
    var $body_type;
    var $engine;

    function initialize($body_type, $engine) {
        $this->body_type = $body_type;
        $this->engine = $engine;
    }
}
?>
```

Comments

The extends statement tells PHP to make a new class and automatically inherit the parent class's variables and methods. The extended or derived class can have all the variables and methods of the base class, and you can add or override variables and methods in its definition (known as overriding):

```php
<?php
class Pet {
    var $food = array();
    var $water;

    function eat() {
        foreach ($this->food as $snack) {
            print $snack;
        }
    }
}
```

```
class Dog extends Pet {
    function set_food() {
        $this->food = array('Iams', 'Meat', 'Alpo');
    }
}

$obj = &new Dog;
$obj->set_food();
$obj->eat();
?>
```

Notice that there is no eat() method in the Dog class because the Dog class extends the Pet class, and so it inherits the methods from the Pet class. Therefore, the eat() method is inherited from the Pet class.

Note that when you inherit constructors, the parent class's constructor is not called if the inherited class is a constructor. For more information, see recipe 9.5.

9.4 Making Variables or Functions Public and Private

You want to make certain variables or functions inaccessible to the person accessing your class.

Technique

There is no way of declaring functions and variables private to a class without putting them within the scope of a function. However, as a standard naming convention, you should always start private methods and variables with an underscore (_):

```
<?php
class Car {
    var $_name; // private
    var $brandname;

    function analyze() {
        if ($this->_name == "Corolla") {
            $this->brandname = 'Toyota';
        } else {
            $this->_delete();
        }
    }
}
```

```php
    function _delete() {
        $this->name = '';
        $this->brandname = '';
    }
}
?>
```

Comments

In languages such as C++ and Java, you can set certain variables accessible to only the methods of the same class. However, PHP does not offer this functionality. Therefore, you must trust that users of the class will make use of only public variables and functions. One way of labeling a variable or function as private to most programmers is by putting an _ before the variable or function name. This is also a good reminder of what is public and what is private if you have to work on your class in a couple of months and you don't remember much about it.

Another thing to keep in mind about scope and class data is that variables declared within a class are not global. They are part of a class and therefore accessible only via an object created from that class. To be global, a variable must be outside of the class definition. The same also holds true with constants: As a rule, you should define your constants outside the scope of the class in order to access them within the class.

9.5 Creating a Constructor

You want to create a function that is called when an instance of a class is created via the new statement; this is known as a constructor.

Technique

Give your constructor function the same name as the class you are calling:

```php
<?php
class Human {
    var $name;

    function Human ($na) {
        print "Wake up $na, you have been initialized";
        $this->name = $na;
    }
}
```

```
$obj = &new Human('Stephen Hughes');
?>
```

Comments

In PHP, a constructor is defined as a method that has the same name (case-sensitive) as the class. The constructor can take arguments, which allows for customization of the object at the initialization time. Also note that if a parent class also has a constructor, the parent class's constructor will not be called when a child class is instantiated. So, you have to do a bit of a manual work. Suppose that you have the following child class to the class Human specified earlier:

```
<?php
class SuperHuman extends Human {
    var $power;

    function SuperHuman($power) {
        Human::Human();
        $this->$power = $power;
    }

    function use_power() {
    /* this should do something interesting */
    }
}
?>
```

Here the SuperHuman constructor will be called, but the Human constructor will not automatically be called. So, you have to call it manually using :: notation (see recipe 9.6).

9.6 Returning a Different Object from a Constructor

You want to return a new object from an object's constructor, but return won't allow you to do this (at least not in a constructor).

Technique

Assign the new object to the $this variable:

```
<?php
class PHP_QA {
    var $name;
```

```php
    function std_response () {
        print "Sorry " . $this->name;
        print ", That's a feature not a bug\n";
    }
}

class BUG {
    var $type;
    function BUG ($type) {
        if ($type == "Invalid Bug") {
            $this = &new PHP_QA;
            return;
        }
        $this->type = $type;
    }

    function std_response () {
        print "Wow, thanks for reporting a " . $this->type;
        print " error!!";
    }
}
?>
```

Comments

If you want to return a different object from a constructor, you must assign the $this variable the new object. The $this variable is the default return value from a constructor; it contains a pointer to the methods and properties of the current class. Overriding the $this variable enables you to change the object returned from the constructor. Note, however, that you lose all the current class's methods and properties when you assign a new value to the $this variable.

9.7 Creating a Class Destructor

You want to create a destructor for your current class.

Technique

Use PHP's register_shutdown_function() function and register a function that frees your object:

```php
<?php

$CLASSNAME_OBJECT_LIST = array();

function classname_destructor () {
    global $CLASSNAME_OBJECT_LIST;

    if (count($CLASSNAME_OBJECT_LIST)) {
        reset($CLASSNAME_OBJECT_LIST);
        while (list(, $obj) = each($CLASSNAME_OBJECT_LIST)) {
            $obj->destroy();
        }
        $CLASSNAME_OBJECT_LIST = null;
    }
}

class Tree {
    var $type;

    function Tree ($type='oak') {
        $this->type = $type;
        global $CLASSNAME_OBJECT_LIST;
        array_push ($CLASSNAME_OBJECT_LIST, &$this);
    }

    function destroy () {
        $this->type = null;
    }
}
register_shutdown_function("classname_destructor");
?>
```

Description

In the preceding example, we register a shutdown function with the `register_shutdown_function()` function. This function will be called when your script is finished executing. Then this function calls the destructor method (`destroy()` in this case, but it could be any other method that you choose) on every object in the global `$CLASSNAME_OBJECT_LIST` variable. An object is added to the object list in the class's constructor by adding a reference to the special `$this` variable to the array.

9.8 Using Functions in a Class Without Initializing an Object

You want to use functions in a certain class without initializing an object via the new statement.

Technique

Use the :: notation, which enables you to access functions in a class without using an object:

```php
<?php
class Conversion {
    function feet_to_meters($feet) {
        return $feet * 0.3054;
    }
}

$average_height = Conversion::feet_to_meters(6);
?>
```

Comments

The :: notation enables you to access function in classes without an object, but how do you access variables from within a class without an object? You don't. At the time this book was written, PHP supports only the capability to access methods—not variables—without using an object. However, after you have an object, you can access both variables and functions via that object.

9.9 Indirectly Accessing a Method of the Parent Class

You want to access a method of a parent class without explicitly naming the class you want to access.

Technique

Use the special parent class to access the method of a parent class:

```php
<?php

class Computer {
    var $is_on = 1;
```

```php
    function turn_on () {
        $this->is_on = 1;
        print "You turned me on";
    }

    function turn_off () {
        $this->is_on = 0;
        print "You turned me off";
    }
}

class HP extends Computer {
    var $processor = 0;
    var $hard_drive = 0;

    function turn_on() {
        parent::turn_on();
        $this->processor = 1;
        $this->hard_drive = 1;
    }

    function turn_off() {
        $this->hard_drive = 0;
        $this->processor = 1;
        parent::turn_off();
    }
}
?>
```

Comments

The parent class is a special class that can be accessed only by using the :: notation. It enables you to access methods from the parent class of the current class. This is useful in the example because the turn_on() and turn_off() methods are defined in both the parent (Computer) and the child (HP) class. Therefore, if we accessed turn_on() or turn_off() through $this, we would get the current turn_on() and turn_off() methods, not the methods in the parent class.

If you don't have a namespace collision between the two classes, you can directly access parent methods by using the $this object. Accessing parent methods via the $this object preserves the current object's properties. Consider the following example, which works only when you use the $this object:

```php
<?php

class Parent {
    var $parent_name;

    function print_parent_name () {
        print $this->parent_name . "\n";
    }
}

class Child extends Parent {
    var $child_name;

    function print_child_name () {
        print $this->child_name . "\n";
    }
}

$obj = &new Child;
$obj->child_name = "Sterling";
$obj->parent_name = "Leslie";

print "Parent name: ";
$this->print parent_name();
print "Child name: ";
$this->print_child_name();

?>
```

9.10 Returning an Error Object on Failure

You want to return a valid object from your class on success, and an error object on failure.

Technique

Create an is_error method in your class, which will find out whether you are returning an error object:

```php
<?php

class SomeClass {
    var $somevar;

    function some_method ($var) {
        $this->somevar = $var;
        if ($this->somevar != $var) {
            $errobj = new SomeClassError;
            $errobj->_code = -2;
            $errobj->_message = 'Couldn't assign $var to $somevar';
            return($errobj);
        } else {
            return(1);
        }
    }

    function is_error ($val) {
        return is_object($val) &&
                (get_class($val) == "SomeClassError" ||
                 is_subclass_of($val, "SomeClassError");
    }
}

class SomeClassError {
    var $_code;
    var $_message;

    function getCode() {
        return($this->_code);
    }

    function getMessage() {
        return($this->_message);
    }
}

$obj = &new SomeClass;
$ret = $obj->some_method("Aqualung");
if (SomeClass::is_error($ret)) {
    die(sprintf('Error [%d]: %s', $ret->getCode(), $ret->getMessage()));
}
```

9.10 Returning an Error Object on Failure

```
// .. Manipulate the SomeClass object here
?>
```

Comments

Returning an error object from a class enables you to return a more specific message to the programmer using your class than just a simple error code or a message. In turn, that enables the programmer to print out a more useful message to the end user.

CHAPTER 10

Maintaining Sessions with PHP

"The true art of memory is the art of attention."

Samuel Johnson

This chapter is all about maintaining state—the process of preserving variable values across script invocations. First, we discuss PHP 4's new session management features, and then round out the section with a small, to the point, shopping cart system. Then we investigate PHP's serialization functions (WDDX included), which are efficient ways to store PHP variables.

10.0 Introduction

HTTP is a stateless protocol, meaning that after a user leaves your Web page or your application ends, the computer loses all memory of the transactions that have occurred (unless you count the Web server's log files). Starting with Netscape 3.0, Netscape addressed this problem with cookies. Cookies are files that are stored on the user's computer, and are accessible to the script that sent them. They enable you to save and access information about past visits a user might have made to your Web site.

By combining cookies and databases, you could save every bit of information you have about a user on your computer and access it by using a unique ID that you assigned to the user and put in a cookie that was stored on the user's computer. However, this was very programming intensive and required a lot of time to start up. Therefore, to make your life easier, the PHP development group came out with a tightly integrated set of session management utilities for PHP. What used to take anywhere from twenty to hundreds of lines of code now takes, at most, a few lines of well-crafted code.

How It Works

Sessions work in the following manner. When the session_start() or session_register() function is called, PHP loads the saved session data from the session store. During a script's execution, you can register variables to be saved into the session store by calling the session_register() function. When your PHP script finishes execution, the session variables are saved to the session store in the path specified by the session.save_path entry in the php.ini file. A unique ID that is associated with the session is put in a cookie and given to the user, but this happens only the first time a session is started.

Serially Though

One way of maintaining state is by using the sessions module. But in some cases, you don't need the power of the sessions module—you just need to save and retrieve certain variables. If this is the case, you can use either PHP's serialization functions (serialize() and unserialize()) or you can use the bundled WDDX extension, which places PHP variables in a standard format that can then be read and used by other languages.

10.1 Creating a Session Variable with PHP

You want to create a session variable by using PHP.

Technique

Use the session_register() function to register a session variable:

```php
<?php
session_register('session_variable');

$session_variable = $session_variable ? $session_variable + 1 : 20;

echo $session_variable;
?>
```

Comments

In PHP, there are currently 3 types of variables, all with different scopes and purposes. The first type of variable and the one with the most limited scope is the local variable. A local variable is any variable that is within the scope of a function, and it lasts only for the time of the function. Consider the following:

```php
<?php
srand((double)microtime() * 1000000);

function get_number($num) {
    $num *= rand();
    return ($num);
}

$number1 = get_number(rand());
$number2 = get_number(5);
$number3 = get_number(5);

print "Number 1 is $number1\n<br>\n
       Number 2 is $number2\n<br>\n
       Number 3 is $number3\n<br>\n";
?>
```

In this example, the $ret variable is locally scoped; that is, its value is not accessible outside the scope of the get_number() function.

The next type of variable is a global variable, which is any variable that is declared outside of a class or function (or declared by the global statement or declared through the $GLOBALS array). Global variables last for the duration of the script's execution.

The last type of variable added in PHP 4 is the session variable. Session variables can (in theory) last forever, unless you or the user explicitly deletes them. (They can be automatically deleted after a certain time by setting configuration options correctly.)

So, session variables are simply regular variables that are declared using the session_register() function. They can be of any PHP-supported type: arrays, strings, numbers, even objects. The behavior of session_register() depends on the value of the register_globals PHP configuration parameter. If register_globals is on, session_register('foo') will save a global variable $foo in the session store. If it's off, it will look inside $HTTP_SESSION_VARS[] array, so $HTTP_SESSION_VARS['foo'] will be saved.

Keep these considerations in mind while you read the rest of this chapter. A list of the topics we'll discuss is

- Saving session variables in databases
- Maintaining browser sessions from page to page
- Setting and getting session names
- Unsetting session variables
- Finding the path where a session ID is saved

10.2 Saving Sessions Using a Database

You want to save your session data in a database rather than saving it in the filesystem.

Technique

Use the `session_set_save_handler()` function to register functions that are working with the database:

```php
<?php
//
// 'sessions' table schema
// create table sessions (
//    session_id char(32) not null,
//    session_data text not null,
//    session_expiration int(11) unsigned not null,
//    primary key (session_id));
//

include_once 'DB.php';

// Global Variables
$dbh = NULL;

function on_session_start ($save_path, $session_name) {
    global $dbh;
```

```
    $dbh = DB::connect('mysql://user:secret@localhost/SITE_SESSIONS',
                        true);

    if (DB::isError($dbh)) {
        die(sprintf('Error [%d]: %s',
                    $dbh->getCode(), $dbh->getMessage()));
    }
}

function on_session_end ()
{
    // Nothing needs to be done in this function
    // since we used persistent connection.
}

function on_session_read ($key)
{
    global $dbh;

    $stmt = "select session_data from sessions";
    $stmt .= " where session_id = '$key'";
    $stmt .= " and session_expiration > now()";

    $sth = $dbh->query($sth);
    $row = $sth->fetchRow(DB_FETCHMODE_ASSOC);
    return $row['session_data'];
}

function on_session_write ($key, $val)
{
    global $dbh;

    $val = addslashes($val);

    $insert_stmt = "insert into sessions values('$key', '$val', now() + 3600)";
    $update_stmt = "update sessions set session_data = '$val', ";
    $update_stmt .= "session_expiration = now() + 3600 ";
    $update_stmt .= "where session_id = '$key'";

    // First we try to insert, if that doesn't succeed, it means
    // session is already in the table and we try to update
    if (DB::isError($dbh->query($insert_stmt)))
        $dbh->query($update_stmt);
```

```php
    }

    function on_session_destroy ($key)
    {
        global $dbh;

        $stmt = "delete from sessions where session_id = '$key'";
        $dbh->query($stmt);
    }

    function on_session_gc ($max_lifetime)
    {
        global $dbh;

        // In this example, we don't use $max_lifetime parameter
        // We simply delete all sessions that have expired
        $stmt = "delete from sessions where session_expiration < now()";
        $dbh->query($stmt);
    }

    session_start ();

    // Register the $counter variable as part
    // of the session
    session_register ("counter");

    // Set the save handlers
    session_set_save_handler ("on_session_start",   "on_session_end",
                              "on_session_read",    "on_session_write",
                              "on_session_destroy", "on_session_gc");

    // Let's see what it does
    $counter++;

    print $counter;

    session_destroy();

?>
```

Comments

The `session_set_save_handler()`function enables you to set up handler functions that the session system will call to perform the work of starting, ending, loading, and saving sessions.

The first argument of `session_set_save_handler()` is a function called by the session system when a session is first initialized. This function gets two arguments—first the path where the session was stored (which is the same as the `session.save_path` setting) and then the name of the session cookie that was set (default is `PHPSESSID`).

The next argument is the function called when the session is over (usually at the end of the script execution), and should be used to clean things up. This function receives no arguments.

The third argument to `session_set_save_handler()` is the function to execute when the session data needs to be read from the session store. The function receives the session ID as a function argument (that is, it receives something like `f08b925af0ecb52bdd2de97d95cdbe6b`). The *session id* is a random number that is generated in order to make it harder for hackers to guess a session id (and therefore have access to a user's data).

The fourth argument of `session_set_save_handler()` is the function to execute when the session needs to save the data to the session store. The function specified in this argument is passed both the value of the current session ID (refer to the previous paragraph) and the session data as one string.

The fifth argument of `session_set_save_handler()` is the function to execute when the value of the session needs to be destroyed. The function specified in this argument is passed the value of the current session ID.

The sixth and last argument of `session_set_save_handler()` is the garbage collection function. It is called periodically by the session system to clean up old sessions that have expired. The function specified in this argument is passed the number of seconds after which the session data should be seen as stale and cleaned up.

The `session_set_save_handler()` function is the crux of customizing the session management features of PHP. Although it might not seem easy, play with it a little bit. Try some trivial scripts with the `session_set_save_handler()`, and you will see how easy it becomes.

10.3 Setting the Session Name

The session name is the name that is stored in users' browsers, and the name that is shown when users visit your Web site who have warnings enabled for cookies. You want to change the name of your session from the one specified in the configuration file.

Technique

Use the session_name() function to change the name of the session cookie. Remember to call this function before the session_register() and session_start() functions:

```php
<?php
$old_session = session_name('WebsiteTracker');
//
// when called with no parameters session_name
// simply returns the current session name
//
$new_session = session_name();

// register a new session variable
session_register('session_variable');

print "The old session name was: $old_session, ";
print "the new session name is $new_session";
?>
```

Comments

The default value for the name of the cookie stored in the user's Web browser is PHPSESSID, but that is not very descriptive name for a cookie. In fact, when most end users who have warnings enabled for cookies are prompted to accept a cookie named PHPSESSID, they will probably be hesitant to accept it. The session_name() function enables you to change the name of the cookie at runtime, so you don't have to make sitewide changes by altering the session.name parameter in php.ini.

When calling the session_name() function, there are a couple rules. First, the new session name must be alphanumeric. No question marks, tildes (~), and so on. Second, the session_name() function must be called before the session_start() function or session_register() function for it to have any effect.

When called with parameters, the session_name() function modifies the session name variable and returns the old session name. However, if the session_name() function is called in void context, it simply returns the name of the current session as a string.

10.4 Setting and Getting Cookie Parameters

You want to get or set cookie parameters at runtime instead of in your php.ini file.

Technique

To set parameters, use the session_set_cookie_params() function, which enables you to set the lifetime of the cookie, the path of the cookie, and the domain of the cookie:

```
<?php
session_set_cookie_params(time()+8600,
                    '/cookiepath',
                    'designmultimedia.com');
?>
```

To get the session cookie parameters, use the session_get_cookie_params() function:

```
<?php
$cookie_params = session_get_cookie_params();
print "Cookie Lifetime:   $cookie_params[lifetime]\n<br>\n
       Cookie Path:       $cookie_params[path]\n<br>\n
       Cookie Domain:     $cookie_params[domain]";
?>
```

Comments

The session_set_cookie_params() function has the following syntax:

```
int session_set_oookie_params(int lifetime,[ string path, [string domain]]);
```

It enables you to modify at runtime the cookie parameters in the php.ini file. The lifetime parameter is how long until the cookie will expire. The optional path parameter is the path where the cookie will be stored and the domain is the domain that will be allowed to access the cookie. The function returns 1 on success and 0 on failure; if no arguments are given, the function returns an array of the current settings.

Even though all these parameters can be set in the php.ini file, it often helps to be able to modify session options at runtime, especially when dealing with something as specific as cookies.

The `session_get_cookie_params()` function returns an array containing the lifetime, path, and domain settings of the cookie, meaning that you can use the `session_get_cookie_params()` function to make sure that the `session_set_cookie_params()` function actually succeeded:

```php
<?php
$lifetime = time() + 8600;
$path     = '/cookiepath';
$domain = 'php.net';
if (session_set_cookie_params ($lifetime, $path, $domain)) {
    $cookie_params = session_get_cookie_params ();
    if ($cookie_params[lifetime] == $lifetime &&
        $cookie_params[path] == $path           &&
        $cookie_params[domain] == $domain) {
        print "Congrats, the session_set_cookie_params()";
        print " function really worked";
    }
}
?>
```

10.5 Unregistering a Variable in a Session

You need to remove a session variable or unregister it before script execution ends.

Technique

Use PHP's `session_unregister()` function instead of `unset()` to remove the variable from the session:

```php
<?php
session_register('somevar');
if (session_is_registered('somevar')) {
    session_unregister('somevar')
        or die('Could not unregister somevar');
}
?>
```

Comments

The `session_unregister()` function removes the specified variable from the session registry, so that when the session is saved, it will not contain the newly unregistered variable. This function does not delete the variable's contents, however.

10.6 Deleting All the Session Variables

You want to clear all the variables in the current session.

Technique

Use the `session_destroy()` function to wipe out the session:

```php
<?php

session_start();

session_register("foo");
session_register("foobar");
session_register("foobarina");

$foo        = array ("banana", "apple", "orange", "mango");
$foobar     = "fruits";
$foobarina  = "vegetables";

session_destroy();

print $foobar;
?>
```

Comments

The `session_destroy()` function will delete the session data from the session store. Note that it will not delete session variables' contents. For that, you need to use the `session_unset()` function to go through all session variables and remove them from the symbol table.

10.7 Using Objects As Session Variables

You're having trouble loading objects from sessions.

Technique

Remember that you must always include the class definition in every place you use the object.

std_class.inc:

```php
<?php
//
// File:  std_class.inc
//   Contains the class definition necessary to let an object be a session
//   variable.
//
class Foo
{
    var $name;
    var $email;

    //
    // A simple function to illustrate the point
    //
    function normalize_name ()
    {
        $name = preg_replace("/h(.)+/i", "\\1", $this->name);
        return substr($name, 0, 15);
    }
}
?>
```

main.php:

```php
<?php
//
// File:  main.php
//   Here is where we save and retrieve the object
//
include_once 'std_class.inc';

session_register('foobar');

if (!$foobar) {
    $foobar = new Foo;
    $foobar->name = "Sterling Hughes";
    $foobar->email = "sterling@php.net";
    $foobar->normalize_name();
}
?>
<a href="nextPage.php">Click Here</a>
```

nextPage.php:

```php
<?php
//
//  File: nextPage.php
//    Print out the name without initializing the
//    class and setting the variables
//
include_once 'std_class.inc';

session_register('foobar');
print $foobar->name;
?>
```

Comments

At the time of this writing, for PHP's session module to work properly with objects, you must include the class definition before you start the session. This needs to be done for every object stored in the session. This might change in later versions of PHP, but right now it is required. If you don't include the class definition, every time you access an object's property or method, PHP will print a warning saying that you should include class definition first.

10.8 Encode That Data

You want to save all the current session variables in string format and extract them back into variables at a later point.

Technique

Use the session_encode() and session_decode() functions:

write.php:

```php
<?php
session_register("monkey");
$monkey = array("see", "do");

$string_monkey = session_encode();
$fp = @fopen ("save_monkey.txt", "w")
              or die ("Cannot open save_monkey.txt");
@fwrite ($fp, $string_monkey);
```

```php
@fclose ($fp)
    or die ("Cannot close save_monkey.txt");
print "Actions Written";
?>
```

read.php:

```php
<?php
$fp = @fopen("save_monkey.txt", "r")
            or die("Cannot open save_monkey.txt");
$data = fread($fp, filesize ($fp));
@fclose ($fp)
     or die ("Cannot close save_monkey.txt");

session_decode($data);
foreach ($monkey as $action) {
    print "$action\n<br>\n";
}
?>
```

Description

The `session_encode()` function takes all the current session information and encodes it in to a string that can be parsed by the `session_decode()` function. The `session_decode()` function then parses that string and creates the session variables from the information contained within that string.

10.9 Creating a Shopping Cart Using Sessions and PHP

The next section of this chapter deals with storing variables and data, but before we go into that, I think the sessions part of this chapter should be culminated with a script. Therefore, I've written a small shopping cart script that contains all the necessary features (add items, take away items, view items). Please note that this script does not contain a checkout portion because that is off the topic.

site_lib.inc:

```php
<?php
//
// site_lib.inc -->
```

```
//   Contains the LoadProducts() function.
//


// Global Array with all the products,
// we fill up $master_products_list with
// the LoadProducts() function.
$master_products_list = array();


//
// void LoadProducts (void)
//   Load all of the products for this shopping cart into the global
//   $master_products_list array.
//
function LoadProducts() {
    global $master_products_list;
    $filename = 'products.txt';

    $fp = @fopen($filename, "r")
        or die("Cannot open $filename");

    // Acquire a shared lock, precautionary,
    // would be important if we were also writing to
    // the file
    @flock($fp, 1)
        or die("Cannot acquire a shared lock on $filename");

    while ($line = fgets($fp, 1024)) {
        list($id, $name, $desc, $price) = explode('|', $line);
        $id = trim($id); // Cut away the fat
        $master_products_list[$id] = array("name" =>  $name,
                                           "desc" => $desc,
                                           "price" => $price);
    }

    @fclose($fp)
        or die("Cannot close $filename");
}
?>
```

products.txt:

```
2kd230 | Bicycle | The coolest bicycle in the world | 23.83
dksk21 | Sony Playstation | Video game excitement | 123.00
```

cart.php:

```php
<?php
//
// cart.php:  The main file
//
require 'site_lib.inc';

session_register('cart'); // Register our session


// Initialize the Cart if it is not already initialized
if (!isset($cart[num_items])) {
    $cart = array("num_items" => 0,
                  "products"  => array());
}

// From site_lib.inc, Loads the $master_products_list array
LoadProducts();
?>

<html>
<head>
    <title>Sterling's Toy Shop</title>
</head>

<body>

<h1>Welcome to Sterling's Toy Shop</h1>

<?php
if ($cart[num_items]) { // If there is something to show
?>
<h2>Items Currently in your shopping cart</h2>
<br>
<table border="2" cellpadding="5" cellspacing="2">
<tr>
    <th>
        Product Name
```

```
    </th>
    <th>
        Short Description
    </th>
    <th>
        Price
    </th>
    <th>
        Quantity
    </th>
    <th>
         
    </th>
</tr>
<?php
    // Loop through the products
    foreach ($cart[products] as $i => $product) {
        $product_id = $product[0];
        $quantity   = $product[1];

        $total += $quantity *
                (double)$master_products_list[$product_id][price];
?>
<tr>
    <td>
        <?php echo $master_products_list[$product_id][name]; ?>
    </td>
    <td>
        <?php echo $master_products_list[$product_id][desc]; ?>
    </td>
    <td>
        <?php echo $master_products_list[$product_id][price]; ?>
    </td>
    <td>
        <form action="change_quant.php" method="GET">
        <input type="hidden" name="id" value="<?php echo $i; ?>">
        <input type="text" size="3" name="quantity"
                value="<?php echo $quantity; ?>">
    </td>
    <td>
        <input type="submit" value="Update Quantity">
        </form>
    </td>
```

```php
    </tr>
<?php
    }
?>
<tr>
    <td colspan="2">
        <b>Total: </b>
    </td>
    <td colspan="2">
        $<?php echo $total; ?>
    </td>
</tr>
</table>
<br>
<br>
<?php
}
?>

<h2>Toys for sale at Sterling's toy shop</h2>
<br>
<i>
    We offer the following toys for sale:
</i>
<br>
<table border="2" cellpadding="5" cellspacing="2">
<tr>
    <th>
        Product Name
    </th>
    <th>
        Product Description
    </th>
    <th>
        Price
    </th>
    <th>
         
    </th>
</tr>
<?php
    // Show all of the products
    foreach ($master_products_list as $product_id => $item) {
```

10.9 Creating a Shopping Cart Using Sessions and PHP

```
?>
<tr>
    <td>
        <?php echo $item[name]; ?>
    </td>
    <td>
        <?php echo $item[desc]; ?>
    </td>
    <td>
        $<?php echo $item[price]; ?>
    </td>
    <td>
        <a href="add_item.php?id=<?php echo $product_id; ?>">
            Add This item to your shopping cart
        </a>
    </td>
</tr>
<?php
    }
?>
</table>
```

add_item.php:

```
<?php
//
// add_item.php:
//   Add an item to the shopping cart.
//
require 'site_lib.inc'; // LoadProducts()

LoadProducts(); // Load products in $master_products_list

// Make $curr_product global
$curr_product = array();

// Loop through all the products and pull up the product
// that we are interested in

foreach ($master_products_list as $prod_id => $product) {
    if (trim($prod_id) == trim($id)) {
        $curr_product = $product;
    }
```

```php
    }

    // Register our session
    session_register('cart');

    if ($ordered) { // If they have chosen the product
        array_push($cart[products], array(trim($id), $quantity));
        $cart[num_items] += $quantity;
    }
?>

<html>
<head>
    <title>
    <?php if ($ordered) { ?>
        Added <?php echo $curr_product[name]; ?> to your shopping cart
    <?php } else { ?>
        Add <?php echo $curr_product[name]; ?> to your shopping cart
    <?php } ?>
    </title>
</head>
<body>
<?php if ($ordered) { ?>
    <h1><?php echo $curr_product[name]; ?>
        Was successfully added to your shopping cart</h1>

    Go <a href="cart.php">back</a> and continue shopping.
<?php } else { ?>
    <h1>Add <?php $curr_product[name]; ?> to your shopping cart</h1>

    <form action="<?php echo $PHP_SELF; ?>" method="GET">
    Product Name: <?php echo $curr_product[name]; ?>
    <br>
    Product Description: <?php echo $curr_product[desc]; ?>
    <br>
    Product Price: $<?php echo $curr_product[price]; ?>
    <br>
    Product Quantity: <input type="text" size="7" name="quantity">
    <input type="hidden" name="id" value="<?php echo $id; ?>">
    <input type="hidden" name="ordered" value="1">

    <input type="submit" value="Add to cart">
    </form>
```

10.9 Creating a Shopping Cart Using Sessions and PHP

```php
<?php } ?>
</body>
</html>
```

change_quant.php:

```php
<?php
//
// change_quant.php:
//    Change the quantity of an item in the shopping cart.
//
session_register('cart'); // register the session

// Typecast to int, making sure we access the
// right element below
$i = (int)$id;

// Save the old number of products for display
// and arithmetic
$old_num = $cart[products][$i][1];

if ($quantity) {
    $cart[products][$i][1] = $quantity; //change the quantity
} else {
    unset($cart[products][$i]); // Send the product into oblivion
}

// Update the number of items
$cart[num_items] = ($old_num > $quantity) ?
                    $cart[num_items] - ($old_num-$quantity) :
                    $cart[num_items] + ($quantity-$old_num);
?>

<html>
<head>
    <title>
        Quantity Changed
    </title>
</head>
<body>
    <h1> Quantity Changed from <?php echo $old_num; ?> to
        <?php echo $quantity; ?></h1>
```

```
    Go <a href="cart.php">back</a> and shop some more.
</body>
</html>
```

10.10 Serialization

You want to save variable contents as a string.

Technique

Create functions that implement the serialize() and unserialize() functions, and
then read and write data to a file:

```php
<?php
//
// File: loadsave.inc
//   Library functions for saving and
//   loading data to and from a file.
//


//
// int save (string varname):
//   Save the value of varname to file.
//
function save($var) {
    global $$var;
    $data = serialize($$var); // String Rep. of $$var
    $filename = "php_serialized_vars/" . $$var . ".txt";
    $fp = @fopen($filename, "w")
            or die("Cannot open $filename for write access");

    fwrite($fp, $data);
    @fclose($fp)
      or die("Cannot close $filename");
    return(true);
}


//
// int load (string varname)
//   Load the value of varname from a file.
```

```
//
function load($var)
{
    global $$var; // Put the saved variable in the global
                  // namespace
    $filename = "php_serialized_vars/" . $$var . ".txt";
    $fp = @fopen($filename, "r")
            or die("Cannot open $filename for read access");

    $data = fread($fp, filesize($filename));
    @fclose($fp)
      or die("Cannot close $filename");

    $$var = unserialize($data);
    return(true);
}
?>
```

Then you can call these newly created functions, like this:

save.php:

```
<?php
$foo = "hello";
save('foo');
?>
<a href="load.php">Click here</a>
```

load.php:

```
<?php
load('foo');
print $foo;
?>
```

Comments

The serialize() function creates a string representation of PHP data, whether that data is an array, object, plain string, or number. The unserialize() function will read this string and bring back the original data, much like a compression and decompression program such as bzip or gzip. Note that when unserializing an object, you need to have the object's class definition loaded first, just as for sessions.

10.11 WDDX Serialization

You want to serialize many variables at once, not just one variable at a time. Or, perhaps you want to share your variables with other languages or processes.

Technique

Use the WDDX functions, which serialize data according to the WDDX standard at `http://www.wddx.org/`.

```php
<?php
$ice_cream = array("Mint Chocolate Chip",
                   "Vanilla",
                   "Chocolate",
                   "Coffee");
$packet_id = wddx_packet_start("PHP");
wddx_add_vars($packet_id, "ice_cream");
$packet = wddx_packet_end($packet_id);
?>
```

Comments

The WDDX, or Web Distributed Data eXchange, format is a "...mechanism for exchanging complex data structures between application environments." (`http://www.wddx.org/DTD.htm`) Basically, when you serialize data with the WDDX functions, the WDDX function creates data "packets" that contain information about your variables.

These packets can be stored and then read back into your program, as we did with the `serialize()` and `unserialize()` functions in recipe 10.10. Another popular use of WDDX is to serialize variables in the WDDX format for other programs or languages to read and then use them.

10.12 WDDX Deserialization

You have a WDDX-encoded string and you want to get your data back from it.

Technique

Use the `wddx_deserialize()` function to decode a WDDX string into a PHP variable:

```php
<?php
```

```
$favorite_tv_shows = array("M*A*S*H", "Seinfeld", "The Simpsons");
$text = wddx_serialize_vars($favorite_tv_shows);
$favorite_tv_shows_again = wddx_deserialize($text);

foreach ($favorite_tv_shows_again as $show) {
    print "$show\n<br>\n";
}

?>
```

Comments

The `wddx_deserialize()` function takes a WDDX packet and converts it to an array of equivalent PHP variables. One neat use of `wddx_deserialize()` is to take WDDX packets generated by other languages and translate them into PHP variables.

CHAPTER 11

Interacting with Web Pages and Servers

11.0 Introduction

Interacting with Web pages and Web servers is at the very heart of what PHP is designed to do.

In this chapter we'll discuss everything from fetching a Web page to searching your Web site for outdated links to extracting all the URLs from a Web page.

11.1 Fetching a Web Page

You have the URL of a Web page and you want to manipulate it as you would a file.

Technique

Use fopen(), which supports the capability of opening URLs:

```php
<?php
$fp = @fopen($url, 'r')
    or die("Cannot Open $url via Get method");
while ($line = @fgets($fp, 1024)) {
    $contents .= $line;
}
fclose($fp);
?>
```

Or, use the `readfile()` function:

```
$contents = readfile($url);
```

Or use PHP's `Net_Curl` module:

```php
<?php
$conn = new Net_Curl($url);
$data = $conn->execute();
print $data;
?>
```

Comments

PHP's filesystem functions enable you to read via HTTP and FTP, meaning that you can open URLs and read from them. However, please be aware that the file stat functions are executed through system calls. Therefore, functions such as `stat()` and `filesize()` will not work on URLs.

You must also be aware that PHP does not support HTTP redirects. Therefore, if you give PHP a URL such as `http://www.designmultimedia.com/programming`, it will not work. However, if you give PHP a URL such as `http://www.designmultimedia.com/programming/`, it will work. Put simply, you must put trailing slashes on directories for PHP to be able to fetch a Web page.

If you want to access a page that requires password authentication, you must use the following form of the URL:

```
http://user:password@www.designmultimedia.com/protected_dir/
```

where *user* is the username for the protected directory and *password* is the corresponding password.

The `readfile()` function shown in the solution implements the same function as `fopen()` as far as opening a URL is concerned. However, note that if you use `readfile()` on a large URL, there is a larger chance that a URL will hang than if you read the file into memory one line at time.

The `Net_Curl` module from PEAR interfaces with the `curl` module. To use the `Net_Curl` module, you need to compile PHP `--with-curl` support. The `Net_Curl` extension provides a more powerful interface for accessing the content of Web pages than do the other methods. For example, with `Net_Curl`, you can connect with SSL servers and connect through proxies.

11.2 Performing an SSL Transaction

You want to use PHP to connect to an SSL server.

Technique

Use the `Net_Curl` module from PEAR, which interfaces with PHP's `curl` extension:

```php
<?php
include_once 'Net/Curl.php';

// Initialize the transfer
$conn = new Net_Curl('https://secureserver.com');
if (Net_Curl::isError($conn)) {
    die(sprintf('Error [%d]: %s',
                $conn->getCode(), $conn->getMessage()));
}

// Set the transfer options
//(optional)
$conn->sslVersion = 3;
$conn->sslCert = 'file_name_of_certificate';
$conn->sslCertPasswd = 'secret';

// Execute the transfer
$data = $conn->execute();
if (Net_Curl::isError($conn)) {
    die(sprintf('Error [%d]: %s',
                $data->getCode(), $data->getMessage()));
}

print "The results of your transaction were: \n<br>\n";
print $data;
?>
```

Comments

The `curl` extension to PHP interfaces with an external library, libcurl, which is freely available from `http://curl.haxx.se`. In the solution, we use the `Net_Curl` package, which is freely available from PEAR at `http://pear.php.net/`. `Net_Curl` provides an easy interface to perform transactions with PHP's `curl` extension.

If you don't want to use PEAR's `Net_Curl` package, you can also directly interface with
the `curl` extension:

```php
<?php

// Initialize the transfer
$ch = curl_init('https://secureserver.com');
if (!$ch) {
    die(sprintf('Error [%d]: %s',
                curl_errno($ch), curl_error($ch)));
}

//Set the transfer options
//(optional)
curl_setopt($ch, CURLOPT_SSLVERSION, 3);
curl_setopt($ch, CURLOPT_SSLCERT, 'ssl_certificate');
curl_setopt($ch, CURLOPT_SSLCERTPASSWD, 'secret');
curl_setopt($ch, CURLOPT_HEADER, 0);
curl_setopt($ch, CURLOPT_RETURNTRANSFER, 1);

// Execute the transfer
$data = curl_exec($ch);
if (!$data) {
    die(sprintf('Error [%d]: %s',
                curl_errno($ch), curl_error($ch)));
}

// Close the transfer
curl_close($ch);

print "The results of your transfer were:\n<br>\n";
print $data;
?>
```

11.3 Performing an HTTP POST Request

You want to use PHP to perform an HTTP POST operation on a remote Web site.

Technique

Use the `Net_Curl` class from PEAR and set the `type` property to `"post"`. Then just fill
in the `fields` property with the array of post fields you want to send:

```php
<?php
// Initialize
$conn = new Net_Curl('http://www.designmultimedia.com/php/form.php');
if (Net_Curl::isError($conn)) {
    die(sprintf('Error [%d]: %s',
                $conn->getCode(), $conn->getMessage()));
}

// Set the transfer options
$conn->type = 'POST';
$conn->fields = array("name"     => "Sterling Hughes",
                      "email"    => "sterling@php.net",
                      "comments" => "Nice site.");

// Execute the transfer
$data = $conn->execute();
if (Net_Curl::isError($data)) {
    die(sprintf('Error [%d]: %s',
                $data->getCode(), $data->getMessage()));
}

print "The results of your transfer were: \n<br>\n";
print $data;
?>
```

Comments

Using the curl extension in conjunction with the Net_Curl package makes HTTP POST operations easy. The basic flow is you initialize the transfer, and then you tell PHP that the method of transfer will be HTTP POST by setting the type property to "POST". After you've told PHP that this will be a POST transfer, you give it an associative array of the information you want to POST to the remote script. Finally, you execute the transfer and receive the results in an array.

Using the Net_Curl package is the best way to perform cURL transfers, but if you want to use the curl extension itself for this, do the following:

```php
<?php
$ch = curl_init('http://www.designmultimedia.com/php/form.php');
if (!$ch) {
    die(sprintf('Error [%d]: %s',
                curl_errno($ch), curl_error($ch)));
}
```

```php
$submit = array("name"     => "Sterling Hughes",
                "email"    => "sterling@php.net",
                "comments" => "Love the site.");

curl_setopt($ch, CURLOPT_POST, 1);
curl_setopt($ch, CURLOPT_POSTFIELDS, $submit);
curl_setopt($ch, CURLOPT_RETURNTRANSFER, 1);

$data = curl_exec($ch);
if (!$data) {
    die(sprintf('Error [%d]: %s',
                curl_errno($ch), curl_error($ch)));
}

print "The results of your transfer were: \n<br>\n";
print $data;
?>
```

11.4 Performing an HTTP File Upload

You want to upload a file to a remote site with PHP by using the PUT method.

Technique

Use the Net_Curl class from PEAR, which interfaces with PHP's curl extension:

```php
<?php

// Initialize the transfer
$conn = new Net_Curl('http://yoursite.com/');
if (Net_Curl::isError($conn)) {
    die(sprintf('Error [%d]: %s',
                $conn->getCode(), $conn->getMessage()));
}

// Set transfer options
$conn->type = "PUT";
$conn->file = "sterling.jpg";

// Execute the transfer
$res = $conn->execute();
```

```php
if (Net_Curl::isError($res)) {
    die(sprintf('Error [%d]: %s',
                $res->getCode(), $res->getMessage()));
}

print "The results of the transfer were:\n<br>\n";
print $res;
?>
```

Comments

Here we use the Net_Curl module, which is a simple wrapper around the curl extension. The crux of this recipe lies in setting the $conn->type variable to "PUT", which tells PHP that we will be using the HTTP PUT method instead of the default HTTP GET method. We then set $conn->file to the name of the file that we want to upload when PHP performs the transfer.

If you want to use a purely PHP implementation (and not use the simpler Net_Curl package), you can do the following:

```php
<?php

// Initialize the cURL transfer
$ch = curl_init('http://yourserver.com');
if (!$ch) {
    die(sprintf('Error [%d]: %s',
                curl_errno($ch), curl_error($ch)));
}

// Set transfer options
curl_setopt($ch, CURLOPT_PUT, 1);
curl_setopt($ch, CURLOPT_INFILE, 'filename');
curl_setopt($ch, CURLOPT_INFILESIZE, filesize('filename'));
curl_setopt($ch, CURLOPT_HEADER, 0);
curl_setopt($ch, CURLOPT_RETURNTRANSFER, 1);

// Execute transfer
$res = curl_exec($ch);
if (!$res) {
    die(sprintf('Error [%d]: %s',
                curl_errno($ch), curl_error($ch)));
}
```

```
// Free resources
curl_close($ch);

print "The results of your transfer were: \n<br>\n";
print $res;
?>
```

11.5 Sending Cookies with Your Request

You want to send an HTTP cookie to a remote server when performing a transaction.

Technique

Set the cookies property of the Net_Curl PEAR class:

```
<?php
// Initialize
$conn = new Net_Curl('http://www.zend.com/');
if (Net_Curl::isError($conn)) {
    die(sprintf('Error [%d]: %s',
                $conn->getCode(), $conn->getMessage()));
}

// Set transfer options
$conn->cookies = array(name  => 'Sterling',
                       email => 'sterling@php.net');

// Execute transfer
$data = $conn->execute();
if (Net_Curl::isError($data)) {
    die(sprintf('Error [%d]: %s',
                $data->getCode(), $data->getMessage()));
}

print "The results of your transfer were: \n<br>\n";
print $data;
?>
```

Comments

When setting the `cookies` property of the `Net_Curl` class, you can provide an array of key/value pairs; a file containing the cookie data in Netscape format or regular HTTP; colon-delimited data; or the raw cookie data itself (in Netscape or HTTP format).

11.6 Excluding or Including the Header from a cURL Transfer

You want to exclude or include the header from a cURL transfer.

Technique

If you are using the `Net_Curl` class from PEAR, the header is automatically not included. To change this, set the `header` property to `true`:

```php
<?php
// Initialize the transfer
$conn = new Net_Curl('http://www.php.net/index.php');
if (Net_Curl::isError($conn)) {
    die(sprintf('Error [%d]: %s',
                $conn->getCode(), $conn->getMessage()));
}


// Include the header
$conn->header = true;


// Execute the transfer
$res = $conn->execute();
if (Net_Curl::isError($res)) {
    die(sprintf('Error [%d]: %s',
                $res->getCode(), $res->getMessage()));
}


print "The output of your transfer was:\n<br>\n";
print $res;
?>
```

If you want to exclude the header from a transfer and you aren't using the `Net_Curl` class from PEAR, set the `CURLOPT_HEADER` option to `0`:

```php
<?php
// Initialize the Curl transfer
$ch = curl_init('http://www.ispi.net/index.html');
```

```php
if (!$ch) {
    die(sprintf('Error [%d]: %s',
                curl_error($ch), curl_errno($ch)));
}

// Set transfer options
curl_setopt($ch, CURLOPT_HEADER, 0);
curl_setopt($ch, CURLOPT_RETURNTRANSFER, 1);

// Execute transfer
$res = curl_exec($ch);
if (!$res) {
    die(sprintf('Error [%d]: %s',
                curl_errno($ch), curl_error($ch)));
}

// Free resources
curl_close($ch);

print "The results of your transfer were:\n<br>\n";
print $res;
?>
```

Comments

The Net_Curl class from PEAR automatically sets the CURLOPT_HEADER option to 0, so if you want to include the header in the results of your transfer, you must set the $header property to a nonfalse value. If you are using the PHP extension interface, the header is included by default, so you are required to set the CURLOPT_HEADER option to a nontrue value manually to exclude the header in the results.

11.7 Connecting Through a Proxy Server

You want to use the Net_Curl class from PEAR and set the proxyUser and proxyPassword properties.

Technique

Use the following code:

```php
<?php
// Initialize
```

```
$conn = new Net_Curl('http://qa.php.net/');
if (Net_Curl::isError($conn)) {
    die(sprintf('Error [%d]: %s',
                $conn->getCode(), $conn->getMessage()));
}

// Set transfer options
$conn->proxyUser     = 'sterling';
$conn->proxyPassword = 'secret';

// Execute transfer
$data = $conn->execute();
if (Net_Curl::isError($data)) {
    die(sprintf('Error [%d]: %s',
                $data->getCode(), $data->getMessage()));
}

print "The results of your transfer were: \n<br>\n";
print $data;
?>
```

Comments

If you need to interact with a proxy server to fetch a URL with the `Net_Curl` class, set the `proxyUser` and `proxyPassword` properties to appropriate values and execute the transfer.

11.8 Getting Information Regarding a cURL Transfer

For some reason your cURL transfers aren't succeeding.

Technique

Set the `$progress`, `$mute`, and `$verbose` properties in the `Net_Curl` class:

```
<?php
//Initialize the CURL transfer
$conn = new Net_Curl('http://www.webtechniques.com/');
if (Net_Curl::isError($conn)) {
    die(sprintf('Error [%d]: %s',
                $conn->getCode(), $conn->getMessage()));
}
```

```php
// Set transfer options
$conn->verbose = 1;
$conn->progress = 1;
$conn->mute = 0;

// Execute the transfer
$data = $conn->execute();
if (Net_Curl::isError($data)) {
    die(sprintf('Error [%d]: %s',
                $data->getCode(), $data->getMessage()));
}

print "The Results of your transfer were:\n<br>\n";
print $data;
?>
```

Comments

Setting the verbose and progress properties to nonfalse values tells PHP to report all its actions to STDERR (the standard error stream). Setting the mute property to 0 tells PHP not to suppress any warnings or errors.

If you want PHP to fail when a bad error code (< 300) is returned from a Web site, set the fail property to a nonfalse value:

```php
<?php

$conn = new Net_Curl('http://www.mcp.com/index.cfm');
if (Net_Curl::isError($conn)) {
    die(sprintf('Error [%d]: %s',
                $conn->getCode(), $conn->getMessage()));
}

$conn->fail = true;

$data = $conn->execute();
if (Net_Curl::isError($data)) {
    die(sprintf('Error [%d]: %s',
                $data->getCode(), $data->getMessage()));
}

print "The Results of your transfer were: \n<br>\n";
print $data;
?>
```

11.9 Interacting with Frames

You are accessing a Web site that uses frames and you want to fetch the contents of an individual frame.

Technique

Use the Snoopy class (available from `http://snoopy.sourceforge.net/`), which supports fetching individual frames:

```php
<?php
include_once 'Snoopy.class.inc';

$snoopy = new Snoopy;
$snoopy->maxframes = 3;
$snoopy->fetch('http://www.ispi.net/');

print "The middle frame has the following contents: ";
print "\n<br>\n<br>\n<br>\n";
print htmlentities($snoopy->results[1]);
?>
```

Comments

Snoopy, available from `http://snoopy.sourceforge.net/`, fetches frames for you. In the example, we initialize the Snoopy class, set the `maxframes` property to the maximum number of frames to fetch (3), and then use the `fetch()` method to fetch the page. After we've fetched the page, we access the middle frame (the frames are stored in a numerically indexed array), and print its contents.

11.10 Extracting All the URLs from a Web Page

You want to extract all URLs from a Web page.

Technique

Use a regex expression and strip the URLs as you read the file line by line:

```php
<?php
$fp = fopen('http://www.yahoo.com/', 'r') or die('Cannot connect');
while ($line = fgets($fp, 1024)) {
    if (preg_match_all('/<.*?a.*?href=\s*?[\'"](.+)[\'"].*?>.*?<\/.*?a.*?>/i',
        $line, $matches)) {
```

```
        array_shift($matches);
        foreach ( $matches as $match ) $url_list[] = $match;
    }
}
fclose($fp)
    or die("Cannot Close File");
?>
```

Comments

The optimal way to get all links from a Web page is by looping through the file line by line, and then matching every occurrence of the links on a Web page. After we match the URL, we can add it to our final array ($url_list). However, $matches is an array and the first item of the array contains the entire match, and we are not interested in that. So, we kick out the first item of the $matches array and loop through the entire array adding it element by element to $url_list.

To achieve this effect, you can also use the Snoopy class, available from http://snoopy.sourceforge.net/. Snoopy extracts all the links on a Web page for you:

```
<?php
include_once 'Snoopy.class.inc';

$snoopy = new Snoopy;
$snoopy->fetchlinks('http://www.internet.com/');

foreach ($snoopy->results as $link) {
    print "Link: $link\n";
}
?>
```

11.11 Finding Stale and Fresh Links

You want to find all links on a certain page and see which ones work and which ones don't.

Technique

Roll your own engine. First, find all the links on the page and then check each one to make sure that it works:

```
<?php
include_once 'Snoopy.class.inc';
```

```php
$good_urls = array();
$bad_urls  = array();

// Use snoopy to fetch all the links on yahoo.com
$snoopy = new Snoopy;
$snoopy->fetchlinks('http://www.yahoo.com/');
$links = $snoopy->results;

//Expand URL's that are not fully qualified
$links = expand_links($links, 'http://www.yahoo.com');
foreach ($links as $link) {
    if (check_link($link))
        array_push($good_urls, $link);
    else
        array_push($bad_urls, $link);
}

print "The Ok urls are:\n" . implode("\n", $good);
print "\n\nThe Bad urls are:\n" . implode("\n", $bad);

// Check to make sure the link works
function check_link($url) {
    $snoopy = new Snoopy;
    $snoopy->fetch($url);

    // A response code of 404 means that the
    // file was not found.
    if (intval($snoopy->response_code) == 404) {
        return(false);
    } else {
        return(true);
    }
}

// Expand links into their full paths
function expand_links($links, $base_url) {
    foreach ($links as $link) {
        if (!preg_match('!^([a-z ])*\://!i', $link)) {
            $link = ($link[0] ==='/') ?
                    $baseurl . $link :
                    $baseurl . '/' . $link;
        }
```

```
        $ret[] = $link;
    }
    return($ret);
}
?>
```

Comments

Here we use the Snoopy class, available from `http://snoopy.sourceforge.net/`. We will use Snoopy's `fetchlinks` method to fetch all the links from `http://www.yahoo.com/` into an array. We then use the `expandLinks()` function to expand all URLs into fully qualified URLs. Then we try to open each URL. If the connection is successful, we add the URL to the `$good_urls` array and then close the connection; otherwise, we add the URL to the `$bad_urls` array.

11.12 Getting New Links from a Web Page

You want to get the latest links for your favorite Web page.

Technique

Save the links in a file, and every time you check the Web page, have the file add new links and report them to you:

```php
<?php
include_once 'Snoopy.class.inc';

$url_list = array();
$snoopy = new Snoopy;

$snoopy->fetchlinks('http://www.yahoo.com/');
$links = $snoopy->results;

$links = expand_links($links);

$fp = @fopen('yahoo_links', 'r');
if (!$fp) {
    die('Cannot open yahoo_links in read mode');
}
```

```
while ($link = @fgets($fp, 1024)) {
    $link = trim($link);
    if (!in_array($link, $links))
        array_push($url_list, $link);
}

print "<b>New URL's on Yahoo:</b>\n<br>\n";
for ($idx = 0; $idx < count($url_list); $idx++) {
    print "<a href=\"$url_list[$idx]\">$url_list[$idx]</a>\n<br>\n";
}

@fclose($fp);

$fp = @fopen('yahoo_links', 'w');
if (!$fp) {
    die('Cannot open yahoo_links in write mode');
}

@fwrite($fp, implode("\n", $links));

@fclose($fp);

function expand_links($links, $base_url) {
    foreach ($links as $link) {
        if (!preg_match('!^([a-z])*\://!i', $link)) {
            $link = ($link[0] == '/') ?
                    $baseurl . $link   :
                    $baseurl . '/' . $link;
        }
        $ret[] = $link;
    }
    return($ret);
}
?>
```

Comments

Creating a list of new links on your Web site can be useful for everything from
creating a what's new script to sending an email to yourself every time Yahoo updates
its content. To do this, we create a plain text file that keeps track of all the URLs we
have already seen. We then extract all the URLs from the current page and put them
in the $links array. After we have all the URLs from the page in the $links array, we

loop through them. If the link does not already exist in the preexisting link file, we add the link to the `$url_list` array. We then loop through all the new links (contained in the `$url_list` array) and print them. Finally, we write the links in the `$links` array to the link file (yahoo_links).

11.13 Mirroring a Web Page

You want to mirror a Web page on your server.

Technique

Simply use the `readfile()` function:

```php
<?php
    readfile('http://www.designmultimedia.com/');
?>
```

Comments

The `readfile()` function takes a URL and writes the output to the browser. So, every time your page is requested, it simply outputs the page that it fetches from another server.

11.14 Parsing and Formatting a Log File

The following program will parse your standard Web server's log file and print the results in a formatted HTML table. An example log file entry might be the following:

```
212.27.53.112 - - [25/March/2000:05:10:29 +100] "GET /site.htm HTTP/1.0"
                200 1892
```

The program:

```php
<?php
$fp = @fopen($logfile_location, "r")
    or die("Cannot Open $logfile_location");

while ($line = fgets($fp, 1024)) {
    $line = trim($line);
    preg_match("/^(\S+)\s+(\S+)\s+(\S+)\s+\[(.*)\]
                \s+\"(.*)\"\s+(\S+)\s+(\S+)$/x", $line, $matches);
    array_shift($matches);
```

11.14 Parsing and Formatting a Log File

```php
    $host = $matches[0];
    $identity = $matches[1];
    $user = $matches[2];
    $time = $matches[3];
    $url = $matches[4];
    $success = $matches[5];
    $bytes = $matches[6];

    preg_match("@(..)/(...)/(....):(..):(..):(..)@", $time, $matches);
    array_shift($matches);

    $day = $matches[0];
    $mon = $matches[1] + 1;
    $year = $matches[2];
    $hour = $matches[3];
    $minutes = $matches[4];
    $seconds = $matches[5];

    preg_match("/\S+\s+(\S+)/", $url, $matches);
    $url = $matches[1];
    if ($success == 200) {
        $success[$i++] = array($host,
                               $identity,
                               $user,
                               array($day, $mon, $year,
                                     $hour, $minutes, $seconds),
                               $url,
                               $bytes);
    } else {
        $failure[$x++] = array($host,
                               $identity,
                               $user,
                               array($day, $mon, $year,
                                     $hour, $minutes, $seconds),
                               $url,
                               $bytes);
    }
}
?>
<html>
<head>
    <title> Here is the results of your access logs </title>
</head>
```

```html
<body>
<h1> Reports on your Access logs </h1>
    <h2> Successful Accesses </h2>
<br>
<table border="1" cellpadding="2" cellspacing="1">
<tr>
    <th> Host </th>
    <th> Identity </th>
    <th> User </th>
    <th> Time </th>
    <th> Url </th>
    <th> Bytes </th>
</tr>

<?php
for ($idx = 0; $idx < count($success); $idx++) {
?>
<tr>
    <td> <?php echo $success[$idx][0]; ?> </td>
    <td> <?php echo $success[$idx][1]; ?> </td>
    <td> <?php echo $success[$idx][2]; ?> </td>
    <td> <?php
     echo "On: " . $success[$idx][3][1] . "/";
     echo $success[$idx][3][0] . "/";
     echo $success[$idx][3][2] . ", ";
     echo "at: " . $success[$idx][3][3] . ":";
     echo $success[$idx][3][4] . ":" . $success[$idx][3][5];
    ?>
    </td>
    <td> <?php echo $success[$idx][4]; ?> </td>
    <td> <?php echo $success[$idx][5]; ?> </td>
</tr>
<?php } ?>
</table>
<br><br>
    <h2> Failures </h2>
<br>
<table border="1" cellpadding="2" cellspacing="1">
<tr>
    <th> Host </th>
    <th> Identity </th>
    <th> User </th>
    <th> Time </th>
```

```
    <th> Url </th>
    <th> Bytes </th>
</tr>

<?php
for ($idx = 0; $idx < count($failure); $idx++) {
?>
<tr>
    <td> <?php echo $failure[$idx][0]; ?> </td>
    <td> <?php echo $failure[$idx][1]; ?> </td>
    <td> <?php echo $failure[$idx][2]; ?> </td>
    <td> <?php
     echo "On: " . $failure[$idx][3][1] . "/";
     echo $failure[$idx][3][0] . "/";
     echo $failure[$idx][3][2] . ", ";
     echo "at: " . $failure[$idx][3][3] . ":";
     echo $failure[$idx][3][4] . ":" . $failure[$idx][3][5];
    ?>
    </td>
    <td> <?php echo $failure[$idx][4]; ?> </td>
    <td> <?php echo $failure[$idx][5]; ?> </td>
</tr>
<?php } ?>
</table>
</body>
</html>
```

PART II

Databases

CHAPTER

12 Creating a Database-Independent API
with PHP

CHAPTER 12

Creating a Database-Independent API with PHP

"If money is your hope for independence you will never have it. The only real security that a man will have in this world is a reserve of knowledge, experience, and ability."

Henry Ford

12.0 Introduction

One of the most powerful features of PHP is its capability to connect to a database, whether it be MySQL or Oracle. It's the reason why most people use PHP: to take the data in databases and bring it to the Web.

In PHP, programmers traditionally make database-specific calls to connect to a different database. For example, you would use `mysql_connect()` to connect to a MySQL database, whereas you would have to use the `OCILogon()` function to connect to an Oracle database.

Using different functions to connect to different databases was a drag for many PHP programmers, especially converted Perl programmers who were used to Perl's DBI, which allows for portability when changing databases. For example, examine the following two pieces of code. One uses PHP's API to connect to MySQL and the other uses Perl's DBI to connect to MySQL:

PHP:

```php
<?php
$dbh = mysql_connect($host, $user, $password);
mysql_select_db($dbname);
$stmt = "SELECT * FROM table";
$sth = mysql_query($stmt, $dbh);
```

```
while ($row = mysql_fetch_array($sth, MYSQL_ASSOC)) {
    echo $row["firstName"];
    echo $row["lastName"];
}
mysql_free_result ($sth);
mysql_close ($dbh);
?>
```

Perl with DBI:

```
use DBI;

my $dbh = DBI->connect("dbi:mysql:$dbname", $user, $password);
my $sth = $dbh->do ("SELECT * FROM table");

while (my $row = $sth->fetchrow_hashref)) {
    print $row->{firstName};
    print $row->{lastName};
}
$sth->finish;
$dbh->disconnect;
```

As you can see, they are both of approximately the same complexity, but the Perl example is more portable. In PHP, if you wanted to change the database from MySQL to Oracle, you would have to use an entirely different set of functions. However, in the Perl example, you need to change only one line:

```
$dbh = DBI->connect("dbi:oracle:$dbname", $user, $pass);
```

Perl's DBI uses an object-oriented approach to creating a database-independent API, but this is not the only way to achieve database independence. In fact, we aren't going to use the object-oriented approach.

"Why not use the object-oriented approach? It works so well for Perl, why not for PHP?" For one thing, in the words of Zeev Suraski, one of the designers of PHP, "PHP is not an OO language." That doesn't mean that PHP doesn't have object-oriented features—in fact, PHP does have most of the major object-oriented constructs, but it does mean that the OO solution will not be as fast or elegant.

What other choices are there? There's really only one viable choice, and that is the function-oriented approach to creating a database-independent API with PHP. In the function-oriented approach, we have a set of generic "wrapper" functions, which are substitutes for the database-specific function calls. For example, instead of `mysql_connect()`, we have `db_connect()`.

Consider the following example of connecting to a database and fetching a row by using the function-oriented API:

```php
<?php
include_once("DB/mysql.php");

$dbh = db_connect(array($host,$user,$pass));
if (!$dbh){
    die("Cannot connect to database");
}
db_select_db(array("sampleDB"));
$sth = db_query("SELECT * FROM sampleTable", $dbh);
if (!$sth) {
    die("Cannot execute query");
}
while ($row = db_fetch_row(array($sth))) {
    echo $row["firstname"];
    echo $row["lastname"];
}
db_free_result(array($sth));
db_close(array($dbh));
?>
```

That's it—no complex interfaces. At the top of the script, you include the file that contains the appropriate wrapper functions, and you use those generic functions instead of the database-specific functions.

In this chapter, we discuss how to implement this database-independent API by using PHP. In the next chapter, we talk about how to use the API, as well as related concepts.

12.1 The Glue

If we were using the object-oriented approach to database independence with PHP, we would need a whole lot of code to tie everything together. However, with the function-oriented interface, the code becomes simpler. Just include the right header file and you're set. For example, to use a MySQL database the include line would be include_once("DB/mysql.php"), and to include and work with an Oracle database, the line would be include_once("DB/oracle.php").

Also note that all function calls will accept only one parameter—an array that contains the real parameters. This is used so that your function take an optional number of arguments, in case the function call for one database requires more arguments than a function call for another database. (It is also done this way for compatibility with PHP 3; in PHP 4, you can use a combination of `func_num_args()`, `func_get_arg()`, and `func_get_args()` to achieve the same effect.)

One thing that's always nice, and not too hard to implement, is a standard set of often-needed functions. These can be API functions (such as `db_fetchall()` in the following code), or they can be internal functions (such as `db_simulate_prepare()`, also in the following code). We're going to place these functions into a file called DB/standard.php, and then include them in all the different modules so that they will be available to the user.

DB/standard.php

```php
<?php
function &db_fetchall($args=array()) {
    $rows = array();
    while ($row = db_fetchrow($args[0], DB_GETMODE_NUM)) {
        array_push($rows, &$row);
    }
    return($rows);
}


function &db_fetchall_assoc($args=array()) {
    $rows = array();
    while ($row = db_fetchrow($args[0], DB_GETMODE_ASSOC)) {
        array_push($rows, &$row);
    }
    return ($rows);
}



function db_simulate_prepare($args=array()) {
    return array_shift($args);
}


function db_simulate_execute($args=array()) {
    $stmt     = array_shift($args);
    $prepArgs = array_shift($args);

    if (!is_array($prepArgs)) {
        return($stmt);
    }
```

```
    $parts = explode('?', $stmt);
    foreach ($parts as $part) {
        $new_stmt .= $part . array_shift($args);
    }

    return($new_stmt);
}
?>
```

The `db_fetchall()` and `db_fetchall_assoc()` functions use the database-independent API that we've created to implement commonly needed and useful functions for manipulating result sets using PHP. Both functions build an array of all the rows in the result set (given by the first argument). You can use these functions like so:

```
<?php

include_once("DB/mysql.php");
$dbh = db_connect(array("localhost", "username", "password"));
if (!$dbh) {
    die(sprintf("An error occurred, %s: %s", db_errno(), db_error()));
}
$sth = db_query("SELECT * FROM some table");
if (!$sth) {
    die(sprintf("Couldn't execute query, %s: %s", db_errno(), db_error()));
}
$rows = db_fetchall_assoc($sth);
foreach ($rows as $row)
{
    print $row[firstname];
    print $row[lastname];
    print $row[occupation];
}

db_free_result($sth);
db_close($dbh);
?>
```

The `db_simulate_prepare()` and `db_simulate_execute()` functions will simulate the prepare and execute functions for databases where those features are not supported. The method we use is quite easy. The `db_simulate_prepare()` function is simply a dummy; it takes the query that needs to be prepared and returns it to the user.

The db_simulate_execute() function is a little more advanced. First, it splits the string by the '?' delimiter (using the explode() function), and then it concatenates the appropriate string from the user's array. The db_simulate_execute() function then returns the query that should be executed.

12.2 The MySQL Module

Now that we have a basic idea of the concept behind our database-independent API, it's time to implement the wrapper functions for the different databases. The first database for which we are implementing a wrapper is MySQL. MySQL is a lightweight, fast database put out by T.c.X. Because of its speed and simplicity, MySQL is an ideal complement to PHP. That is why, as of PHP version 4, MySQL support is bundled with PHP. More information about MySQL can be found at http://www.mysql.com/.

DB/mysql.php

```php
<?php
include_once("DB/standard.php");

function db_connect($args=array()) {
    switch (count($args)) {
        case 0:
            return @mysql_connect();
        case 1:
            return @mysql_connect($args[0]);
        case 2:
            return @mysql_connect($args[0], $args[1]);
        default:
            return @mysql_connect($args[0], $args[1], $args[2]);
    }
}

function db_pconnect($args=array()) {
    switch (count($args)) {
        case 0:
            return @mysql_pconnect();
        case 1:
            return @mysql_pconnect($args[0]);
```

Explanation

The MySQL API is very easy to create wrappers for because like the mSQL and the MSSQL modules, it is fairly standard. It has most functions that the other databases have, and it doesn't have many critical functions that the other databases don't have.

For arguments that can take a varying number of arguments (such as `mysql_connect()`), we use a `switch..case` loop to determine how many arguments to pass to the function. Something to notice is that for the maximum number of arguments, we don't use the argument number, but rather we use the default statement. This ensures that if we are moving from a database that requires a greater number of arguments to a database that requires fewer arguments, the database that requires fewer arguments still gets the arguments it needs.

12.3 The mSQL Module

Now we cover how to create the mSQL module for PHP. This module, like the MySQL module, is very simple to implement. In fact, the function calls for mSQL are almost identical to those of the MySQL module. This is because MySQL is really an enhanced version of mSQL, which is a fast, lightweight database available from `http://www.Hughes.com.au/`.

DB/msql.php
```php
<?php
include_once("DB/standard.php");

function db_connect($args=array()) {
    return @msql_connect($args[0]);
}


function db_pconnect($args=array()) {
    return @msql_pconnect($args[0]);
}


function db_select_db($args=array()) {
    if (isset($args[1])) {
        return @msql_select_db($args[0], $args[1]);
    }
    return @msql_select_db($args[0]);
}
```

```php
function db_close($args=array()) {
    return @msql_close($args[0]);
}

function db_query($args=array()) {
    if (isset($args[1]) {
        return @msql_query($args[0], $args[1]);
    }
    return @msql_query($args[0]);
}

function db_db_query ($args=array()) {
    if (isset($args[2])) {
        return @msql($args[0], $args[1], $args[2]);
    }
    return @mysql_db_query($args[0], $args[1]);
}

function db_prepare($args=array()) {
    return db_simulate_prepare($args);
}

function db_execute ($args=array()) {
    $stmt = db_simulate_execute(&$args);
    return db_query(array($stmt, array_shift($args)));
}

function db_fetchrow($args=array()){
    if ($args[1] == DB_GETMODE_ASSOC) {
        return @msql_fetch_array($args[0], MSQL_ASSOC);
    } elseif ($args[1] == DB_GETMODE_REG) {
        return @msql_fetch_array($args[0], MSQL_NUM);
    }
    return @msql_fetch_array($args[1]);
}

function db_num_rows($args=array()) {
    return @msql_num_rows($args[0]);
}

function db_commit($args=array()) {
    return(true);
}
```

```
function db_rollback($args=array()) {
    return(false);
}

function db_autoCommit($args=array()) {
    return(true);
}

function db_free_result($args=array()) {
    return @msql_free_result($args[0]);
}

function db_errno($args=array()) {
    return @msql_errno();
}

function db_error($args=array()) {
    return @msql_error();
}
?>
```

Explanation

This module is the same as the MySQL module except for one fundamental difference. `msql_connect()` takes only one argument: the hostname to which you want to connect to execute your query. Therefore, only the first argument is used. This is the good thing about passing all the arguments in array form.

In the previous module, MySQL, `db_connect()` takes three arguments: hostname, username, and password. If we didn't take the arguments in an array form, it would cause a problem when you switch from MySQL to mSQL. But because the arguments are passed as an array, you can leave the username and password in the argument list and it will not cause anything to break.

12.4 The Oracle Module

The past two modules have been kind of straightforward to implement, so why not throw in a hard one? Oracle is an industrial-strength database used on all the major Web sites, including Yahoo and Amazon.com. More information about Oracle can be found at `http://www.oracle.com/`.

DB/oracle.php

```php
<?php
include_once("DB/standard.php");

function db_connect($args=array()) {
    array_shift($args);
    $conn = @ora_logon($args[0], $args[1]);
    $dbh = @ora_open($conn);
    return($dbh);
}

function db_pconnect($args=array()) {
    array_shift($args);
    $conn = @ora_plogon($args[0], $args[1]);
    $dbh = @ora_open($conn);
    return($dbh);
}

function db_db_query($args=array()) {
    return db_query($args);
}

function db_query($args=array()) {
    if (@ora_parse($args[0], $args[1]) < 0) {
        return(false);
    }
    @ora_exec($args[0]);
    return($args[0]);
}

function db_fetchrow($args=array()) {
    switch ($args[1]) {
        case DB_GETMODE_ASSOC:
            $cols = @ora_fetch_into($args[0], &$rows, ORA_FETCHINTO_ASSOC);
            break;
        case DB_GETMODE_NULL:
            $cols = @ora_fetch_into($args[0], &$rows, ORA_FETCHINTO_NULLS);
            break;
        default:
            $cols = @ora_fetch_into($args[0], &$rows);
            break;
    }
```

```php
    if ($cols) {
        return($rows);
    }
    return(false);
}

function db_prepare($args=array()) {
    return db_simulate_prepare($args);
}

function db_execute($args=array()) {
    $stmt = db_simulate_execute(&$args);
    return db_fetchrow(array($stmt, array_shift ($args)));
}

function db_num_rows($args=array()) {
    return @ora_numrows($args[0]);
}

function db_commit($args=array()) {
    return @ora_commit($args[0]);
}

function db_rollback($args=array()) {
    return @ora_rollback($args[0]);
}

function db_autoCommit($args=array()) {
    return $args[1] ? @ora_commiton($args[0]) : @ora_commitoff($args[0]);
}

function db_free_result($args=array()) {
    return @ora_close($args);
}

function db_close($args=array()) {
    return @ora_logoff($args[0]);
}
?>
```

Explanation

In the preceding extension we use PHP's Oracle extension, not the OCI8 extension, to create our module. We do this because the Oracle extension, although not as powerful as the OCI8 extension, is more akin to the rest of the PHP extensions.

The structure of an Oracle call sequence goes something like this:

Connect → Open → Query → Fetch → Close → Disconnect

This is different from most other databases, which have the following sequence of operations:

Connect → Query → Fetch → Disconnect

Therefore, we must combine the Connect and Open stages as well as the Close and Disconnect stages in order for the Oracle module to work.

When creating a database-independent API, the feature set is limited because PHP and other databases don't support some of the features that Oracle supports. If you need the advanced features of Oracle, I suggest that you check out the documentation for the Oracle and OCI8 modules.

12.5 The MSSQL Module

SQL Server is a powerful relational database system put out by the folks at Microsoft. Because of its speed and power, SQL Server is a popular choice among many Windows NT developers. It is used with PHP on large applications, such as Marriot's m3 extranet system.

```
DB/mssql.php
<?php
include_once("DB/mssql.php");

function db_connect($args=array()) {
    switch (count($args)) {
        case 0:
            return mssql_connect($args[0]);
        case 1:
            return mssql_connect($args[0], $args[1]);
        case 2:
            return mssql_connect($args[0], $args[1], $args[2]);
    }
}
```

```php
function db_pconnect($args=array()) {
    switch (count($args)) {
        case 0:
            return @mssql_connect();
        case 1:
            return @mssql_connect($args[0]);
        case 2:
            return @mssql_connect($args[0], $args[1]);
        default:
            return @mssql_connect($args[0], $args[1], $args[2]);
    }
}

function db_select_db($args=array()) {
    if (isset($args[1])) {
        return @mssql_select_db($args[0], $args[1]);
    }
    return @mssql_select_db($args[0]);
}

function db_close($args=array()) {
    if (isset($args[1])) {
        return @mssql_close ($args[0]);
    }
    return @mssql_close();
}

function db_query($args=array()) {
    if (isset($args[1])) {
        return @mssql_query($args[0], $args[1]);
    }
    return @mssql_query($args[0]);
}

function db_db_query($args=array()) {
    return db_query($args[0], $args[1]);
}

function &db_fetchrow($args=array()) {
    return @mssql_fetch_array($args[0]);
}
```

```php
function db_prepare($args=array()) {
    return db_simulate_prepare($args);
}

function db_execute($args=array()) {
    $stmt = db_simulate_execute(&$args);
    return db_query(array($stmt, array_shift ($args)));
}

function db_num_rows($args=array()) {
    return @mssql_num_rows($args[0]);
}

function db_free_result($args=array()) {
    return @mssql_free_result($args[0]);
}

function db_commit($args=array()) {
    return(true);
}

function db_rollback($args=array()) {
    return(false);
}

function db_autoCommit($args=array()) {
    return($args[1]);
}
?>
```

Explanation

The MSSQL extension for PHP is about as straightforward as it gets. It's a simple wrapper for the `mssql*` functions, and is identical to the MySQL module.

12.6 The ODBC Module

ODBC is a Microsoft specification that enables developers to access many different databases through a single API (similar to what we're doing). You can also use PHP's ODBC functions to access IBM's DB2 databases directly.

DB/odbc.php

```php
<?php

function db_connect($args=array()) {
    if (isset($args[3])) {
        return @odbc_connect($args[0], $args[1]. $args[2], $args[3]);
    }
    return @odbc_connect($args[0], $args[1], $args[2]);
}

function db_pconnect($args=array()) {
    if (isset($args[3])) {
        return @odbc_pconnect($args[0], $args[1], $args[2], $args[3]);
    }
    return @odbc_pconnect($args[0], $args[1], $args[2]);
}

function db_select_db($args=array()) {
    return(true);
}

function db_close($args=array()) {
    return @odbc_close($args[0]);
}

function db_query($args=array()) {
    return @odbc_do($args[0], $args[1]);
}

function db_db_query($args=array()) {
    return db_query($args[0], $args[2]);
}
function &db_fetchrow($args=array()) {
    if ($args[1] == DB_GETMODE_ASSOC) {
        $rows = @odbc_fetch_array($args[0]);
    } else {
        @odbc_fetch_into($args[0], &$row);
    }
    return($row);
}
```

```php
function db_prepare($args=array()) {
    return @odbc_prepare($args[0], $args[1]);
}

function db_execute($args=array()) {
    if (isset($args[1])) {
        return @odbc_execute($args[0], $args[1]);
    }
    return @odbc_execute($args[0], $args[1]);
}

function db_num_rows($args=array()) {
    return @odbc_num_rows($args[0]);
}


function db_free_result($args=array()) {
    return @odbc_free_result($args[0]);
}

function db_commit($args=array()) {
    return @odbc_commit($args[0]);
}

function db_rollback($args=array()) {
    return @odbc_rollback($args[0]);
}

function db_autoCommit($args=array()) {
    return @odbc_autocommit($args[0], $args[1]);
}
?>
```

Explanation

The ODBC module is a pretty straightforward module to implement because it
contains most of the common features (more than any of the other modules, actually).
In fact, we don't even need to implement any of the functionality ourselves.

12.7 The PostgreSQL Module

PostgreSQL is one of the first industrial-strength RDBMS, offering features comparable to those of all the major players at absolutely no cost. You can find more information about PostgreSQL at http://www.postgresql.org/.

DB/pgsql.php

```php
<?php

function db_connect($args=array()) {
    return @pg_connect($args[0], $args[1], $args[2], $args[3], $args[4]);
}

function db_pconnect ($args=array()) {
    return @pg_pconnect($args[0], $args[1], $args[2], $args[3], $args[4]);
}

function db_close($args=array()) {
    return @pg_close($args[0]);
}

function db_select_db($args=array()) {
    return(true);
}

function db_query($args=array()) {
    return @pg_exec($args[0], $args[1]);
}

function db_db_query($args=array()) {
    return db_query($args[0], $args[2]);
}

function db_fetchrow($args=array()) {
    if ($args[2] == DB_GETMODE_ASSOC) {
        return @pg_fetch_array($args[0], $args[1], PGSQL_ASSOC);
    } elseif ($args[2] & DB_GETMODE_REG) {
        return @pg_fetch_array($args[0], $args[1], PGSQL_NUM);
    } else {
        return @pg_fetch_array($args[0], $args[1]);
    }
}
```

```php
function db_prepare($args=array()) {
    return db_simulate_prepare($args);
}

function db_execute($args=array()) {
    $stmt = db_simulate_execute(&$args);
    return db_query(array($stmt, array_shift ($args)));
}

function db_num_rows($args=array()) {
    return @pg_numrows($args[0]);
}

function db_free_result($args=array()) {
    return @pg_freeresult($args[0]);
}

function db_commit($args=array()) {
    return(true);
}

function db_rollback($args=array()) {
    return(true);
}

function db_autoCommit($args=array()) {
    return($args[1]);
}
?>
```

Explanation

The PostgreSQL module—like the MSSQL, MySQL, and mSQL modules before it—is a simple wrapper for the PostgreSQL functions of the same names.

12.8 The InterBase Module

InterBase has until recently been a closed source database developed by Borland. But InterBase has lately joined the open source movement. More information about InterBase can be found at http://www.interbase.com/.

DB/interbase.php

```php
<?php

function _db_ibase_connect($args=array(), $connfunc) {
    switch (count($args)) {
        case 1:
            return @$connfunc($args[0]);
        case 2:
            return @$connfunc($args[0], $args[1]);
        case 3:
            return @$connfunc($args[0], $args[1], $args[2]);
        case 4:
            return @$connfunc($args[0], $args[1], $args[2], $args[3]);
        case 5:
            return @$connfunc($args[0], $args[1], $args[2], $args[3],
                              $args[4]);
        case 6:
            return @$connfunc($args[0], $args[1], $args[2], $args[3],
                              $args[4], $args[5]);
        default:
            return @$connfunc($args[0], $args[1], $args[2], $args[3],
                              $args[4], $args[5], $args[6]);
    }
}

function db_connect($args=array()) {
    _db_ibase_connect($args, "ibase_connect");
}

function db_pconnect($args=array()) {
    _db_ibase_connect($args, "ibase_pconnect");
}

function db_select_db($args=array()) {
    return(true);
}

function db_close($args=array()) {
    return @ibase_close($args[0]);
}
```

```php
function db_query($args=array()) {
    return @ibase_query($args[0], $args[1]);
}

function db_db_query($args=array()) {
    return @ibase_query($args[0], $args[1]);
}

function &db_fetchrow ($args=array()) {
    if ($args[1] == DB_GETMODE_ASSOC) {
        return (array)@ibase_fetch_object($args[0], IBASE_ASSOC);
    }
    return (array)@ibase_fetch_object($args[0]);
}

function db_prepare ($args=array()) {
    if (isset($args[1])) {
        return @ibase_prepare($args[0], $args[1]);
    }
    return @ibase_prepare($args[0]);
}

function db_execute($args=array()) {
    if (isset($args[1])) {
        return @ibase_execute($args[0], $args[1]);
    }
    return @ibase_execute($args[0]);
}

function db_num_rows ($args=array()) {
    return @ibase_num_fields($args[0]);
}

function db_commit($args=array()) {
    if (isset($args[1])) {
        return @ibase_commit($args[0], $args[1]);
    }
    return @ibase_commit($args[0]);
}
```

```php
function db_rollback($args=array()) {
    if (isset($args[1])) {
        return @ibase_rollback($args[0], $args[1]);
    }
    return @ibase_rollback($args[0]);
}

function db_autoCommit($args=array()) {
    return $args[1];
}
?>
```

Explanation

The InterBase module is just like all the other modules we've discussed—except for one oddity: It doesn't have a fetch_array() function. Therefore, in the db_fetchrow() function, we cast the return value of ibase_fetch_object() to an array that converts the object's properties into the indexes of an associative array.

12.9 The Sybase Module

Sybase is an industrial-strength database rivaling other big databases such as Oracle and IBM's DB2. You can also use the Sybase functions to access an MS SQL 6.5 server.

DB/sybase.php

```php
<?php

function db_connect($args=array()) {
    return @sybase_connect($args[0], $args[1], $args[2]);
}

function db_pconnect($args=array()) {
    return @sybase_pconnect($args[0], $args[1], $args[2]);
}

function db_select_db($args=array()) {
    return @sybase_select_db($args[0], $args[1]);
}
```

```php
function db_close ($args=array()) {
    return @sybase_close($args[0]);
}

function db_query ($args=array()) {
    return @sybase_query($args[0], $args[1]);
}

function db_fetchrow($args=array()) {
    if ($args[1] == DB_GETMODE_ASSOC) {
        return @sybase_fetch_array($args[0]);
    }
    return @sybase_fetch_row($args[0]);
}

function db_prepare ($args=array()) {
    return db_simulate_prepare($args);
}

function db_execute($args=array()) {
    $stmt = db_simulate_execute(&$args);
    return db_query(array($stmt, array_shift($args)));
}

function db_numrows($args=array()) {
    return @sybase_num_rows($args[0]);
}

function db_commit($args=array()) {
    return(true);
}

function db_rollback($args=array()) {
    return(false);
}

function db_autoCommit($args=array()) {
    return(true);
}
?>
```

Explanation

This is similar to all the other database-independent APIs. We simply wrap the Sybase functions with their generic counterparts.

PART III

Going Outside PHP

CHAPTER

13 Interfacing with Other Programs and Languages

14 Communicating with Sockets

15 Handling E-mail

16 Working with SNMP Objects

17 LDAP

CHAPTER 13

Interfacing with Other Programs and Languages

"Skill in the art of communication is crucial to a leader's success. He can accomplish nothing unless he can communicate effectively."

Norman Allen

13.0 Introduction

Sometimes PHP can't get the job done, or it can get the job done, but not quickly or efficiently enough for the needs of your program. Perhaps you simply need to get the output of another program for manipulation. In any of these situations, you need to perform *interprocess communication*, which is when you communicate and work with another program (known as a *process*).

But before we go on, a disclaimer: Most of the information in this chapter is meant either solely for a UNIX system or solely for a Windows NT system. Interprocess communication (IPC) is not as universal as strings, arrays, and numbers because it deals with other processes, not just PHP. Some examples here will work fine on NT but not on UNIX (such as recipe 13.5), and vice versa. When using interprocess communication, you are not dealing with PHP itself; you are going outside the program, where everything is more dependent on the OS.

This chapter mainly deals with a concept known as *process creation*, which is opening a new program to do your work. Whether this is achieved by using backticks to capture output into a variable or by the `system` and `exec` commands, process creation is the basis of interprocess communication.

We also do, however, discuss how to use PHP 4's exciting new features such as more integrated COM support and the integrated Java support.

13.1 Capturing the Output of Another Program

You want to capture the output of another program, such as the output of the date program or the whereis program.

Technique

The simplest solution is to use backticks to capture the output of a program into a variable:

```php
<?php
$current_date = `date`;
?>
```

Or, open a pipe to the program from which you want to capture output:

```php
<?php
$pp = popen('date', 'r');
while ($line = fgets($var, 1024)) {
    $output .= $line;
}
pclose($pp);
?>
```

Comments

The miracle of backticks is that they provide a convenient and easy way to assign the output of a program to a variable. Perhaps some of you are saying that they are too good to be true. No, that's all there is to it. However, there's one catch: Using backticks takes considerably longer than other related procedures simply because the backticks format the output of the program and place it all in the variable to which the output is being assigned.

In the second method, we open a pipe to the program. We can then manipulate this pipe as if it were a file, meaning that not only can we get output from the pipe as if it were a file, but we can also send data through the pipe via fputs().

There is another method of collecting the output of your program with PHP, which is via the exec() function. The exec() function will open a pipe to a program and place all the output of the program into an array of lines (the array to fill is the second argument):

```php
<?php
exec('date', $output);
print implode("\n", $output);
?>
```

> **Gotcha**
> I want to stress this: Whenever interprocess communication is involved, if you are collecting data from your users and executing it on the shell, always use the EscapeShellCmd() function. The EscapeShellCmd() function escapes all the characters that might cause your system harm.

13.2 Printing the Output of a Program

You want to send the output of a program directly to standard output without any intermediate steps or extra garbage.

Technique

Use the passthru() function, which will print the results of your shell command directly to standard output:

```php
<?php
passthru('date');
?>
```

Comments

If you simply need to execute a command and display the output to the browser, use the passthru() function, which frees you from worrying about the intermediate steps. (This is similar to fpassthru() and readfile(), which act on files.)

> **Gotcha**
> I stressed this in the previous recipe, but I will also stress it here: Always use the EscapeShellCmd() function when accepting data from your users. In that way, harmful shell characters are escaped.
>
> ```php
> passthru(EscapeShellCmd($submitted_data));
> ```

13.3 Opening a Pipe to Another Program

You want to open a pipe to a process and read or write data to it.

Technique

Use the `popen()` and `pclose()` functions as substitutes for `fopen()` and `fclose()`. You can then treat the pipe just like a file:

```php
<?php
$pp = popen("/usr/sbin/sendmail -t", "w") or die("Cannot Fork Sendmail");
fputs($pp, "To: sterling@designmultimedia.com\r\n");
fputs($pp, "Reply-to: $senders_email\r\n");
fputs($pp, "From: $senders_email\r\n");
fputs($pp, "Subject: The Results of your form\r\n\r\n");
fputs($pp, "$senders_email sent the following comments:\r\n");
fputs($pp, $comments);
pclose($pp) or die("Cannot close pipe to Sendmail");
?>
```

Comments

In this example, we open a pipe to the sendmail process, and then print the information we want sendmail to deal with to the pipe handle ($pp). Perl programmers might have noticed that this is a PHP version of the classic way of sending form results by e-mail through Sendmail.

When working with pipes, all data must be in the format in which the other program wants it, because pipes are relatively low level. For example, we terminate each line in the example with both a carriage return and a newline so that the mail sent is compatible with both DOS- and UNIX-based systems.

Pipes allow for the two way exchange of data, meaning you can both write to a pipe and then retrieve data from a pipe. This makes them a powerful addition to PHP's set of functions for IPC. Examine the following, which reads the output of a Perl script and prints it to the Web browser:

```php
<?php
$pp = popen("./some_perl_script.pl", "r")
    or die("cannot fork");
while ($line = fgets($pp, 1024)) {
    print $line;
}
?>
```

13.4 Working with Sockets

You want to open a socket to either a local port or a remote server.

Technique

Use the `fsockopen()` function, which opens a socket to the specified server. Subsequently, you send to and retrieve information from that socket via the `fgets()`, `fgetss()`, and `fputs()` functions:

```php
<?php
$sp = fsockopen($hostname, $port, &$errno, &$errstr, $timeout);
if (!$sp) {
    print "$errstr  [$errno]<br>\n";
} else {
    fputs($fp,"GET / HTTP/1.0\r\n\r\n");
    while ($line = fgets($fp, 1024)) {
        print $line;
    }
fclose($sp);
}
?>
```

Comments

The `fsockopen()` function provides a simple API for using sockets. For more information on `fsockopen()` and some of PHP's more advanced socket features, see Chapter 14, "Communicating with Sockets."

13.5 Working with COM Objects

You are an ASP programmer, and you want to have the same ability to handle COM objects in PHP that you had in ASP.

Technique

With the advent of PHP 4, you can now manipulate COM objects with unparalleled ease:

```php
<?php
$word = new COM("word.application")
  or die("Unable to instanciate Word");
```

```php
print "Loaded Word, version {$word->Version}\n";
$word->Visible = 0;
$word->Documents->Add();
$word->Selection->TypeText("Testing, testing… 1,2,3");
$word->Documents[1]->SaveAs("some_tst.doc");
$word->Quit();
?>
```

Comments

For a long time, one of strongest arguments for ASP was the ability for programmers to access prebuilt COM objects from the Web inside the code, meaning that you really didn't need to do that much programming in ASP. You could write the application end of your Web site in C, C++, or Visual Basic, and then interface it to the Web with ASP and COM objects. Now that PHP supports this feature, I don't really see a reason ever to use ASP. PHP is cross-platform, and much easier to work with or learn, if you have programmed in a language such as C, Perl, or Java. Take the following example in PHP, and compare it to the same example in ASP:

```php
<?php
require("DB.php");
$excel_handle = new COM("excel.application");
$excel_handle->Visible = false;
$worksheet = $excel_handle->workbooks->add();
$values = array("Name", "Salary", "Time of Employment");
for ($i = 1; $i < 4; ++$i) {
    $cell = &$worksheet->Cells(1, $i);
    $cell->value = $values[$i - 1];
}

$dbh = new DB;
$dbh->connect("mssql://username:password@localhost/empreports");
$sth = $dbh->query("SELECT * FROM empnames WHERE salary='salary'");

$idx = 2;
    while ($row = $dbh->fetchRow($sth, DB_GETMODE_ASSOC)) {
    $values = array($row['name'], $row['Salary'], $row['toe']);
    for ($i = 0; $i < 4; ++$i) {
        $cell = &$worksheet->Cells($idx, $i);
        $cell->value = $values[$i - 1];
    }
}

$dbh->disconnect();
$worksheet->SaveAs("emp_reports-$salary.xls");
$excel_handle->quit();
?>
```

Here is the same example in ASP:

```
<%
Dim excel_handle, worksheet, FileName 'Manipulating the xls file
Dim dbh, sth, stmt                    'Database related
Dim i, x                             'For looping and assigning
Dim Salary                           'From user input

set Salary = request.queryString("salary")

set excel_handle = server.createObject("excel.application") 'COM Object
excel_handle.visible = False
excel_handle.workbooks.Add
set worksheet = excel_handle.Worksheets(1)

' START DATABASE CONNECTION AND ADD RECORDS

set dbh = server.createObject("ADODB.Connection")
dbh.Open "DSN=empreports;uid=username;pwd=password"
set stmt = "SELECT * FROM empnames WHERE salary='"
stmt = stmt & Salary & "'"

set x=2
For i=0 to sth.eof
    Worksheet.Cells(x,1) = sth(i).name
    Worksheet.Cells(x,2) = sth(i).salary
    Worksheet.Cells(x++, 3) = sth(i).toe
    sth.movenext
next

dbh.close

worksheet.SaveAs "emp_reports-" & Salary & ".xls"
excel_handle.quit

set worksheet = Nothing
set excel_handle = Nothing
%>
```

Judge for yourself.

13.6 Accessing Predefined Java Methods and Classes

You want to access methods and classes from Java's set of built-in methods and classes (that is, java.io.lang).

Technique

No problem! As of PHP 4, Java support is built in:

```php
<?php
$formatter = new Java("java.text.SimpleDateFormat",
                      "EEEE, MMMM dd, yyyy 'at' h:mm:ss a zzzz");
print $formatter->format(new Java("java.util.date"));
?>
```

Comments

Here we create a special object, the Java object. The first argument to the constructor is the class we want to work with (in this case, it is `java.text.SimpleDateFormat`), and the second argument (as well as the third, fourth, and so on) are the arguments we want to pass to the class specified in the first argument.

Having the ability to interface with Java is tremendously useful. For example, much of the XML and XSL functionality in the Open Source world is available only through Java classes. The PHP-Java connection enables you to harness this power for your applications. For example, you could generate XML in PHP and then pass it to a Java XSL formatter class to generate HTML.

13.7 Accessing Your Own Custom Java Methods and Classes

You want to write your components and then call your predefined class.

Technique

Create your class, place it in your Java lib file, and then call the class file with the syntax described in recipe 13.6.

The Java class: `SimpleClass`

```
public class SimpleClass {
    public string get_greeting(string name) {
        return "Hello, there, " + name + ".";
    }
}
```

The PHP script to access `SimpleClass`:

```php
<?php
$jclass = new Java("SimpleClass");
print $jclass->get_greeting ("Joe");
?>
```

Comments

We created our own simple Java class (`SimpleClass`) with a method (`get_greeting`), and then called that class from within our PHP program. That is basically how you do it, but remember that your class must be in a special directory where all the predefined classes for the JVM are stored (for me, it is `windows\java\trustlib`). Consult your Java documentation for more information.

This is a simple example; nothing is accomplished that we couldn't have accomplished in PHP. So, how is this useful? Assume that we have a mainframe that we need Java to connect to, and we need to connect that mainframe to the Internet. We might be able to use something like a Java applet or Java servlets, but a much simpler solution is to use PHP to connect to Java, which in turn would connect to the mainframe. We are done!

This is such an important feature that it certainly deserves a more powerful example. Therefore, I wrote the following Java class, `Zipper`, which zips files into *.zip files that can then be distributed from your Web site. Interfacing with this class enables us to create zip files on-the-fly and give them to our users. (I am not doing tar.gz files because PHP already offers this functionality. See `http://www.php.net/manual/html/_ref.zlib.html` for more information.)

First, the Java source file: `Zipper.java`

```java
import java.io.*;
import java.util.zip.*;

public class Zipper {
    public int chunk = 8192;
```

```java
public string Zipem ( String files, String zipped ) {
    String this_file = '';

    if (files.length() < 1) {
        return "You need to have some files to Zip";
    }

    // Output stream
    try {
        FileInputStream foward = new FileInputStream(zipped);
        ZipOutputStream final = new ZipOutputStream(foward);
    } catch (IOException e) {
        return "Cannot create " + zipped + " an error occurred";
    }

    do {
        if (files.indexOf("|" != -1) {
            this_file = files.substring(0, files.indexOf("|") );
            try {
                ZipEntry ent;
                if (this_file.indexOf("/") != -1) {
                    ent = new ZipEntry(this_file.substring(
                        this_file.lastIndexOf("/") +1,
                        this_file.length())
                        );
                } else {
                    ent = new ZipEntry(this_file.substring(
                        this_file.lastIndexOf("\\") +1,
                        this_file.length())
                        );
                }
                final.putNextEntry(ent);
            } catch (IOException e) {
                return "Cannot prepare " + zipped +
                    "Unable to add" + this_file;
            }
            files.substring( files.indexOf("|")+1 );
            byte[] buf = new byte[chunk];

            //Compress that file
            try {
                FileInputStream reader = new FileInputStream(this_file);
```

13.7 Accessing Your Own Custom Java Methods and Classes

```
                int length;
                while ((length = reader.read(buf, 0 chunk)) != -1) {
                    final.write(buf, 0, length);
                }
                reader.close();
            } catch (IOException e) {
                return "Can't compress " + this_file;
            }
        }
    } while (files.indexOf("|") != -1);

    try {
        ZipEntry ent;
        if (files.indexOf("/") != -1) {
            ent = new ZipEntry(files.substring(
                    files.lastIndexOf("/") + 1,
                    files.length())
                );
        } else {
            ent = new ZipEntry(files.substring(
                    files.lastIndexOf("\\") + 1,
                    files.length())
                );
        }
        final.putNextEntry(ent);
    } catch (IOException e) {
        return "Cannot prepare " + zipped + " unable to add " + this_file;
    }

    byte[] buf = new byte[chunk];

    try {
        FileInputStream reader = new FileInputStream(files);
        int length;
        while ((length = reader.read(buf,0,chunk)) != -1) {
            final.write(buf,0,length);
        }
        reader.close();
    } catch (IOException e) {
        return "Cannot compress " + files;
    }

    try {
```

```
            final.close();
        } catch (IOException e) {
            return "Cannot create" + zipped;
        }

        return zipped + " has been created";
    }
}
```

Now the PHP script that interfaces with this class:

```php
<?php
$zipObj = new Java("Zipper");
$files = array("/home/designmm/designmultimedia-logs/access_log",
                "/home/designmm/designmultimedia-logs/error_log");

$ret_val = $zipObj->ZipEm(implode("|", $files), "logs.zip");
if ($ret_val == "logs.zip has been created") {
    header("http://www.designmultimedia.com/logs/logs.zip");
} else {
?>
<html>
<head>
    <title> Sorry there was an error <?php echo $ret_val; ?></title>
</head>
<body>
    <h1> I'm Sorry there seems to have been an error </h1>
<br>
    <b> <?php echo $ret_val; ?> </b>
<br><br>
  Please try again some other time.
</body>
</html>
<?php
}
?>
```

CHAPTER 14

Communicating with Sockets

"Communication with an engineer is only slightly more difficult than communication with the dead."

Lorren 'Rus' Stiles, Sr.

14.0 Introduction

Much of what you do in programming is communication between different interfaces—whether it's opening a file and reading data or opening a socket and sending data. In this chapter, we cover some of the trickier points of communication with PHP. We discuss topics such as SSL transactions and creating a small HTTP Web server with PHP.

14.1 A TCP Client

You want to connect to a socket on a remote machine.

Technique

To connect to a remote machine by using a TCP connection, use PHP's fsockopen() function:

```php
<?php
$fp = fsockopen("www.zend.com", 80, $errno, $errstr, 30);
if (!$fp){
    die($errstr);
}

fputs($fp, "HEAD /HTTP/1.0 \r\n\r\n");
```

```
while (!feof($fp)) {
    $line = fgets($fp, 2048);
    echo $line;
}
fclose($fp);
?>
```

Or, for more control, use PHP's sockets module (you must compile with `--enable-sockets` for this to work):

```
<?php
$url = 'www.zend.com';

$serv_port = getservbyname('www', 'tcp');
$address = gethostbyname($url);

$sock = socket(AF_INET, SOCK_STREAM, 0);
if ($sock < 0) {
    die(strerror($sock));
}

$res = connect($sock, $address, $serv_port);
if ($res < 0) {
    die(strerror($res));
}

$data = "HEAD / HTTP/1.0\r\n\r\n";

write($sock, $data, strlen($data));

while (read($sock, $response, 2048)) {
    print $response;
}

close($sock);
?>
```

Comments

The two programs in the solution do the same thing, but the first one uses the standard `fsockopen()` function, and the second uses the `sockets` module distributed with PHP.

The `fsockopen()` function provides a generic, simple interface to connecting to a socket. However, if you want more control, you can use PHP's `sockets` module, which gives you more direct access to the lower-level C APIs.

14.2 A TCP Server

You want to create a simple TCP server with PHP.

Technique

Use PHP's lower-level socket functions along with the `set_time_limit()` function to create a simple server:

```php
<?php
set_time_limit(0);

$addr = "127.0.0.1";
$port = 5000;

$sock = socket(AF_INET, SOCK_STREAM, 0);
if ($sock < 0)
    die(strerror($sock));

if (($ret = setsockopt($sock, SOL_SOCKET, SO_REUSEADDR, 1)) < 0)
    print strerror($ret);

if (($ret = bind($sock, $addr, $port)) < 0)
    die(strerror($ret));

if (($ret = listen($sock, 10)) < 0)
    die(strerror($ret));

while (($csock = accept_connect($sock)) >= 0) {
    // .. manipulate $csock here.
}

close($sock);
?>
```

Comments

To create a TCP server, you must first create a new socket with a domain of AF_INET and a type of SOCK_STREAM (most similar to a UNIX pipe). Then you bind() that socket to an address and port. Following that, you have to tell PHP to listen() on that socket, with a maximum number of connections specified by the second argument. (For portable applications, the number of connections should be a maximum of five because BSD and BSD-derived systems support no more than that.) Finally, you have to accept new connections to the socket. For that, you can use PHP's accept_connect() function, which will accept a new socket that can be both read from and listened to. When you close this socket, a new socket will be accepted.

If you just want to open a socket with a given port (with an IP address of 0.0.0.0), you can use the open_listen_sock() function:

```php
<?php
$sock = open_listen_sock(230);

while (($msock = accept_connect($sock)) >= 0) {
    // .. Manipulate $msock
}

close($sock);
?>
```

14.3 Reading and Writing to Sockets

You want to know how to read and write to sockets.

Technique

If you are using the high-level, abstracted interface (sockets opened with fsockopen() and pfsockopen()), you can use the same functions you would use for regular files (fread() and fwrite()):

```php
<?php
$data = fread($sock, 1024);
fwrite($sock, $data);
?>
```

If you are using the low-level interface with a SOCK_STREAM connection, you should use the read() and write() functions:

```php
<?php
if (($ret = read($sock, $buf, $len)) < 0)
    die(strerror($ret));

if (($ret = write($sock, $buf, $len)) < 0)
    die(strerror($ret));
?>
```

If you are using the low-level functions with a SOCK_DGRAM socket (datagram), you need to use the sendto() and recvfrom() functions:

```php
<?php
if (($ret = recvfrom($sock, $data, $len, $flags, $name, $port)) < 0)
    die(strerror($ret));

if (($ret = send($sock, $data, $len, $flags, $to, $port)) < 0)
    die(strerror($ret));
?>
```

Comments

When you use the high-level functions, you can use PHP's file I/O functions to manipulate the socket. No special considerations are necessary (but you can't read from SOCK_DGRAM sockets, either).

When dealing with the lower-level socket functions for SOCK_STREAM sockets, you need to use the read() and write() functions. For SOCK_DGRAM (datagram) sockets, you need to use the sendto() and recvfrom() functions.

When dealing with the lower-level socket functions, it is especially important to be aware of buffering issues. Buffering is done at the operating system level, under a strategy called the *Nagle algorithm*. The Nagle algorithm specifies that when a packet of data has been sent, but the remote server has not acknowledged it, the data that would be sent next is placed into a buffer and queued. This data is sent only when another complete packet is present in the buffer or the acknowledgement is received. If you want to determine whether a socket has unread data, you can use the select() function:

```php
<?php

$readset = fd_alloc();
fd_set($sock, $readset);
select($readset, 0, 0, 0, 5);
```

```php
if (fd_isset($sock, $readset)) {
    // .. There is data to be read
}
?>
```

The `select()` function takes five arguments. The first argument is a file descriptor set indicating which file descriptors to check for unread data. The second argument is a file descriptor set containing the file descriptors to check for nonblocking write safety. The third argument is a file descriptor set on which to check for special conditions. The fourth argument is the number of microseconds to wait, and the fifth argument is the number of seconds to wait.

If the fourth and fifth arguments to `select()` are set to 0, the `select()` function will *poll* the socket, or check the socket without blocking. If those arguments are set to NULL, the socket will never time out.

14.4 A UDP Client

You want to create a UDP client.

Technique

For an easy-to-use, abstracted interface, use the `fsockopen()` function:

```php
<?php
$fp = fsockopen("udp://127.0.0.1", 13, $errno; $errstr);
fwrite($fp, $msg);
while ($line = fread($fp, $len)) {
    print $line;
}
fclose($fp);
?>
```

Or, you can use the more advanced, low-level functions:

```php
<?php
$addr = gethostbyname('127.0.0.1');
$port = 50;

$sock = socket (AF_INET, SOCK_DGRAM, getprotobyname('udp'));
if ($sock < 0)
    die(strerror($sock));
```

```
if (($ret = sendto($sock, $data, $dlen, 0, $addr, $port)) < 0)
    die(strerror($sock));

while (recvfrom($sock, $buf, $blen, 0, $addr, $port) > 0)
    print $buf;
```

Comments

There are two types of sockets you can use with PHP: stream sockets (SOCK_STREAM) and datagram sockets (SOCK_DGRAM). Stream sockets are more like files; they give the illusion of a stable connection in which data streams from the socket and to the socket. Although streaming sockets are more expensive on your system resources, what they lack in speed, they make up in ease of use and reliability.

Datagram sockets provide no such reliability or ease of use. Datagrams are meant for speed; they offer no assurances that your data will arrive, or that your data will arrive in the proper order.

It might seem odd to use datagram sockets if they are so unreliable. Surely, the speed increase is surely not worth the lack of reliability?

In some applications, such as streaming audio, where it's more important that the whole is preserved than that individual packets get through, datagram sockets make more sense because of their speed. Datagram (udp) sockets are also a widely used method for broadcasting where the data is sent, but it isn't particularly imperative that the target accepts it.

14.5 A UDP Server

You want to create a UDP server.

Technique

Simply bind the created socket to a port and then you receive data by using the recvfrom() function:

```
<?php
set_time_limit(0);

$addr = "127.0.0.1";
$port = 500;
```

```php
$sock = socket(AF_INET, SOCK_DGRAM, 0);
if ($sock < 0)
    die(strerror($sock));

if (($ret = bind($sock, $addr, $port)) < 0)
    die(strerror($ret));

while (($read = recvfrom($sock, $buf, $buflen, 0, $name, $port)) > 0) {
    // .. $name contains your socket.
}

close($sock);
?>
```

Comments

Creating a UDP server is much easier than creating a TCP server because when UDP requests come in, we don't have to create a whole new socket connection. We simply get the data from the user as well as his address, and then we can do what we want to do with that data. Examine the following simple script, which will receive data and then send a message based on that data:

```php
<?php
set_time_limit(0);

$addr = "127.0.0.1";
$port = 500;

$sock = socket(AF_INET, SOCK_DGRAM, 0);
if ($sock < 0)
    die(strerror($sock));

if (($ret = bind($sock, $addr, $port)) < 0)
    die(strerror($ret));

while (($read = recvfrom($sock, $buf, strlen($buf), 0, $name, $port)) > 0)
{
    // is_valid_packet() is a custom function which
    // validates the packet sent to the server.
    if (is_valid_packet ($buf)) {
        $resp = "Well it looks like your packet was valid";
        $resp .= "Here is the contents of your packet $buf";
```

```
    } else {
        $resp = "Sorry, Invalid packet";
    }
    sendto($socket, $resp, strlen($resp), 0, $name, $port);
}

close($sock);
?>
```

14.6 UNIX Domain Sockets

You want to connect to a UNIX domain socket because you are communicating to processes only on the local machine.

Technique

For servers:

```
<?php
$sock = socket(AF_UNIX, SOCK_STREAM, 0);
if ($sock < 0)
    die(strerror($sock));

unlink("/tmp/sterlingsock");

if (($ret = bind($sock, "/tmp/sterlingsock")) < 0)
    die(strerror($ret));

if (($ret = listen($sock, 5)) < 0)
    die(strerror($ret));

while (($csock = accept_connect($sock)) < 0) {
    // .. Manipulate client socket, $csock here
}

close($sock);
?>
```

For clients:

```
<?php
$sock = socket(AF_UNIX, SOCK_STREAM, 0);
```

```php
if ($sock < 0)
    die(strerror($sock));

if (($ret = connect($sock, "/tmp/sterlingsock")) < 0)
    die(strerror($ret));

if (($ret = write($sock, $data, $data_len)) < 0)
    die(strerror($ret));

while (($ret = read($sock, $buf, $buflen)) < 0) {
    print $buf;
}

close($sock);
?>
```

Comments

Most UNIX domain sockets have names for the filesystem, just like any ordinary file. In fact, they are considered to be a type of file, so you can perform stat operations on them.

In the preceding example, we use the stream method of connecting to the local socket, but we could have just as easily used the datagram (udp) method:

For servers:

```php
<?php
$sock = socket(AF_UNIX, SOCK_DGRAM, 0);
if ($sock < 0)
    die(strerror($sock));

unlink("/tmp/sterlingsock");

if (($ret = bind($sock, "/tmp/sterlingsock")) < 0)
    die(strerror($ret));

while (recvfrom($sock, $buf, $buflen, $addr, $port) > 0) {
    // .. manipulate $addr & $port here.
}
?>
```

For clients:

```php
<?php
$addr = '127.0.0.1';
$port = 67;

$sock = socket(AF_UNIX, SOCK_DGRAM, 0);
if ($sock < 0)
    die(strerror($sock));

sendto($sock, $data, $datalen, $addr, $port);

if (($ret = recv($sock, $buf, $buflen, $newaddr, $newport)) < 0)
    die(strerror($ret));
?>
```

14.7 Handling Multiple IP Addresses

You want to write a server that is aware that the machine on which it runs on has multiple IP addresses, and it should do different things for different addresses.

Technique

Bind your server to INADDR_ANY instead of a specific address, and then get the server's address and port using the getsockname() function:

```php
<?php
$sock = socket(AF_INET, SOCK_STREAM, 0);
if ($sock < 0)
    die(strerror($sock));

if (($ret = setsockopt($sock, SOL_SOCKET, SO_REUSEADDR, 1)) < 0)
    die(strerror($ret));

if (($ret = bind($sock, INADDR_ANY, $port)) < 0)
    die(strerror($ret));

while (($csock = accept_connect($sock)) >= 0) {
    if (($ret = getsockname($csock, $name, $port)) < 0)
        return;
```

```php
    // Manipulate Hostname, $name and with Port, $port, here.
}
?>
```

Comments

To bind your socket to all the available IP addresses on your system, use the `bind()` function along with the `INADDR_ANY` option. When you receive a new connection, you can use the `getsockname()` function to get the current socket's name and information. That way you know what IP address the user connected to and you can treat the connection accordingly.

14.8 Nonblocking Sockets

You don't want your sockets to wait around forever trying to connect to a given server.

Technique

If you are using the high-level socket functions, use the `socket_set_blocking()` function:

```php
<?php
$fp = fsockopen('www.webtechniques.com', 80, $errno, $errstr, 30);
if (!$fp) {
    die(sprintf('Error [%d]: %s',
                $errno, $errstr));
}

socket_set_blocking($fp, false);

fwrite($fp, "GET / HTTP/1.0\r\n\r\n");
while ($line = fgets($fp, 1024)) {
    print $line;
}
fclose($fp);
```

Or, if you are using the lower-level socket functions, you can use the `set_nonblock()` function:

```php
<?php
$sock = socket(AF_INET, SOCK_STREAM, 0);
if ($sock < 0)
    die(strerror($sock));
```

```
if (($ret = set_nonblock($sock)) < 0)
    die(strerror($ret));

if (($ret = connect($sock, $addr, $port)) < 0)
    die(strerror($ret));

if (($ret = write($sock, $data, $len)) < 0)
    print strerror($ret);

while (read($sock, $buf, $buflen) < 0)
    print $buf;
?>
```

Comments

If you do not want your sockets to *block*, or wait for data if data is not available, use the appropriate function to set blocking to zero. When you set blocking to zero, the socket doesn't wait for data, but instead immediately returns if it cannot access data from the stream.

14.9 Reading and Writing I/O Vectors

You want to read and write I/O vectors with PHP.

Technique

Use the readv() and writev() functions along with the vector manipulation functions:

```
<?php
$vector1 = build_iovec(5, 40, 40, 30, 40, 20);

$vector2 = build_iovec(2, strlen($data1), strlen($data2));
set_iovec($vector2, 1, $data1);
set_iovec($vector2, 2, $data2);


$sock1 = socket(AF_INET, SOCK_STREAM, 0);
if ($sock1 < 0)
    die(strerror($sock1));
$sock2 = socket(AF_INET, SOCK_STREAM, 0);
if ($sock2 < 0)
    die(strerror($sock2));
```

```php
if (($ret = bind($sock1, $addr1, $port1)) < 0)
    die(strerror($ret));

if (($ret = connect($sock2, $addr2, $port2)) < 0)
    die(strerror($ret));

if (($ret = listen($sock1, 5)) < 0)
    die(strerror($ret));

while (readv($sock1, $vector1) >= 0)
    writev($sock2, $vector2);
?>
```

Comments

Using vectors is almost the same as using the `read()` and `write()` functions, except that I/O vectors enable you to provide named buffers to specify where to read and where data should be written. You must also use I/O vectors with the `recvmsg()` and the `sendmsg()` functions.

14.10 Controlling Data Transfer Timeout

You want the socket to time out after a certain time if the reading operation is blocked.

Technique

For high-level sockets, use the `socket_set_timeout()` function:

```php
<?php
$sock = fsockopen("www.slashdot.org", 80, $errstr, $errno, 30);
if(!$sock) {
    dir($errstr);
}

socket_set_timeout($sock, 60);
fwrite($sock,"GET / HTTP/1.0\n\n");
$res = fread($sock, 2000);
$status = socket_get_status($sock);
if ($status['timed_out']) {
    print "Timeout\n";
    fclose($sock);
```

```
} else
    print $res;
?>
```

Comments

If you use blocking sockets but still want the read operation to time out after a certain period, you should make use of `socket_set_timeout()` function. It takes the socket descriptor as the first parameter, and number of seconds and microseconds specifying the timeout as the second and third parameters.

After the socket read operation exits, the way to find out whether timeout occurred is to call the `socket_get_status()` function and check the `'timed_out'` entry in the array it returns. If the `'timed_out'` entry is true, the socket read timed out; otherwise, the operation was completed successfully. See the next section for more information about `socket_get_status()`.

14.11 Getting Socket Status

You want to get some information about an existing high-level socket descriptor.

Technique

Use the `socket_get_status()` function:

```php
<?php
$sock = fsockopen("www.slashdot.org", 80, $errstr, $errno, 30);
if(!$sock) {
    dir($errstr);
}
$res = fread($sock, 4000);
var_dump(socket_get_status($sock));
fclose($sock);
?>
```

Comments

`socket_get_status()` returns an array containing information about the specified socket descriptor. Currently, the array contains four entries:

- `timed_out` (Boolean)—True if the socket timed out while waiting for data
- `blocked` (Boolean)—True if the socket was blocked

- `eof` (Boolean)—True if no more data is available from the socket
- `unread_bytes` (integer)—Number of unread bytes in the socket buffer

Chapter 15

Handling E-mail

"I can't send an e-mail. Is the Internet full?"

A Customer

15.0 Introduction

PHP offers support for reading and manipulating e-mail through the IMAP library, which enables you to access IMAP, NNTP, and POP3 servers. If you want to send email, you can either use the built-in `mail()` function, which is compatible with both Windows and UNIX systems, or you can write your own SMTP mailer.

IMAP, or Internet Message Access Protocol, was developed at Stanford University back in 1986. It has been—until its recent introduction into the commercial market—entirely freeware, similar to the more popular and simpler POP, or Post Office Protocol. IMAP, in the most basic sense, provides an interface enabling you to send and receive email. More information about IMAP can be found at `http://www.imap.org`.

PHP has excellent support for IMAP, with (at the time this book was written) more than 50 different functions for manipulating IMAP streams, making it one of most full-featured extensions in PHP.

The IMAP client library allows you to access both POP and NNTP servers. This means that you can not only access all the major mail protocols (SMTP via `Mail_Sendmail`) via PHP, but

you can also access newsgroup servers. For more information on accessing these
different protocols via the IMAP extension, see recipe 15.1.

15.1 Opening an IMAP Mailbox

You want to open a stream to an IMAP mailbox. This technique can also be used when
accessing POP or NNTP mailboxes.

Technique

Use the `imap_open()` function, which enables you to open a stream to a POP, NNTP,
or IMAP server. To open a connection to an IMAP server, do the following:

```php
<?php
$mh = imap_open("{servername.com:143}INBOX", $user, $pass);
?>
```

To open a connection to a POP server, simply specify it in the syntax of the first
argument:

```php
<?php
$mh = imap_open("{servername.com/pop3:110}INBOX", $user, $pass);
?>
```

The same thing applies when accessing an NNTP server:

```php
<?php
$nh = imap_open("{servername.com/nntp:119}comp.lang.perl.misc",
                $username, $password );
?>
```

Comments

The `imap_open()` function takes as its first argument the mailbox name. The server
part of the mailbox name, enclosed in { and }, consists of the server name, a protocol
specification that is separated from the server name with /, and an optional port
specifier beginning with :. The second and third arguments to `imap_open()` are your
username and passwords, respectively.

`imap_open()` is the only place where you need to distinguish between server types (that
is, nntp or pop3). You can manipulate the stream returned by `imap_open()` with any of
the appropriate `imap_*` functions. Of course, because of the difference in the types of
programs, some functions will not work with different server types.

15.2 Checking Whether an IMAP Stream Is Still Active

You want to see whether an IMAP stream is still active. This can be either a method for checking for new messages, or a "keep-alive" technique.

Technique

Use the `imap_ping()` function, which returns true if the stream is active and false if the stream is inactive.

```php
<?php
$mh = imap_open("{localhost:143}INBOX", $user, $pass);
if (imap_ping($mh)) {
    echo "Stream is active";
} else {
    echo "Stream is in-active";
}
?>
```

Comments

The `imap_ping()` function is simply a wrapper for the `mail_ping()` function call (in C). Its purpose is to make sure that the stream is still active, and in doing so, it also prevents a timeout on that stream. It is helpful to think of the `imap_ping()` function as similar to the Check E-mail button on Netscape Communicator. It returns true if there are new messages and therefore the stream is active.

> **Note**
> If you are running your programs at the command line or as a background utility (which is really only possible when PHP is installed as a CGI rather than as a module), you can use this in context of a `while` loop with the `sleep()` function:
>
> ```php
> <?php
> while (1) {
>     if (imap_ping($mh)) {
>         print time() . " NEW MESSAGES\n";
>     }
>     sleep(60); #sleep for 60 seconds
> }
> ?>
> ```

15.3 Converting Messages to a Readable Format

You are getting messages in the standard UTF-7 encoding and you need to change them to UTF-8 encoding.

Technique

Use the `imap_8bit()` function, which takes a UTF-7 encoded string and converts it to a quoted printable string:

```php
<?php
$mh = imap_open("{localhost/pop3:110}INBOX", $user, $pass)
   or die("Cannot Open IMAP Stream");
$body = imap_8bit(imap_body($mh, $msg_num));

imap_close($mh) or die("Cannot Close IMAP Stream");
?>
```

Comments

UUCP, or UNIX-to-UNIX copy, was created as a result of the e-mail system. It was perfectly suited for its original purposes, which at the time were mainly the plain text mediums of Usenet and e-mail messages. However, UUCP was woefully inadequate at handling binary files. To work around this, programmers created uuencoding, which encodes 8-bit character sets to a 7-bit character set so that they can be sent over e-mail. Therefore, you have to use the `imap_8bit()` function to decode messages that are sent using this protocol.

In the solution example, we first open a stream to an IMAP mailbox by using the `imap_open()` function. Then we retrieve the body of a certain message specified in `$msg_num`. However, we must decode this message before printing it to the user, so we use the `imap_8bit()` function to convert the uuencoded string into a quoted printable string.

15.4 Sending E-mail

You want to send an e-mail from your PHP script.

Technique

Use PHP's built-in `mail()` function:

```php
<?php
/* submitted data is $email, $name,$subject, $message and $to */
mail($to,
    $subject,
    $message,
    "From: $email\r\nReply-to: $email\r\n");
?>
```

Comments

The `mail()` function takes three required arguments: the e-mail address to which you want to send the e-mail, the subject of the e-mail, and the body of the message. The fourth argument is optional, but it enables you to give any extra headers, which should be separated by the standard `<CRLF>` (`"\r\n"`).

The preceding script sends an e-mail based on the user's input. A form that might trigger this script would be something like the following (assuming the script in the solution is named mailer.php):

```html
<form action="mailer.php" method="POST">
To: <input type="text" name="to"><br>
From:  <input type="text" name="email"><br>
Subject: <input type="text" name="subject"><br>
Message Body: <br>
<textarea rows="10" cols="40" name="message"></textarea><br>
<input type="submit" value="Send your message">
</form>
```

15.5 Sending Attachments with PHP

You want to send an attachment along with your mail message.

Technique

Use a boundary to separate the body of your message with the attachment:

```php
<?php
$boundary = "b" . md5(uniqid(time()));
$mime =  "Content-type: multipart/mixed; ";
$mime .= "boundary = $boundary\r\n\r\n";
$mime .= "This is a MIME encoded message.\r\n\r\n";
// First the regular message
$mime_message .= "--$boundary\r\n";
```

```php
$mime .= "Content-type: text/plain\r\n";
$mime .= "Content-Transfer-Encoding: base64";
$mime .= "\r\n\r\n" . chunk_split(base64_encode($message)) . "\r\n";
// Now the attachment
$filename = "data.txt";
$attach = chunk_split(base64_encode(implode("", file($filename))));
$mime .= "--$boundary\r\n";
$mime .= "Content-type: text/plain\r\n";
$mime .= "Content-Transfer-Encoding: base64";
$mime .= "\r\n\r\n$attachment_datar\n";

mail($to,
    $subject,
    "",
    $mime);
?>
```

Comments

When sending messages with more than one part, you need a *boundary*—a unique separator that separates the different parts of the message. Unfortunately, you cannot work with this boundary in the body of a message. Therefore, as in the preceding example, you must specify an empty body and then write out the entire message according to RFC 821.

The message is encoded using base 64 encoding. This isn't really necessary for text files, but if you want to send binary files, it is vital. The `chunk_split()` breaks up the blobs into 76 character lines terminated by `"\r\n"` in accordance with the RFC 2045 guidelines.

15.6 Sending Binary Attachments

You want to send binary attachments, not just the plain text attachments described in recipe 15.5.

Technique

All that is necessary is to change the content-type declaration, but I'm getting tired of retyping the same formatting for the messages. So, I think I will create a class that will do it for me:

```php
<?php
mt_srand((double)microtime()*1000000);

/**
 *  MIME class for building muiltipart MIME messages.
 *
 * @author Sterling Hughes <sterling@php.net>
 */
class MIME {
    // {{{ properties

    var $attachments = array();
    var $to = "";
    var $from = "";
    var $subject ="";
    var $body = "";

    // }}}
    // {{{ MIME()

    /**
     * Constructor class that adds the values of the
     * required parts.
     *
     * @param $to string Who to send the message to.
     * @param $from string Who sent the message.
     * @param $subject string subject of the message
     * @param $body string the body of the message.
     *
     * @return object the new MIME object.
     */
    function MIME ($to, $from='', $subject='', $body='') {
        $this->to = $to;
        $this->from = $from;
        $this->subject = $subject;
        $this->body = $body;
    }

    // }}}
    // {{{ attachment()
```

```php
/**
 *  Add an attachment to the message
 *
 * @param $name string Name of the attachment.
 * @param $body string Body of the attachment.
 * @param $type string Content-type of the attachment.
 * @param $encoding string encoding of the attachment.
 *
 * @return null
 */
function attachment ($name = "",
                     $contents = "",
                     $type = "application/octet-stream",
                     $encoding = "base64")   {
    $this->attachments[] =
                     array("filename" => $name,
                           "type"     => $type,
                           "encoding" => $encoding.
                           "data"     => $contents);
}


// }}}
// {{{ _build()

function _build () {
    $boundary = 'b' . md5(uniquid(mt_rand())) + getmypid();

    if ($this->from != "")
        $ret = "From: " . $this->from . "\r\n";

    $ret .= 'Content-type: multipart/mixed; ';
    $ret .= "boundary = $boundary\r\n\r\n";
    $ret .= "This is a MIME encoded message.\r\n\r\n";
    $ret .= "--$boundary";

    $ret .= "Content-type: text/plain\r\n";
    $ret .= "Content-Transfer-Encoding: 7bit\r\n\r\n";
    $ret .= $this->body . "\r\n--$boundary";

    foreach ($this->attachments as $attachment) {
        $attachment[data] = base64_encode($attachment[data]);
        $attachment[data] = chunk_split($attachment[data]);
```

```
            $data =
                "Content-type: $attachment[type]" .
                $attachments[filename] ?
                  "; name = \"$attachments[filename]\"" : "" .
                "\r\n" .
                "Content-Transfer-Encoding: $attachments[encoding]" .
                "\r\n\r\n$attachment[data]\r\n";

            $ret .= "\r\n--$data--$boundary";
        }
        $ret .= "--\r\n";

        return($ret);
    }


    // }}}
    // {{{ send()

    /**
     * Send the prebuilt message
     *
     * @return bool true on success, false on failure.
     */
    function send () {
        return @mail($this->to,
                    $this->subject,
                    '',
                    $this->_build());
    }
}
?>
```

You would use this class like this:

```
<?php
//posted data is $to, $email, $subject, $body

$mm = new MIME($to, $email, $subject, $body);
$mm->attachment("picture.jpg",
                $contents,
                "image/jpeg");
$mm->send();
?>
```

Comments

The MIME class will take all the standard email information and send a mail message to the specified recipient. Let's go over the basic methods and functions of this class.

The first interesting method is the MIME() method. This method is a constructor, meaning that it is called when an instance of the class is created. The purpose of this function is to set the $to, $from, $subject, and $body attributes, which will be used when sending the e-mail.

The next method is the attachment() method. This method adds an attachment to a 2D array that looks like the following:

```
attachments -  element-array [filename => name of file to send with the
                                          attachment
                            type => content type of file
                            encoding => type of file encoding,
                                        defaults to base64
                            data => the content of the attachment]
```

Next we have the _build() method. This method builds the entire message and returns the contents. The attachments to the message are all encoded with base 64 encoding and the body of the message is in the standard 8-bit encoding.

Finally, the send() method uses the built-in mail() function to send an email to the specified address with the content made with the _build method. One thing that should be noted is that the mail() function specifies the entire message in the additional headers function and leaves the body argument empty.

15.7 Sending HTML E-mail

You want to send HTML-enabled e-mail with PHP.

Technique

HTML-enabled messages are simply MIME-encoded messages in which the attachment is of type text/html. So, create a new class that inherits from the one in recipe 15.6:

```php
<?php
/**
 * A class for sending HTML e-mails
 *
 * @author Sterling Hughes <sterling@php.net>
```

```php
 */
class HTML_Email extends MIME {

    // {{{ HTML_Email()

    /**
     *  Constructor adds the To From and Subject
     *  fields of your e-mail
     *
     * @param $to string Who your sending the message to.
     * @param $from string Who the message is from.
     * @param $subject string The subject of the message
     *
     * @return object A new HTML_Email object.
     */
    function HTML_Email ($to, $from, $subject) {
        $this->MIME($to, $from, $subject);
    }

    // }}}
    // {{{ html_data()

    /**
     *  Add your HTML message to the e-mail
     *
     * @param $html string The HTML message.
     *
     * @return null
     */
    function html_data ($html) {
        $this->attachment("", $html, "text/html");
    }

    // }}}
    // {{{ plain_data()

    /**
     * Add your Plain text message to the e-mail
     *
     * @param $data string The Plain text message.
     *
     * @return null
     */
```

```php
    function plain_data ($data) {
        $this->body = $data;
    }


    // }}}
}
?>
```

Comments

Sending an HTML-enabled e-mail is nearly the same thing as sending any attachment, but the content-type must be text/html and the filename must not be set. Here we create a simple class that will interface with the MIME class (as well as inheriting its core methods) You can use the HTML_Email class like so:

```php
<?php
$mm = new HTML_Email('andrei@php.net',
                     'sterling@php.net',
                     'Annoying HTML Message');
$mm->html_data($html);
$mm->plain_data(strip_tags($html));
$mm->send();
?>
```

As a side note on usability, always make sure that when you send an HTML message, you also send a plain text version for people (like myself) who can't stand receiving HTML e-mails.

15.8 Getting the Size of a Message

You want to get the size of a particular message.

Technique

Use the imap_fetchstructure() function:

```php
<?php
$structure = imap_fetchstructure($mh, $msg_num);
$message_size = $structure->bytes;
$message_size_in_kb = $message_size/1024;
?>
```

Comments

The `imap_fetchstructure()` function fetches the structure as a psuedo-object of an individual message specified by `$msg_num`. One of the attributes of that psuedo-object is the `bytes` attribute, which returns the message size in bytes. Most people work with kilobytes, so to convert from bytes to kilobytes, we need to divide by the number of bytes in a kilobyte, or 1024. For more information about `imap_fetchstructure()` and its other attributes, see the documentation for the function.

15.9 Parsing Mail Headers

You want to parse mail headers manually instead of using the `imap_header()` or `imap_headers()` function.

Technique

Use a regular expression:

```php
<?php
$fp = fopen("mail_message.txt", "r") or die("Cannot open");
while ($line = fgets($fp, 1024)) {
    if (preg_match("/^.*?:.*$/i", $line, $match)) {
        list (, $header_name, $header_value) = $match;
        $headers[trim($header_name)] = $header_value;
    } else if (empty($line)) {
        break;
    }
}
?>
```

Comments

As far as the headers of a message are concerned, the header name and header value are separated by a : sign. This goes on until the end of the message, where there is an empty line before the body of the message. In the solution script, we match all the header names and values and then place name/value pairs into the `$headers` array. When the header section is over, we break out of the `while` loop.

Note that if you have the IMAP library installed, you can simply use the `imap_header()` function, which will return a psuedo-object of the headers for a particular message. For more information, see the documentation for `imap_header()`.

CHAPTER 16

Working with SNMP Objects

16.0 Introduction

In this chapter and in the one following it, we discuss two of PHP's add-on modules that enable you to access two different network protocols: SNMP and LDAP. We will discuss exactly what each protocol is and then move into the functions and their uses.

SNMP, or Simple Network Management Protocol, helps you manage your network, as its name suggests. Developed to provide a common framework for network management, SNMP is the emerging communications and control management standard. Some uses of SNMP include

- Managing databases
- Managing power on a network
- Setting up addresses for devices
- Monitoring printer queues

SNMP works by interfacing with the management information databases (MIDs) of the devices on the network. By issuing SNMP commands, you can monitor and control the network by retrieving information for network devices and issuing control commands.

PHP offers a standard set of functions that enables you to add, delete, get, and read SNMP objects, which are basically wrappers for the C function calls. For more information about what is supported, see the man page on SNMP at `http://www.php.net/manual/ref.snmp.php`.

16.1 Setting an SNMP Object

You want to set the value of an SNMP object.

Technique

Use the `snmpset()` function:

```php
<?php
snmpset("localhost", "public",
        "system.SysContact.0", "s", "sterling@designmultimedia.com")
            or die("Cannot Set SNMP object");
?>
```

Comments

The `snmpset()` function sets an SNMP object (in this case, `"system.SysContact.0"`) of a certain type (in this case, a string `"s"`) on a server (`"localhost"`) with a specified community (in this case, `"public"`) to a certain value (in this case, `"sterling@_designmultimedia.com"`). Because the `snmpset()` function returns true on success and false on failure, we can then check the return value with the `die()` function.

The `snmpset()` function has two optional arguments: the timeout argument and the retry argument. Their meanings are the same as for the `snmpwalk()` function.

16.2 Getting an SNMP Object

You want to get the value of a certain SNMP object.

Technique

Use the `snmpget()` function to retrieve the value of a specified object:

```php
<?php
$contact = snmpget("localhost", "public", "system.SysContact.0");
print "The system contact is $contact";
?>
```

Comments

The `snmpget()` function gets the value of an SNMP object (in this case, `"system.SysContact.0"`) for a specified community (in this case, `"public"`) on a specified server (in this case, `"localhost"`).

The same two optional arguments discussed earlier—timeout and number of retries—can be supplied to this function as well.

16.3 Fetching All SNMP Objects into an Array

You want to fetch all the SNMP objects from an agent into an array.

Technique

Use the `snmpwalk()` function, which does exactly that:

```php
<?php
$obj_array = snmpwalk("localhost", "public", "");
while ($idx < count($obj_array)) {
    echo "$idx. $obj_array[$idx]\n";
}
?>
```

Comments

The `snmpwalk()` function returns an array of SNMP object values starting from the object ID. (If the third argument is left as an empty string `""`, all objects are fetched.)

If you want to fetch all objects into an associative array where the object ID is the key and the value is the corresponding SNMP object value, use the `snmpwalkoid()` function:

```php
<?php
$obj_array = snmpwalkoid("localhost", "public", "");
while (list($object_id, $object_value) = each($obj_array)) {
    echo "Object ID: $object_id\n<br>\n";
    echo "Object Value: $object_value\n<br>\n<br>\n";
}
?>
```

Please note that the `snmpwalk()` and `snmpwalkoid()` functions have two optional arguments: the timeout argument and the retry argument. The timeout argument, as its name suggests, is an integer value of how long to wait before timing out. If this argument is not set, it defaults to `SNMP_DEFAULT_TIMEOUT` or, in other words, it never times out. The retry argument is the number of times to retry the operation until giving up and reporting an error. If no argument is supplied, the default is `SNMP_DEFAULT_RETRIES`; or, in other words, one strike and you're out.

CHAPTER 17

LDAP

17.0 Introduction

LDAP, or Lightweight Directory Access Protocol, is a protocol that enables you to access X500-compliant directory servers. So, what are *directory servers*? They work much like your hard drive, except that they store user information in a hierarchical tree structure rather than storing files in a hierarchical tree structure. The terms are slightly different as well: In your filesystem, the top-level directory is known as the *root*, but when we are discussing LDAP, the top-level directory is known as the *world*.

PHP offers almost full support for the LDAP C API; it enables you to add, delete, get, modify, and search LDAP servers. The process of connecting to an LDAP server is simple with PHP— just open a connection, log on, do your voodoo, and then close the connection.

17.1 Adding an Entry to an LDAP Server

You want to add an entry to an LDAP server. In the following example, we will add Doc Brown.

Technique

Use the ldap_add() function after binding with write access to the LDAP server:

```php
<?php
// connect and bind
$lh = ldap_connect("localhost") or die("Cannot connect to the LDAP server");
ldap_bind($lh, "cn=root, o=Sterling's Company, c=US", "password")
        or die("Cannot Bind");

// build the data
$data["cn"] = "Doc Brown";
$data["objectclass"] = "Person";

// add the data and close the connection
ldap_add($lh, "cn=Doc Brown, o=Sterling's Company, c=US", $data);
ldap_close($lh);
?>
```

Comments

In this example, we add an entry for Doc Brown, who is an employee of the company named Sterling's Company, which is located in the United States. We achieve this by first connecting to the LDAP server on localhost. Then we bind the server and specify a password, which is necessary if we want to add, delete, and modify entries. We then build the data for Doc Brown into an associative array and use ldap_add() to add him to the directory.

Make special note of the ldap_bind() function in which you need to specify a password when you want to have write access to the LDAP server. Also note that ldap_close() is really an alias for ldap_unbind() and the two different functions can be used interchangeably. Therefore, we could have written

```php
ldap_unbind($lh);
```

and it would have achieved the same effect.

If you want to add attributes to a preexisting entry, simply use the ldap_mod_add() function like so:

```php
<?php
// connect and bind, notice the password is specified
// when we bind the connection
$lh = ldap_connect("localhost") or die("Cannot connect to LDAP server");
ldap_bind($lh, "cn=root, o=Sterling's Company, c=US", "password")
            or die("Cannot Bind to LDAP Server");
```

```
// Build the data
$data["sn"] = "Brown";
$data["mail"] = "sterling@designmultimedia.com";

// Add the data and close the connection
ldap_mod_add($lh, "cn=Doc Brown, o=Sterling's Company, c=US", $data);
ldap_close($lh);
?>
```

This would add the attributes of sn (surname) and mail (email address) to the Doc Brown entry in the LDAP server.

17.2 Removing an Entry from an LDAP Server

You want to delete an entry from an LDAP server.

Technique

Use the ldap_delete() function to delete object-level entries on your LDAP server:

```
<?php
// connect and bind, notice the password is specified
// when we bind the connection
$lh = ldap_connect("localhost") or die("Cannot connect to LDAP server");
ldap_bind($lh, "cn=root, o=Sterling's Company, c=US", "password")
        or die("Cannot Bind");

// delete and close
ldap_delete($lh, "cn=Doc Brown, o=Sterling's Company, c=US");
ldap_close($lh);
?>
```

Comments

In this script, we delete the person Doc Brown from our directory. Doing so removes not only his entry but also all attributes associated with his entry. This is achieved by using the ldap_delete() function, which enables you to delete object-level entries from an LDAP server.

If you want to delete attributes from a specific dn, use the ldap_mod_del() function instead:

```
<?php
$lh = ldap_connect("localhost") or die("Cannot connect to LDAP server");
```

```php
ldap_bind($lh, "cn=root, o=Sterling's Company, c=US", "password")
        or die("Cannot Bind to LDAP server");
$delete_data = array("sn", "mail");
ldap_mod_del($lh, "cn=Doc Brown, o=Sterling's Company, c=US", $delete_data);
ldap_close($lh);
?>
```

17.3 Executing a Query and Getting the Results

You want to execute a query and get back the relevant results in an array for easy processing and extraction.

Technique

Use `ldap_list()` for a quick, single-level search. You can then use the `ldap_get_entries()` function to extract the results into an array:

```php
<?php
// connect and bind
$lh = ldap_connect("localhost")
    or die("Cannot connect to LDAP server");
ldap_bind($lh) or die("Cannot Bind");

// perform query
$sth = ldap_list($lh,"o=Sterling's Company, c=US","cn=S*");
if (!$sth) {
    die(sprintf("Error [%d]: %s",
                ldap_errno($lh), ldap_error($lh)));
}
$entries = ldap_get_entries($lh, $sth);

// loop and print
for ($idx = 0; $idx < $entries["count"]; $idx++) {
    print "The distinguished name (dn) is: {$entries[$idx]}\n<br>\n";
    print "The common name (cn) of the first entry is:";
    pri {$entries[$idx]['cn'][0]}";
    print "\n<br>\n";
}

// Close the connection
ldap_close($lh);
?>
```

Comments

In this example, we use the `ldap_list()` function in conjunction with the `ldap_get_entries()` function to perform a search query and then load the results into an array that we then process using a `for` loop. It is important to note that we do not specify a maximum value in the `for` loop by the standard `"count($entries)"`, but rather use the special `"count"` element of the associative array, which accurately gives the number of matching results.

Note that we search the directory at only a single level. If you want to search entire LDAP directory subtrees, see recipe 17.5.

17.4 Freeing an LDAP Result Set

You want to free the results of an LDAP query so that you don't have large result sets in memory.

Technique

Use the `ldap_free_result()` function to free result sets:

```php
<?php
// Open and bind a connection
$lh = ldap_connect("localhost") or die("Cannot connect to LDAP");
ldap_bind($lh) or die("Cannot Bind");

// criteria
$bdn = "o=Sterling's Company, c=US";
$criteria = array("ou");

// perform query and free result
$sth = ldap_list($lh, $bdn, "ou=*", $criteria);
$data = ldap_get_entries($lh, $sth);
ldap_free_result($sth);

// loop through results
while ($idx < $data["count"]) {
    print $data[$idx++]["ou"][0] . "\n<br>\n";
}

// close the connection
ldap_unbind($lh);
?>
```

Comments

The `ldap_free_result()` function simply takes a handle of a result set and frees the memory allocated internally for that result set. In this example, we search the current level (`ldap_list()`) with our criteria, and then get the results and put them into a variable (which happens to be an array because that is what `ldap_get_entries()` returns). Then we free the result set because it is no longer needed.

With the advent of PHP4 and Zend's garbage collection feature, `ldap_free_result()` might seem redundant. However, for backward compatibility and for good programming practices, it is best to free result sets explicitly.

17.5 Performing a Tree Search

You want to search more than just the current directory level, as `ldap_list()` does.

Technique

Use the `ldap_search()` function, which will search the entire LDAP tree of the specified directory:

```php
<?php
// connect and bind
$lh = ldap_connect("localhost")
  or die("Cannot Connect");
ldap_bind($lh)
  or die("Cannot Bind");

// Build the search and attributes we want
$search_query = "sn=bro*";
$attributes = array("cn", "objectclass", "mail");

// Perform that thar query and load the results into an array
$sth = ldap_search($lh, "o=Sterling's Company, c=US",
                   $search_query, $attributes);
$entries = ldap_get_entries($lh, $sth);
ldap_free_result($sth);

// Print out all the good information that we have collected
echo "$entries[count] matching entries were found";
```

```
while ($idx < $entries[count]) {
    echo 'Well ' . $entries[$idx][cn] . ' seems to have matched;';
    echo ' if you want to talk to him his e-mail is ';
    echo $entries[$idx][mail] ."\n<br>\n";
    $idx++;
}


// close the connection
ldap_close($lh);
?>
```

Comments

The `ldap_search()` function searches an entire LDAP directory tree, as opposed to `ldap_list()`, which searches only the current directory. In this example, we connect to the LDAP server (`ldap_connect()`), and then bind for read access (`ldap_bind()` without dn and password). We then build up our search query (`$search_query`) and the attributes that we want to collect from the matches. After all this is done, we are ready to use the `ldap_search()` function to find the relevant entries, which we then retrieve with the `ldap_get_entries()` function. Finally, we have the results in an array for manipulation, and we simply use a `while` loop to process the array and print the relevant entries. When it is all done, the connection is closed.

Note in the synopsis that when it comes time to loop through the result array, we use `$entries[count]` instead of `count($entries)`. This is because the `ldap_get_entries()` function has a special key, `count`, that holds the number of entries in the array to process.

17.6 Sorting Search Results

You want to sort the results of an LDAP search.

Technique

Use the `usort()` function on your result set:

```
<?php

// ldap sort function
// sort by common name length (cn)
function ldap_sort_func($a, $b) {
    if (!is_array($a) || !is_array($b) ||
```

```php
        $a[cn] == $b[cn]) return 0;
    return strlen($a[cn]) > strlen($b[cn]) ? 1 : -1;
}

// connect and bind
$lh = ldap_connect("localhost")
  or die("Cannot Connect");
ldap_bind($lh)
  or die("Cannot Bind");

// Build the search and attributes we want
$search_query = "sn=bro*";
$attributes = array("cn", "objectclass", "mail");

// Perform that thar query and load the results into an array
$sth = ldap_search($lh, "o=Sterling's Company, c=US",
                   $search_query, $attributes);
$entries = ldap_get_entries($lh, $sth);
ldap_free_result($sth);

// Print out all the good information that we have collected
echo "$entries[count] matching entries were found";

// now sort the results
usort($entries, 'ldap_sort_func');

while ($idx < $entries[count]) {
    echo 'Well ' . $entries[$idx][cn] . ' seems to have matched;';
    echo ' if you want to talk to him his e-mail is ';
    echo $entries[$idx][mail] ."".\n<br>\n";
    $idx++;
}

// close the connection
ldap_close($lh);
?>
```

Comments

To sort a list of LDAP results, we first fetch all the results of our search into a two-dimensional array as described in recipe 17.5. Then we use the usort() function to custom sort the two-dimensional array returned by ldap_get_entries().

PART IV

Generating Other Languages

18 Creating and Managing Images

19 HTML

20 XML

CHAPTER 18

Creating and Managing Images

"If God created us in his image we have certainly returned the compliment."

Voltaire (1694-1778)

The purpose of a Web site is to interact with your users, whomever they might be. An extremely effective way of interacting with users is through the use of visuals. As the saying goes, "A picture is worth a thousand words." However, with the Web more than any other medium, pictures have become vital, mainly because your customers don't always speak the same language that you do and visuals might be your only means of communication. Also the careful use of images can inspire trust in both a product and a company, despite any language barriers.

PHP offers an interface to the GD module by Thomas Boutell, which in turn currently supports the creation and management of JPEGs and PNGs. By using the functions provided, you can create, add text to, draw pictures on, and modify preexisting PNG and JPEG images.

Perhaps the observant reader has noticed that there is no mention of GD supporting the creation of probably the most popular format on the Web: GIF. As of GD 1.4, GD no longer supports the creation and management of GIF images because of the licensing restrictions placed on the LZW algorithm by Unisys. More information about this matter can be found in Lincoln Stein's excellent article for Webtechniques, "Fugitive from Justice." You can view arguments online at http://www.webtechniques.com/archives/1999/12/webm/index.shtml.

In this chapter, we cover how to create and manipulate PNG, JPEG, and GIF images. (You can use GIFs, illegally, if you compile with GD 1.3 or earlier.)

18.1   Creating an Image with GD

You want to create a new image, whether it is in GIF, PNG, or JPEG format.

Technique

Use the `ImageCreate()` function and then use the `ImagePng()`, `ImageJpeg()`, or `ImageGif()` function, depending on your system:

```php
<?php

header("Content-type: image/gif");
$im = ImageCreate(100,20);

$red = ImageColorAllocate($im, 255, 0, 0);
$white  = ImageColorAllocate($im, 255, 255, 255);

ImageString($im, 3, 3, 3, "YES!", $white);
ImageGif($im);

ImageDestroy($im);   #Free memory
?>
```

Comments

If you run the preceding script, you should see something like the following (although the font might be different):

YES!

But what exactly are we doing? Let's go over this line by line:

Line 3—Print the header telling the Web browser that this is a GIF image.

Line 4—Create a GD image stream that can be manipulated by any of the other GD functions. The format of this image is not determined until we tell GD that it is a GIF and print it out on Line 10.

Line 6—Create the background color for the image and set it to red using the `ImageColorAllocate()` function.

Line 7—Create the foreground color for the image and set it to white by using the `ImageColorAllocate()` function.

Line 9—Draw a string to image `$im` using a built-in font at x-pixel location of 3 and a y-pixel location of 3. The contents of the string is `"YES!"` and the color of the string is white, denoted by the variable `$white`.

Line 10—Convert the image to a GIF and output it to the browser.

Line 12—Destroy the memory allocated for the GIF. This is done when the script executes anyway.

In the example, we use the `ImageGif()` function to convert the image, `$im`, to a GIF and then output it to the browser (STDOUT). However, if we want to save it to a file, we can provide an optional second argument, like so:

```
<?php
$filename = "some_image.gif";

$im = ImageCreate(150,40);

$red = ImageColorAllocate($im, 255, 0, 0);
$white  = ImageColorAllocate($im, 255, 255, 255);

ImageString($im, 3, 4, 3, "Saved to $filename with GD", $white);
ImageGif($im, $filename);

ImageDestroy($im);   # Free memory associated with image
?>
The image was written to <?php echo $filename; ?>
```

18.2 Opening a Preexisting Image

You want to open a preexisting image for manipulation rather than creating an image from scratch.

Technique

Use the `ImageCreateFrom*` functions instead of the combination of the `ImageCreate` and `Image*` functions:

```php
<?php
// Opening a pre-existing PNG
$im_ping = ImageCreateFromPng("someimage.png");

// Opening a pre-existing GIF
$im_gif = ImageCreateFromGif("someimage.gif");

// Opening a pre-existing JPEG
$im_jpeg = ImageCreateFromJpeg("someimage.jpg");
?>
```

Comments

The ImageCreateFrom* functions enable you to open preexisting images as GD streams so that you can then manipulate them. Note that to use the ImageCreateFromGif() function, you must have GD 1.6 or earlier; to access the ImageCreateFromJpeg() function, you must have GD 1.8 or greater; for PNG support, you need GD 1.3 or greater.

After you have a GD stream to the image, manipulations of the image are done the same way as if you had created an image by using the ImageCreate() function. Consider the following script, which adds text to the middle of this image:

```php
<?php
header("Content-type: image/png");
if (($im = ImageCreateFromPng("generic.png")) == "") {
    echo "Error, could not open generic.png for manipulation!";
    exit;
}

$red = ImageColorAllocate($im, 255, 0, 0);
ImageString($im, 3, 20, 10, "Home", $red);
ImagePng($im); // Print the Image out to the browser
?>
```

18.3 Getting the Size of an Image

You want to get the size of an image. For example, you might want to generate width and height tags for images automatically.

Technique

Use the `GetImageSize()` function, which returns an array of information about an image, including prebuilt width and height tags:

```php
<?php

$image_info = GetImageSize("someimage.gif");
list($image_width, $image_height,
     $image_type, $image_width_height_string) = $image_info;
print "<img src='someimage.gif' $image_width_height_string>";

?>
```

Comments

The `GetImageSize()` function is part of the standard PHP library, meaning that you do not need GD support enabled to use this function. `GetImageSize()` returns a numerically indexed array with the first element equal to the width of the image in pixels, and the second element equal to the image's height. The third element contains the type of the image (1 is GIF, 2 is JPG, 3 is PNG), and the fourth and final element is the width and height string, which you can embed in image tags.

If you pass it a JPEG, the `GetImageSize()` function also returns two elements in associative array form. One element is the number of bits in the image and the other is the number of channels. You can access the items of the associative array like so:

```php
<?php
$image_info = GetImageSize("someimage.jpg");
print "someimage.jpg has {$image_info['channels']} channels ";
print "as well as {$image_info['bits']} bits\n";
?>
```

18.4 Adding Text to Images

You want to add text to your images.

Technique

There are quite a few functions that enable you to write text to your images. The "Discussion" section contains a list of all the different functions. For information on drawing TrueType fonts to an image, see recipe 18.14.

Comments

The following sections comprise a list of the different functions that you can use to draw text to images with PHP's gd functions.

ImageChar

```
int ImageChar(int im, int font, int x, int y, string c, int col);
```

Draw a character horizontally.

Example

```php
<?php
header("Content-type: image/jpeg");
$im = ImageCreate(140, 50);
$str = "Hello";
$bgcol = ImageColorAllocate($im, 234, 122, 99);
$txtcol = ImageColorAllocate($im, 0, 0, 0);
for ($i=0, $x=10; $i < strlen($str); $i++, $x+=15) {
    ImageChar($im, 5, $x, 20, $str[$i], $txtcol);
}
ImageJpg($im);
ImageDestroy($im);
?>
```

ImageCharUp

```
int ImageCharUp(int im, int font, int x, int y, string c, int col);
```

Draw a character vertically.

Example

```php
<?php
header("Content-type: image/gif");
$str = "Hello";
$im = ImageCreate(50, 140);
$bgcol = ImageColorAllocate($im, 234, 122, 99);
$txtcol = ImageColorAllocate($im, 0, 0, 0);
for ($i=0, $y=20; $i < strlen($str); $i++, $y+=15) {
    ImageCharUp($im, 5, 10, $y, $str[$i], $txtcol);
}
```

```php
ImageGif($im);
ImageDestroy($im);
?>
```

ImageLoadFont

```
int ImageLoadFont(string file);
```

Load a user-defined font.

Example

```php
<?php
header("Content-type: image/png");
$im = ImageCreate(140, 50);
$font = ImageLoadFont("myfont.ft");
$bgcolor = ImageColorAllocate($im, 222, 4, 232);
$txt_color = ImageColorAllocate($im, 23, 3, 32);
ImageString($im, $font, 20, 10, "Some Str", $txt_color);
ImagePng($im);
ImageDestroy($im);
?>
```

ImagePsLoadFont

```
int ImagePsLoadFont(string file);
```

Load a PostScript 1 font.

Example

```php
<?php
header("Content-type: image/png");
$im = ImageCreate(140, 50);
$black = ImageColorAllocate($im, 0, 0, 0);
$white = ImageColorAllocate($im, 255, 255, 255);
$font = ImagePsLoadFont("postscript_font.ttf");
ImagePsText($im, "Hello", $font, 13, $white, $black, 20, 10);
ImagePsFreeFont($font);
ImagePng($im);
ImageDestroy($im);
?>
```

ImagePsText

```
array imagepstext(int image, string text, int font, int size,
                  int foreground, int background, int x, int y,
                  int [space], int [tightness], float [angle],
                  int [antialias_steps]);
```

Draw text with a Postscript 1 type font.

Example

See example for ImagePsLoadFont().

ImagePsFreeFont

```
void ImagePsFreeFont(int fontindex);
```

Free memory associated with a font loaded by ImagePsLoadFont().

Example

See the example for ImagePsLoadFont().

ImagePsEncodeFont

```
int ImagePsEncodeFont(string encodingfile);
```

Change the character encoding vector for a font, which is often useful when dealing with other languages that require characters above ASCII 127.

Example

```php
<?php
header("Content-type: image/gif");
$im = ImageCreate(140, 50);
$blue = ImageColorAllocate($im, 0, 0, 255);
$white = ImageColorAllocate($im, 255, 255, 255);
$font = ImagePsLoadFont("some_postscript_font.ps");
$font = ImagePsEncodeFont("IsoLatin1.enc");
ImagePsText($im, "Hello~", $font, 12, $white, $blue, 20, 10);
ImagePsFreeFont($font);
ImagePng($im);
ImageDestroy($im);
?>
```

ImageString

```
int ImageString(int im, int font, int x, int y, string s, int col);
```

Draw a string horizontally.

Example

```php
<?php
header("Content-type: image/png");
$im = ImageCreate(140,50);
$green = ImageColorAllocate($im, 0, 255, 0);
$white = ImageColorAllocate($im, 255, 255, 255);
ImageString($im, 4, 20, 10, "Hello World", $white);
ImagePng($im);
ImageDestroy($im);
?>
```

ImageStringUp

```
int ImageStringUp(int im, int font, int x, int y, string s, int col);
```

Draw a string vertically.

Example

```php
<?php
header("Content-type: image/jpeg");
$im = ImageCreate(50, 140);
$blue = ImageColorAllocate($im, 0, 0, 255);
$mix = ImageColorAllocate($im, 190, 34, 3);
ImageStringUp($im, 4, 10, 70, "Hello", $mix);
ImageJpeg($im);
ImageDestroy($im);
?>
```

18.5 Getting the Color of a Certain Part of an Image

You want to get the color of a particular part of an image.

Technique

Use the ImageColorAt() function, which will return the color index for the specified pixel, and then translate that into the RGB values by using the ImageColorsForIndex() function:

```php
<?php
$im = ImageCreateFromJpeg("colors.jpg");
$cindex = ImageColorAt($im, 34, 40);
$rgb_color = ImageColorsForIndex($im, $cindex);
echo "colors.jpg has a red value of {$rgb_color ['red']}a green value of ";
echo "{$rgb_color['green']} and a blue value of {$rgb_color['blue']} at ";
echo "a pixel position of 34, 40";
?>
```

Comments

The ImageColorAt() function returns the color index, not the RGB value of the specified pixel location. Therefore, you must use the ImageColorsForIndex() function, which converts a color index into its red, green, and blue values and returns those values as an associative array.

You might be wondering how these functions are useful. Why would someone ever need to find the RGB color of a certain part of an image? There is a good reason for these functions being in here, but first let me explain a bit about images and color palettes.

Every image has a color palette with a limited number of colors. For example, a GIF image has a 256-color palette, meaning that each GIF image can have only 256 unique colors. Also, the fewer colors used by the palette, the smaller the size of the image file. So, a GIF image with 16 colors has a smaller file size than a GIF image with 32 colors, and is much smaller than an image with 256 colors.

Knowing this, it becomes apparent that if you can reuse colors that are already in the image palette, the size of the image file will be smaller. By getting certain colors in an image, you can reuse those colors and reduce the file size of the image.

Another use of this function is to get the background color on which you are drawing your enhancements. For example, if the background is black, you probably will want to draw white text; or, if the background is white, you might want to draw some other color. After you get the colors for a certain area, you can perform some manipulations on the RGB indexes and create a color that matches perfectly with the background:

```php
<?php
header("Content-type: image/png");
$im = ImageCreateFromPng("tst.png");
$cindex = ImageColorAt($im, 50, 100);  // middle of the image
$rgb_color = ImageColorsForIndex($im, $cindex);

if ($rgb_color["red"] > 150) $r = 10;
else $r = 230;
if ($rgb_color["green"] > 150) $g = 10;
else $g = 180;
if ($rgb_color["blue"]  > 150) $b = 10;
else $b = 210;

$color = ImageColorAllocate($im, $r, $g, $b);
ImageString($im, 4, 25, 50, "Hello World", $color);
ImagePng($im);
ImageDestroy($im);
?>
```

18.6 Getting the Total Number of Colors in an Image

You need to find out how many colors there are in an image.

Technique

Use the `ImageColorsTotal()` function, which returns the number of colors allocated for an image:

```php
<?php
$im = ImageCreateFromGif("some_im.gif");
echo 'some_im.gif has ' . ImageColorsTotal($im) . ' colors in its palette';
ImageDestroy($im);
?>
```

Comments

The `ImageColorsTotal()` function returns a long with the total number of colors allocated for the given image stream. This can be useful if you need to have a certain amount of colors in an image and no more (for example, a GIF must have fewer than 256 colors).

18.7 Making a GIF/PNG Transparent

You want to make a GIF or PNG stream transparent. (JPEG doesn't support transparency.)

Technique

Use the `ImageColorTransparent()` function to make the background color transparent:

```php
<?php
header("Content-type: image/png");
$im = ImageCreate(100, 20);
$bgcolor = ImageColorAllocate($im, 255, 255, 255);
$bgcolortrans = ImageColorTransparent($im, $bgcolor);
$black = ImageColorAllocate($im, 0, 0, 0);
ImageString($im, 2, 5, 5, "Hello World");
ImagePng($im);
ImageDestroy($im);
?>
```

Comments

When you set a color to be transparent it means that color morphs into whatever the background color is. For example, assume that you have set the color gray as the transparent color for an image. When you put that image on a red background, every occurrence of that gray color becomes the red color of the background.

If you want to see what color is transparent for a specified image, simply use the `ImageColorTransparent()` function with only one argument like so:

```php
<?php
$im = ImageCreateFromPng('tst.png');
$trans_color = ImageColorTransparent($im);
$rgb_col = ImageColorsForIndex($trans_color);
echo "The transparent color has a red value of {$rgb_col['red']}";
echo "a green value of {$rgb_col['green']} and a blue value of ";
echo $rgb_col['blue'];
?>
```

18.8 Copy One Part of an Image to Another

You want to copy part of one image to another image.

Technique

Use the `ImageCopy()` function to copy part of one image to another image:

```php
<?php
header("Content-type: image/jpeg");
$im1 = ImageCreateFromJpeg('tst1.jpg');
$im2 = ImageCreateFromJpeg('tst2.jpg');
ImageCopy($im1, $im2, 50, 100, 50, 100, 35, 35);
ImageJpeg($im2);
ImageDestroy($im2);
ImageDestroy($im1);
?>
```

Comments

The `ImageCopy()` function has the following prototype:

```
int ImageCopy(int src, int dest, int destX, int destY, int srcX, int srcY,
              int srcW, int srcH);
```

This means that the function takes an image stream `src` and appends the portion of the stream starting at `srcX`, `srcY` with a width of `srcW` and a height of `srcH` to the image stream `dest`, at an X location of `destX` and a Y location of `destY`. In the example, we copy a 35_35 portion of tst1.jpg starting at 50, 100 to tst2.jpg starting at 50, 100.

Here we use the `ImageCopy()` function to copy one portion of one image to another portion of another image. However, if you simply want to move around parts of a single image, specify the same source and destination image:

```
ImageCopy($im1, $im1, 50, 100, 25, 50, 25, 50);
```

But be careful: If the pixel areas overlap, unpredictable things will occur!

If you want to copy part of the image, but resize the part of the image you are copying, use the `ImageCopyResized()` function. Here is a quick example:

```php
<?php
$im = ImageCreateFromJpeg("tst.jpg");
$im1 = ImageCreateFromJpeg("tst1.jpg");
```

```php
ImageCopyResized($im, $im1, 50, 100, 50, 100, 70, 70, 35, 35);
ImageJpeg($im1);
ImageDestroy($im);
ImageDestroy($im2);
?>
```

18.9 Drawing Rectangles

Drawing text to images isn't enough for you—you need to make art!

Technique

Use the `ImageRectangle()` and the `ImageFilledRectangle()` functions to draw rectangles in your images.

Example 1—A simple, filled rectangle:

```php
<?php
header("Content-type: image/png");
$im = ImageCreate(100, 20);
$white = ImageColorAllocate($im, 255, 255, 255);
$light_blue = ImageColorAllocate($im, 20, 93, 233);
ImageFilledRectangle($im, 5, 10, 60, 14, $light_blue);
ImagePng($im);
ImageDestroy($im);
?>
```

Example 2—A simple rectangle (not filled):

```php
<?php
header("Content-type: image/png");
$im = ImageCreate(100, 20);
$white = ImageColorAllocate($im, 255, 255, 255);
$light_blue = ImageColorAllocate($im, 20, 93, 233);
ImageRectangle($im, 5, 10, 60, 14, $light_blue);
ImagePng($im);
ImageDestroy($im);
?>
```

Comments

In example 1, we use the `ImageFilledRectangle()` function to draw a simple, filled rectangle to the image stream, `$im`. This function takes an image stream, `$im`, and draws a rectangle starting at the X coordinate, 5, and the Y coordinate 10, to the X coordinate 60 and the Y coordinate 14, with the color $light_blue.

In example 2, we use the ImageRectangle() function, which draws an unfilled rectangle to image $im, with a border of $light_blue. This function has an argument order identical to that of the ImageFilledRectangle() function discussed earlier.

A line is a rectangle with a nonexistent width. Therefore, the ImageFilledRectangle() function can be used not only to draw rectangles but also to simulate the drawing of lines. But in reality, lines have to be at least one pixel wide, so you need to specify a width of 1 for the rectangle so that it looks like a line:

```php
<?php
header("Content-type: image/png");
$im = ImageCreate(100, 20);
$white = ImageCollorAllocate($im, 255, 255, 255);
ImageColorTransparent($im, $white);
$light_red = ImageColorAllocate($im, 233, 93, 20);
ImageFilledRectangle($im, 5, 10, 60, 11, $light_red);
ImagePng($im);
ImageDestroy($im);
?>
```

18.10 Drawing Polygons

You want to draw a polygon, which is any figure with more than one side.

Technique

Use the ImagePolygon() and the ImageFilledPolygon() functions to draw polygons.

Example 1—A simple polygon (not filled):

```php
<?php
header("Content-type: image/gif");
$im = ImageCreate(100, 20);
$white = ImageColorAllocate($im, 255, 255, 255);
$light_blue = ImageColorAllocate($im, 20, 93, 233);
$points = array(12, 10, 15, 20, 50, 17, 70, 10);
ImagePolygon($im, $points, 4, $light_blue);
ImageGif($im);
ImageDestroy($im);
?>
```

Example 2—A simple, filled polygon:

```php
<?php
header("Content-type: image/gif");
$im = ImageCreate(100, 20);
$white = ImageColorAllocate($im, 255, 255, 255);
$light_blue = ImageColorAllocate($im, 20, 93, 233);
$points = array(12, 10, 15, 20, 50, 17, 70, 10);
ImageFilledPolygon($im, $points, 4, $light_blue);
ImageGif($im);
ImageDestroy($im);
?>
```

Comments

In example 1, we draw a polygon on the image stream, $im, with vertices of (12, 10), (15, 20), (50, 17), and (70, 10) with a border color of light blue. We achieve this by using the ImagePolygon() function which takes an image stream, $im, as its first argument. Its second argument is an array of points (in pairs), followed by the number of vertices there are to be on the polygon, and then finally the color to draw the border of the polygon.

In the example 2, we draw the same polygon as in example 1, but this time we use the ImageFilledPolygon() function which fills in the polygon with the color given by the last argument. The argument order and content are the same for both ImagePolygon() and ImageFilledPolygon().

18.11 Drawing an Arc

You want to draw an arc to your image.

Technique

Use the ImageArc() function to draw an arc to your image:

```php
<?php
header("Content-type: image/gif");
$im = ImageCreate(100, 20);
$white = ImageColorAllocate($im, 255, 255, 255);
ImageColorTransparent($im, $white);
$light_red = ImageColorAllocate($im, 233, 93, 20);
```

```
ImageArc($im, 4, 5, 50, 40, 10, 180, $light_red);
ImageGif($im);
ImageDestroy($im);
?>
```

Comments

The `ImageArc()` function has the following syntax:

```
int ImageArc(int im, int cx, int cy, int w, int h, int s, int e, int col);
```

This means it draws an arc to an image, im, with a start X position of cx and a start Y position of cy. The arc is of width w and height h, with a start angle of s and an end angle of e, all in the color col.

The `ImageArc()` function can be used not only for drawing arcs but also for drawing circles and ellipses and filled circles and ellipses. The following is an example of drawing an ellipse using the `ImageArc()` function:

```
<?php
header("Content-type: image/gif");
$im = ImageCreate(500, 100);
$white = ImageColorAllocate($im, 255, 255, 255);
ImageColorTransparent($im, $white);
$light_red = ImageColorAllocate($im, 233, 93, 20);
ImageArc($im, 40, 50, 50, 40, 0, 360, $light_red);
ImageGif($im);
ImageDestroy($im);
?>
```

The preceding code works because to have an ellipse, you need a 360-degree difference between the start position and the end position. Applying that knowledge, we can also draw a filled circle by using the `ImageFillToBorder()` function. (Note that this is a circle not an ellipse because the width and height parameters have the same value.)

```
<?php
header("Content-type: image/gif");
$im = ImageCreate(500, 100);
$white = ImageColorAllocate($im, 255, 255, 255);
ImageColorTransparent($im, $white);
$light_red = ImageColorAllocate($im, 233, 93, 20);
ImageArc($im, 40, 50, 50, 50, 0, 360, $light_red);
ImageFillToBorder($im, 50, 40, $light_red, $light_red);
```

```
ImageGif($im);
ImageDestroy($im);
?>
```

18.12 Making an Image Interlaced

You want to make an image interlaced, meaning that it will load in multiple scans.

Technique

Use the ImageInterlace() function on an image stream:

```php
<?php
header("Content-type: image/gif");
$im = ImageCreate(100, 20);
ImageInterlace($im, 1);
$white = ImageColorAllocate($im, 255, 255, 255);
ImageColorTransparent($im, $white);
$light_red = ImageColorAllocate($im, 233, 93, 20);
ImageArc($im, 4, 5, 50, 40, 10, 180, $light_red);
ImageGif($im);
ImageDestroy($im);
?>
```

Comments

The ImageInterlace() function enables you to set whether an image stream is interlaced. If the second argument of ImageInterlace() is true (1), the image is interlaced; otherwise, the image is not interlaced. By default, images are not interlaced.

If the second argument is not provided to the ImageInterlace() function, the function simply returns whether the image is currently interlaced.

18.13 Dynamic Buttons

You want to generate a bunch of buttons from the same template.

Technique

This code will create dynamic buttons on-the-fly, given some text and a background image. This saves time if you want to have constantly changing text on images and you don't feel like using Photoshop or GIMP to make each button:

The variables: vars.php

The code:

```php
<?php
//
// The color of the text to be drawn can be either 'r' (red),
// 'g' (green), 'bl' (blue), 'b' (black), 'w' (white).
//

$txtCol = "w";

//
// The Font size of the number, can be from 1 .. 5
//

$defaultFont = 4;

//
// The Starting X position, where to start drawing text.
//

$xStartPos = 0;

//
// The Starting Y position, where to start drawing text.
//

$yStartPos = 0;

//
// The default text message if no text message is given.
//

$genericTxt = "";

//
// The button image, if not already given.
```

```php
    //

    $genImage = "genericButton.gif";
?>
```

The Program: button.php

The Code:

```php
<?php
header("Content-type: image/gif");
include_once("vars.php");

if (!isset($color)) {
    $color = $txtCol;
}

if (!isset($fontsize)) {
    $fontsize = $defaultFont;
}

if (!isset($startX)) {
    $startX = $xStartPos;
}

if (!isset($startY)) {
    $startY = $yStartPos;
}

if (!isset($txt)) {
    $txt = $genericTxt;
}

if (!isset($tmpl_image)) {
    $tmpl_image = $genImage;
}

$im = ImageCreateFromGif($tmpl_image);
switch ($color) {
    case 'w':
        $col = ImageColorAllocate($im, 255, 255, 255);
        break;
```

```php
    case 'b':
        $col = ImageColorAllocate($im, 0, 0, 0);
        break;
    case 'r':
        $col = ImageColorAllocate($im, 255, 0, 0);
        break;
    case 'g':
        $col = ImageColorAllocate($im, 0, 255, 0);
        break;
    case 'bl':
        $col = ImageColorAllocate($im, 0, 0, 255);
        break;
}

ImageString($im, $fontsize, $startX, $startY, $txt, $col);
ImageGif($im);
ImageDestroy($im);
?>
```

Comments

If you are anything like me, doing the same things over and over annoys you. One area where things can become redundant is when creating navigation buttons for your Web site. Every button is the same size and has the same background; the only thing different is the text contained within the button. In the preceding recipe, we remedy this by creating a script in which you fill in a few variable parameters and the script creates all your buttons for you. Of course, this script might need a little modification for your purposes (such as adding more colors for the text to be drawn), but the basic concept remains the same.

18.14 Using TrueType Fonts

You want to draw a string using a TrueType font instead of a built-in or PostScript font.

Technique

Use the ImageTTFText() function:

```php
<?php
header("Content-type: image/gif");
$im = ImageCreate(140, 50);
$black = ImageColorAllocate($im, 0, 0, 0);
```

```
$white = ImageColorAllocate($im, 255, 255, 255);
ImageTTFText($im, 24, 0, 30, 35, $white, "assets/arial.ttf", "Hello");
ImageGif($im);
ImageDestroy($im);
?>
```

Comments

The prototype for the ImageTTFText() function looks like this:

```
array ImageTTFText(int im, int size, int angle, int x, int y, int col,
                   string fontfile, string text)
```

Note that for this function, the x and y arguments represent the coordinates of the lower-left corner of the first character in the string.

ImageTTFText() returns an array of eight elements representing the bounding box of the drawn text, starting from upper left and going clockwise. The bounding box points are relative to the text, so if you draw text at a 90-degree angle, "lower left" will actually be in the lower-right corner of the image. You can also obtain the bounding box information without drawing a string by using the ImageTTFBBox() function, which takes font size, angle, font filename, and text to be measured, and returns the same information as ImageTTFText().

CHAPTER 19

HTML

19.0 Introduction

Have you ever created a rollover script (in JavaScript) for the Web where the engine itself was 6 lines of code, but the script spanned more than 400 lines of code? Have you ever had to create a select list for a form manually?

No, this isn't a marketing pitch (although it very well could be). The scenarios I describe are tedious, time-consuming chores that can be done simply and quickly using PHP.

19.1 Stripping HTML Tags

You want to remove or extract all HTML tags from a document.

Technique

Either use the `strip_tags()` function after you have read the entire file or string:

```php
<?php
$new_str = strip_tags($old_str);
?>
```

Or, when looping through a file line by line, use the `fgetss()` function:

```php
<?php
$fp = @fopen('/path/to/somefile', 'r')
    or die('Cannot Open Somefile');
while ($line = @fgetss($fp, 1024)) {
    $no_html_tags .= $line;
}
fclose($fp);
?>
```

Comments

Sometimes you have HTML documents that you want to convert to plain text—a format accessible to everyone, everywhere. PHP enables you to do this by providing functions that take away all the HTML tags in a document. In other languages, this requires complex regular expressions. But there is one weakness: In HTML, things such as extra spaces and copyright characters (©) are represented with special format specifiers that look something like this:

`&individual_specifier;`

Therefore, we must also eliminate these unwanted specifiers and replace them with their corresponding ASCII characters, To do this, use the `HTML_processor` class from PEAR:

```php
<?php
require("HTML_processor.php");
$processor = new HTML_Processor;
$processor->ConvertSpecial(&$text);
?>
```

19.2 Converting ASCII to HTML

You want to convert your ASCII text files to HTML.

Technique

Use a combination of `htmlentities()` and `nl2br()` to convert the document:

```php
<?php
$doc = implode("", file($conversion_file));
$doc = nl2br(htmlentities($doc));
```

```
print $doc;
?>
```

Comments

The `htmlentities()` function replaces all special HTML characters such as ®,©, and ™ with the equivalent escape character sequences. The `nl2br()` function takes all newline characters and inserts a <br> tag (HTML line break). Converting ASCII to HTML is really that simple!

19.3 Generating <select> Lists

You want to automate the generation of <select> lists from an array.

Technique

Use a `while` loop to loop through your array and print out the <option> tags:

```php
<?php
print "<select name=\"select_list\">";
foreach ($select_array as $name => $value) {
    print "<option value=\"$value\">$name</option>\n";
}
print "</select>";
?>
```

Comments

In PHP, as shown next in recipe 19.4, you can generate JavaScript and HTML with extraordinary ease. One use is generating <select> lists from an associative array. Using this basic theory, you can also generate tables, lists, and even entire Web pages—it just takes a little creativity. The preceding example will suffice for simple needs, but here is a useful function that does the same thing and a lot more:

```php
<?php
function html_options($output,
                      $values   = NULL,
                      $selected = NULL,
                      $first_option_output = false)
{
    // If there is nothing to output, return
```

```php
    if (empty($output))
        return;

    // Cast all arguments to arrays
    settype($values, "array");
    settype($output, "array");
    settype($selected, "array");

    // Count the number of values in arrays
    $num_output = count($output);
    $num_values = count($values);

    $html_output = "";

    if ($first_option_output) {
        $html_output = "<OPTION value=\"\">";
        $html_output .= "$first_option_output</OPTION>\n";
    }

    for ($i=0; $i < $num_output; $i++) {
        // By default, check value against $selected
        $sel_check = $values[$i];
        $html_output .= "<OPTION";
        if ($i < $num_values) {
            $html_output .= " value=\"".$values[$i]."\"";
        } else {
            // If more output than values, check
            // output against $selected.
            $sel_check = $output[$i];
        }

        if (in_array($sel_check, $selected)) {
            $html_output .= " selected";
        }
        $html_output .= ">".$output[$i]."</OPTION>\n";
    }

    return($html_output);
}
?>
```

The first argument to this function is a list of strings you want to display in the select box. That's all that's really needed sometimes. The second argument is a list of option values—one for each string. The third argument enables you to select a certain option automatically when it displays on the page. Finally, your first option string will very often be something like `"--select month--"`. The last argument enables you to pass that string to be displayed as the first option. Here is an example of using this function with all the arguments:

```php
<?php
$colors = array("Red", "Green", "Blue", "Orange");
$color_values = array("#ff0000", "#00ff00", "#0000ff", "#ff8000");
$selected_color = "#ff8000";
print html_options($colors,
                   $color_values,
                   $selected_color,
                   "-- select color --");
?>
```

This would output the following HTML:

```
<OPTION value="">-- select color --</OPTION>
<OPTION value="#ff0000">Red</OPTION>
<OPTION value="#00ff00">Green</OPTION>
<OPTION value="#0000ff">Blue</OPTION>
<OPTION value="#ff8000" selected>Orange</OPTION>
```

19.4 Generating JavaScript Rollovers

You want to have PHP generate your JavaScript for you.

Technique

Use PEAR's `Javascript_Rollover` class:

```php
<?php
$links = array('http://www.internet.com/',
               'http://www.designmultimedia.com/',
               'http://www.redhat.com/');

$rollovers = new Javascript_Rollover($links);
$rollovers->types(ROLLOVER_MOUSEOVER|ROLLOVER_MOUSEOUT);
$rollovers->prefix('somepage');
$rollovers->ending('jpg');
```

```
?>
<html>
<head>
    <title> Somepage </title>
    <script language="javascript">
    <?php
        print $rollovers->genPreloadData();
    ?>
    </script>
</head>
<body>
<!-- Place the images in a table -->
<table border='0' cellpadding='0' cellspacing='3'>
<tr>
<td>
<?php
foreach ($rollovers->genRollovers() as $rollover) {
    print "$rollover\n";
}
?>
</td>
<td>
Page contents here
</td>
</tr>
</table>
</body>
</html>
```

Comments

As I said in the second sentence of this book, PHP is a language that helps you do more. PHP is excellent at generating JavaScript code, saving you the time and the effort of writing all that horrendous HTML and JavaScript. Because a Web page is parsed by PHP and then sent to the browser where the HTML and JavaScript are manipulated, you can easily generate buttons by using PEAR's `Javascript_Rollover` class.

The `Javascript_Rollover` class has two interfaces, the advanced interface shown earlier, which generates rollovers that preload your images (where your images are named prefix*imgNum*.**ending**), and rollovers that will generate an embedded rollover when given an array:

```php
<?php
$rollovers = new Javascript_Rollover;
print $rollovers->genRollover(array('link' => 'http://www.internet.com',
                'mouseOver' => 'image1_on.gif','mouseOut'  =>
                'image1_off.gif'));
?>
```

19.5 Creating HTML Templates

You want to have things such as header files and table of contents automatically included, depending on the page.

Technique

Send `filename` to the page that you are currently on and include the corresponding file:

```php
<?php /* $filename is passed to the webpage */ ?>
<html>
<head>
    <title> Somepage </title>
</head>
<body>
<?php include("$filename.header"); ?>
sometext
<?php include("$filename.footer"); ?>
</body>
</html>
```

Comments

Many people tend to forget that PHP is an embedded scripting language, meaning that you can embed PHP in HTML. Because of this, you can separate work that should be done by the designers (mainly the HTML) and work that should be done by the programmers.

The `include` statement enables you to include PHP files that will be parsed and their output placed in the same place as the statement itself. If you want to include files that are in different languages and you have Apache, use the `virtual()` function (which is equivalent to `<!--#include virtual...-->`). Consider the following example (using Perl as the other CGI language):

```
yahoo.cgi
#!/usr/bin/perl -w
use strict;
use LWP::Simple;
print get 'http://www.yahoo.com';

yahoo.php
<?php
virtual("yahoo.cgi");
?>
```

This would print out the contents of the Yahoo home page. Please note that when you use this function with CGI scripts, you lose the speed advantage that PHP has over CGI scripts.

Alternately you can use PEAR's Template class which allows you to create a template with special "template" variables and then you can assign those variables values using the assign method and parse the template:

```
SampleTemplate.htx
<html>
<head>
    <title>%%PAGE_TITLE%%</title>
</head>
<body>
  %%PAGE_BODY%%
</body>
</html>

SampleProgram.php
<?php
// Template.php along with the template
// class are from PEAR
require_once("Template.php");

$templ = new Template("SampleTemplate.htx");
$templ->assign("PAGE_TITLE", "Hello World");
$templ->assign("PAGE_BODY",  "This is page contents");

print $templ->output();
?>
```

CHAPTER 20

XML

20.0 Introduction

XML seems to be a buzzword in the Web industry these days. No matter what job you're working on, it seems to be a requirement that you know XML. Whether you are a network administrator or HTML coder, you should probably try to learn what XML is (even if it's to just put it on your resume). In this chapter, we discuss how PHP enables you to work with XML.

A Quick Overview of XML

Before I explain how PHP handles XML, perhaps we should talk a little about XML itself. XML, or Extensible Markup Language, enables us to create structured documents. For example

```
<recipe>
    <title>Mom's Meatloaf</title>
    <instructions>
        Pre-heat oven to 400 degrees. Saute chopped onions
till
        almost translucent. Chop celery, carrots and
parsley into
        little pieces. Stir sauted onions into celery,
carrot, parsley
```

```
        mixture. Add meat, tomato sauce, eggs and wine, and spices
        (salt, pepper, garlic, Italian spice). After thoroughly mixed
        add bread crumbs till firm. Cover bottom of baking pan with
        a little tomato sauce and virgin olive oil. Spread meatloaf
        mixture evenly. It cooks faster if in a shallow pan and only
        1-2 inches thick then if in a loaf pan. Cover entire top
        surface with tomato sauce. Lower oven temperature to 350
        degrees and cook until toothpick in center comes out clean
        (and no pink) about a hour to a hour and half.
    </instructions>
    <ingredients>
        <item>
            <name>Onions</name>
            <amount>1 large onion</amount>
        </item>
        <item>
            <name>Celery</name>
            <amount>3 stalks</amount>
        </item>
        <item>
            <name>Carrots</name>
            <amount>Two medium sized carrots</amount>
        </item>
        <item>
            <name>Chopped Sirloin</name>
            <amount>1.75 lbs.</amount>
        </item>
        <item>
            <name>Parsley</name>
            <amount>1/4 cup chopped</amount>
        </item>
        <item>
            <name>Eggs</name>
            <amount>4</name>
        </item>
        <item>
            <name>Tomato Sauce</name>
            <amount>1/2 cup</amount>
        </item>
        <item>
            <name>Salt, Pepper, Garlic, Italian spice</name>
            <amount>As much as necessary</amount>
```

```
        </item>
    </ingredients>
</recipe>
```

This is one way you might represent an entry into a cookbook (this is my mom's recipe). The tags in the document describe the content that is contained within them, rather than describing the way that the content is formatted (as HTML does). That is basically all there is to XML. The simplest description is to say that XML is HTML except that you can use any tags you want, and the tags describe the data rather than the way the data is displayed. There are some markup differences between XML and HTML (for example, empty tags such as <br> must contain a trailing slash: <br/>), but the fundamental conceptual difference is that one (HTML) represents the way to display content, the other (XML) is a way to structure the content.

This book can in no way be a full-fledged tutorial on XML. The subject is too broad for me to do it justice in just one chapter, so for more information on the XML standard, see *XML by Example*, published by Que Publishing.

20.1 Error Handling

When errors occur, you want to know what happens, but the errors given by XML are usually in the form of constants such as XML_ERROR_SYNTAX. You would rather have the messages in plain English.

Technique

Here is a method of converting the error numbers into their corresponding error messages:

```
<?php
print xml_error_string(XML_ERROR_SYNTAX);
?>
```

Comments

Given an error code, the xml_error_string() will return a text description. You can give the xml_error_string() function an error code by either passing it one of the predefined constants or, if you are parsing a document, by using the xml_get_error_code() function like so

```
<?php
print xml_error_string(xml_get_error_code($parser));
?>
```

Note

Throughout the rest of this chapter, I will use the following to catch errors when
`xml_parse()` fails:

```php
<?php
die (sprintf ("XML Error: %s at line %d.",
              xml_error_string (xml_get_error_code ($parser)),
              xml_get_current_line_number ($parser)));
?>
```

This will print out something like

```
XML Error: Malformed Syntax at line 5.
```

This error reporter is great for the small examples in this book, but if you are working on
bigger projects, you might want to make the error output a little nicer. Here is an example
of how you might do that:

```php
<?php
function output_error($parser)
{
    $error_string = xml_error_string (xml_get_error_code ($parser));
    $error_line = xml_get_current_line_number ($parser);
    $error = "An <b>XML Error</b> occurred on line $line: $errstr\n";
    error_log($error, 0);
    print $error;
    exit;
}
/* then call it */
output_error($parser);
?>
```

20.2 Parsing a Simple XML Document

You want to know the steps to parsing a simple XML document.

Technique

Here is an example of an XML document and the steps needed to parse that
document:

```
test.xml -- The XML file we parse.
<?xml version="1.0"?>
<book>
    <chapter id="1">
```

20.2 Parsing a Simple XML Document

```
        <title>Chapter 1</title>
        <contents>
            The Contents of chapter one go here.
        </contents>
    </chapter>
    <chapter id="2">
        <title>Chapter 2</title>
        <contents>
            The Contents of chapter two go here.
        </contents>
    </chapter>
</book>

xml-test.php -- The PHP program to parse the XML file.
<?php
function start_element($parser, $element_name, $element_attrs)
{
    switch ($element_name) {
        case "CHAPTER":
            print "<a name=\"#$element_name{$element_attrs['ID']}\"></a>";
            break;

        case "TITLE":
            print '<h2>';
            break;

        case "CONTENTS":
            print '<font face="arial" size="2">';
            break;
    }
}

function end_element($parser, $element_name) {
    switch ($element_name) {
        case "TITLE":
            echo "</h2>\n";
            break;

        case "CONTENTS":
            echo "</font>\n<br><br>";
            break;
    }
}
```

```
function character_data($parser, $data) {
    echo $data;
}

$parser = xml_parser_create();
xml_set_element_handler($parser, 'start_element', 'end_element');
xml_set_character_data_handler($parser, 'character_data');
$fp = fopen('test.xml', 'r') or die('Cannot open test.xml');

while ($data = fread($fp, 4096)) {
    xml_parse($parser, $data, feof($fp))
        or die(sprintf('XML Error: %s at line %d',
                       xml_error_string(xml_get_error_code($parser)),
                       xml_get_current_line_number($parser)));
}
xml_parser_free($parser);
?>
```

Comments

PHP connects to the Expat C API, so if you have used Expat before, the example in the synopsis should look somewhat familiar. If you haven't used Expat before, let me explain a little bit about the theory involved in parsing XML documents.

Expat uses a SAX-type XML parser, meaning that it uses handlers for the different types of events that may occur. When an event occurs, the data is passed to these different handlers, along with information related to the data. Let's consider the XML document in the preceding "Technique" section: On the start of an element (`<title>` would be an element), PHP sends the element name (that is, the title) and any attributes (in array form) related to the start tag to the `start_element()` function. The `start_element()` function is defined as the handler for start elements by the `xml_set_handler()` function.

After you have defined your handlers, you can use the `xml_parse()` function to parse the XML data either in separate chunks (as done here) or all at once. The `xml_parse()` function returns true on success and false on failure, so you can check whether any errors occurred. When you are done parsing the document, free the parser allocated by the `xml_parser_create()` function.

This is essentially what is done to parse XML documents in PHP with the Expat library. There are a few tricks and a couple more functions, but the idea is basically the same: create the parser, create the handlers, set the handlers, and then parse the document.

20.3 Parsing an XML Document into an Array

You want to load an XML document into an array and examine it that way.

Technique

Use the xml_parse_into_struct() function to place your data into an array:

faq-test.xml:

```
<faqs>
    <faq id="1">
        <title>FAQ 1</title>
        <code>
            zval_dtor(tmp);
        </code>
        <text>
            The above is a piece of code from rand.c in
            <important>ext/standard</important> in the PHP distribution.
        </text>
    </faq>
</faqs>
```

The PHP file:

```php
<?php
$parser = xml_parser_create ();
$data = implode ("", file("faq-test.xml"));
xml_parse_into_struct($parser, $data, $d_ar, $i_ar);

$i = 0;
foreach ($d_ar as $element) {
    if (!preg_match("/^\s+$/", $element[value])) {
        $tag = $element[tag];
        $faq[$i][strtolower($tag)] = $element[value];
    } elseif (isset($element[attributes])) {
        $faq[$i][id] = $element[attributes][ID];
        $i++;
    }
}

?>
```

Comments

In recipe 20.2, you learned how to parse a basic XML document. Now you are exploring how to load an XML document into an array via the `xml_parse_into_struct()` function and then extract the information from that array into a final and permanent array.

In the example, we are parsing an XML file, faq-test.xml. Now, let's go over the steps. First, we create a new parser and assign it to `$parser`. Then we load the file we want to parse, faq-test.xml, into the `$data` variable. After this is done, we call the `xml_parse_into_struct()` function, which loads the XML file into an array specified by the third argument with an index structure specified by the fourth argument (note that you must pass these by reference).

When we have the data loaded into the array, it is simply a matter of extracting the data from that array. The `$d_ar` array has the following format:

```
(
    Array (
        [tag] => "value for tag (ie ID)"
        [type] => (open|close|complete|)
        [value] => "what's inside the tags"
        [attributes] => Array (
                            [attrname] => "Name of the attribute"
                                ...
                        )
        [level] => depth of XML
    )
)
```

We immediately eliminate the outside array via a `foreach` loop, and we focus on the inside array. The first thing we test is whether the value of the element is completely whitespace. If so, we will have nothing to do with it unless it has attributes. If the value of the element contains information, we extract that information and assign it to the appropriate space in the `$faq` array.

The next test is whether current `$element` has an `attributes` parameter. If it does, it must be a `<faq>` tag and therefore contain the `"ID"` attribute (because our document has only one tag that contains attributes). Therefore, we assign the ID to the element in our associative array, and then move on to the next entry in our `$faq` array by incrementing `$i`.

As you can see, it is probably easier to use the `xml_parse()` function rather than the `xml_parse_into_struct()` function, simply because using `xml_parse()` is so much simpler. However, should you need to use the `xml_parse_into_struct()` function, I suggest that you take a quick look at the array of values returned by using the `print_r()` function.

20.4 Mapping XML Tags

You want to convert XML tags into either a singular HTML tag or a set of HTML tags.

Technique

Use an associative array to trigger start elements and end elements:

`html-test.xml`:

```
<faqs>
    <faq id="1">
        <title>FAQ 1</title>
        <code>
            idx = p - str;
        </code>
        <text>
            The above is a piece of code from rand.c in
            <important>ext/standard</important> in the PHP distribution.
        </text>
    </faq>
</faqs>
```

`html-test.php`:

```php
<?php
$start = array('title' => '<h2>',
               'text' => '<font face="arial, helvetica" size="2">',
               'code' => '<pre>',
               'important' => '<b>');

$end = array('title' => '</h2>',
             'text' => '</font>',
             'code' => '</pre>',
             'important' => '</b>');
```

```php
function start_html ($parser, $element_name, $element_attrs) {
    global $start;
    echo $start[strtolower($element_name)];
}

function end_html ($parser, $element_name) {
    global $end;
    echo $end[strtolower($element_name)];
}

function character_data ($parser, $data) {
    echo $data;
}

$parser = xml_parser_create();
xml_set_element_handler ($parser, "start_html", "end_html");
xml_set_character_data_handler ($parser, "character_data");
$fp = fopen ("html-test.xml", "r") or die("Cannot open file");

while ($data = fread($fp, 4096)) {
    xml_parse($parser, $data, feof($fp)) or
        die(sprintf('XML Error: %s at line %d',
                    xml_error_string(xml_get_error_code($parser)),
                    xml_get_current_line_number($parser)));
}

fclose($fp);
xml_parser_free($parser);
?>
```

Comments

In the example, we maintain a global associative array that maps XML elements to their HTML equivalents. Then we parse the XML elements, and replace each recognized tag with the appropriate formatting for that tag. We also maintain an array of end tags for each array because, start tags and end tags can differ by much more than simply a /.

PHP is good for parsing and displaying XML documents on-the-fly. But if you do not need to parse your documents on-the-fly, you are better off using something like XML and DSSSL and then parsing your documents with Jade—they allow for much more power than the techniques described here. By the way, PHP documentation is written using XML and DSSSL as the format (Jade is used to generate the different types of files, such as HTML or PDF).

20.5 Setting Up an External Reference Entity Handler

Many documents have external entities, and you want to have a program to parse those different entities.

Technique

Use the `xml_set_external_ref_handler()` function, and be prepared to parse the extra data.

The XML files:

`xmlref-test.xml`:

```
<!DOCTYPE tst [
<!ENTITY arms SYSTEM "xmlref-test2.xml">
]>
<body>
    <face>
        <nose>
            <size>
                big
            </size>
            <hairs>
                none
            </hairs>
        </nose>
        <mouth>
            <size>
                small
            </size>
            <lips>
                chapped
            </lips>
        </mouth>
        <eyes>
            <size>
                medium
            </size>
```

```
            <color>
                  green
            </color>
        </eyes>
    </face>
    &arms;
</body>
```

xmlref-test2.xml:

```
<arms>
    <biceps>
        <size>
            medium
        </size>
        <veins>
            not huge
        </veins>
    </biceps>
    <triceps>
        <size>
            small
        </size>
        <sore>
            yes
        </sore>
    </triceps>
</arms>
```

The PHP file:

```php
<?php
function start_element($parser, $element_name, $element_attr) {
    switch ($element_name) {
        case "ARMS":
        case "FACE":
            $data = ucfirst(strtolower($element_name));
            print "<h2>Descriptor for $data:</h2>\n<br>\n";
            break;

        case "BICEPS":
        case "SIZE":
        case "TRICEPS":
```

```
        case "EYES":
        case "MOUTH":
        case "LIPS":
        case "NOSE":
        case "HAIRS":
            $data = ucfirst(strtolower($element_name));
            print "\n<br>\n$data";
            break;

        case "VEINS":
            print "\n<br>\nAre they sore from a workout? ";
            break;

        case "COLOR":
     print _\n<br>\nThe color of my eyes is:_;
            break;
    }
}

function end_element($parser, $element_name, $element_attr) {
    // empty
}

function character_data($parser, $data) {
    echo $data;
}

function pi_handler($parser, $type, $data) {
    if ($type == "php") {
        eval($data);
    }
}

function lost_data($parser, $data) {
    echo "<!-- Not Dealt with data (per se): $data -->\n";
}

function xml_conn($file) {
    $parser = xml_parser_create();
    xml_parser_set_option($parser, XML_OPTION_CASE_FOLDING, 1);
    xml_set_element_handler($parser, "start_element", "end_element");
```

```php
        xml_set_character_data_handler($parser, "character_data");
        xml_set_processing_instruction_handler($parser, "pi_handler");
        xml_set_default_handler($parser, "lost_data");
        xml_set_external_entity_ref_handler ($parser, "external_ent_ref");
        if (!($fp = fopen($file, "r"))) {
            die("Cannot Open File, $file");
        }
        return array($fp, $parser);
    }


    function external_ent_ref($parser,
                              $open_ent_names,
                              $base,
                              $system_id,
                              $public_id) {
        if ($system_id != "") {
            list ($fp, $parser) = xml_conn ($system_id);
            while ($data = fread ($fp, 4096)) {
                print $data;
                xml_parse($parser, $data, feof($fp)) or
                    die(sprintf('XML Error: %s at line %d',
                              xml_error_string(xml_get_error_code($parser)),
                              xml_get_current_line_number($parser)));
            }
            xml_parser_free ($parser);
            return true;
        }
        return false;
    }

    list ($fp, $parser) = xml_conn('tst_xmlref.xml');
    while ($data = fread ($fp, 4096)) {
        xml_parse ($parser, $data, feof($fp))
            or die (sprintf('XML Error: %s at line %d',
                            xml_error_string(xml_get_error_code($parser)),
                            xml_get_current_line_number($parser)));
    }
    xml_parser_free ($parser);
    ?>
```

Comments

This code might look significantly more complicated than the rest of the code in this chapter, but I promise that it really isn't. The same theory of creating handlers and then opening and parsing the documents applies, except that there are a couple more levels.

An external entity reference is usually in the form of

```
<!ENTITY foobar SYSTEM "foobar.xml">
```

In plain English, that means, "There's more data to parse, but we put the data in foobar.xml, so I would appreciate it if you go there to find the rest of the data." It is similar to using `include()` or `require()` in PHP—using external entities enables you to break up big files into files of manageable size.

The elements of the solution code that deserve special attention are the `xml_conn()` function and the `external_ent_ref()` function—they are the crux of this recipe.

The `xml_conn()` function is used to create a new XML parser for a specified file. Specifically, it creates a parser (`$parser`), sets all the handlers, and opens a connection to the file specified by the first argument (`$file`). We wrap this in a function because it is used in many places—every time we reach an external entity reference, we have to parse the document pointed to by that external entity reference. It is similar to a Web crawler following links.

The `external_ent_ref()` function is the default handler for external entities, which is defined by the `xml_set_external_entity_ref_handler()` function. For every system entity, the `external_ent_ref()` function opens and parses the document with the same criteria with which we are parsing the main document (that is, using the `start_element` and `end_element` handlers).

Those are the two main functions involved in the code in the solution. All the rest of the code is the standard start element and end element handlers, as well as a few extra-fancy handlers, such as the XML default handler. The XML default handler is similar to the `AUTOLOAD` subroutine in Perl; it takes all the document elements that aren't recognized by the parser.

I neglected to discuss two functions in the explanation because they are really not important to the main idea of external entity references. Those functions are the `pi_handler()` function and the `lost_data()` function.

The `pi_handler()` function takes any processing instructions (in the format `<?target data?>`), and makes decisions about what to do with those processing instructions based on the target (`$type`). In the solution example, if we are given PHP processing instructions (`<?php ?>`), we evaluate the code and call it a night. Any other type of processing instructions go to the `lost_data()` function.

The `lost_data()` function is like a garbage truck—it takes all the data that the XML processor throws away. For example, things such as missing processing instructions or unparsed tags go straight to the `lost_data()` function. From there, we can manipulate the extra bits and pieces.

20.6 Searching XML

You want to query your XML files and return records.

Technique

Here is a case where `xml_parse_into_struct()` really does come in handy:

`sites.xml`:

```
<sites>
    <site>
        <title>PHP.net</title>
        <url>http://www.php.net/</url>
        <description>
            The homepage of PHP.
        </description>
        <keywords>
            MySQL, PHP, Documentation, downloads, articles, books
        </keywords>
    </site>
</sites>
```

`search.php`:

```php
<?php
$parser = xml_parser_create ();
$data = implode ("", file ("sites.xml"));
```

```
xml_parse_into_struct ($parser, $data, &$d_ar, &$i_ar);
xml_parser_free ($parser);

$y = 0;
foreach ($d_ar as $element) {
    $x = 0;
    switch (($tag = strtolower($element[tag]))) {
        case "title":
        case "description":
        case "url":
            $tmp[$x][$tag] = trim($element[value]);
            if (preg_match("/$query/i", trim($element[value])) ||
                isset($matches[$y])) {
                $matches[$y] = $tmp[$x];
            }
            break;

        case "keywords":
            if (preg_match("/$query/i", trim($element[value]))) {
                $matches[$y] = $tmp[$x];
                $y++;
            }
            $x++;
            break;
    }
}
?>
```

Comments

After we load the XML document into an array (as described in recipe 20.3) by using
the xml_parse_into_struct() function, the rest is extremely simple. Loop through the
document, loading each entry into a temporary array, $tmp. We then check whether
the document matches our search criteria. If so, we add the item into the $matches
array; otherwise, we move on to the next entry.

There are many ways to accomplish a goal, and the preceding approach is just one of
those ways. I find it easier to load everything into an array and then display that array,
but it is a little slower than the parsing the document in chunks. It is a matter of
preference.

20.7 Saving Memory

> You don't want to leave inactive parsers lying around. What does the XML API offer in terms of managing your parsers?

Technique

Use the `xml_parser_free()` function, which will free up a parser. This is not needed in PHP 4 because it has support for basic garbage collection, but you should use this with PHP 3:

```php
<?php
    $parser = xml_parser_create();
    // Do your thing
    xml_parser_free ($parser);
?>
```

Comments

The `xml_parser_free()` function will free an already allocated parser. Although this is done for you in PHP 4 because of reference counting, your scripts will leak in PHP 3 if you do not call this function.

20.8 Setting and Getting Options

> You want to control or view certain aspects of the way PHP handles XML processing.

Technique

Use the `xml_parser_set_option()` and the `xml_parser_get_option()` functions:

```php
<?php
$parser = xml_parser_create();

xml_parser_set_option($parser, XML_OPTION_CASE_FOLDING, 0);
// defaults to 1

xml_parser_set_option($parser, XML_OPTION_TARGET_ENCODING, "UTF-8");
// defaults to ISO-8859-1

$skip_white = xml_parser_get_option($parser, XML_OPTION_SKIP_WHITE);
?>
```

Comments

You can get and set four options by using the `xml_parser_get_option()` and
`xml_parser_set_option()` functions. Here is a list of the constants and their values:

`XML_OPTION_CASE_FOLDING`—Whether to change all the elements' cases to uppercase
while parsing. For example, `<title></title>` would become `<TITLE></TITLE>`.

`XML_OPTION_TARGET_ENCODING`—The type of target encoding. It defaults to ISO-
8859-1, but you can set it to either UTF-8 or US-ASCII.

`XML_OPTION_SKIP_WHITE`—None yet

`XML_OPTION_SKIP_TAGSTART`—None yet

These four constants are the only things that you can set, but the rest of the XML API
is pretty flexible, so you shouldn't have to worry about not having enough flexibility or
power.

20.9 Parsing Using the DOM-XML Functions

You want to use the DOM-XML functions to parse a document.

Technique

First, you have to make sure to install PHP using the `--with-dom` configure option.
Then you can parse an XML document like so:

```
XML File: tst.xml
<sites>
    <site>
        <title>PHP.net</title>
        <url>http://www.php.net/</url>
        <description>
            The homepage of PHP.
        </description>
        <keywords>
            MySQL, PHP, Documentation, downloads, articles, books
        </keywords>
    </site>
</sites>
```

PHP File: process.php

```php
<?php

$start = array(title => "<h2>");

$end   = array(title => "</h2><br>",
               keywords => "<br>",
               description => "<br>");

$que[last] = '';

$doc = xmldocfile('tst.xml');

// Root node
$root = $doc->root();

process_node($root);

function process_node($node) {
    global $que, $start, $end;
    switch ($node->type) {
        case XML_ELEMENT_NODE:
            switch (($name = strtolower(trim($node->name)))) {
                case 'site':
                    print '<br>';
                    $que[last] = "";
                    break;
                case 'title':
                    print $start[title];
                    $que[last] = $name;
                    break;
                case 'description':
                case 'keywords':
                    $que[last] = $name;
                    $name = ucfirst($name);
                    print "<b>${name}:</b>: ";
                    break;
                default:
                    $que[last] = "";
                    break;
            }
```

```
        case XML_TEXT_NODE:
            if (!empty($que[last])) {
                print $node->content . $end[$que[last]];
            }
            $que[last] = '';
            break;
    }

    $children = $node->children();
    if (is_array($children)) {
        foreach ($children as $child) {
            process_node($child);
        }
    }
}
?>
```

Description

The recipes before this one use Expat's SAX-based interface for processing XML documents. With SAX-based processors, you register handlers and then parse the XML document. When a particular tag or type of tag is reached, the handler is then called. Starting with PHP 4, PHP offers a Document Object Module (DOM)-based processor (by interfacing with libxml). DOM-based processors will parse an XML document into a tree that you can then access.

In the solution, we traverse a simple XML document, tst.xml, using the DOM-XML functions. The crux of this recipe lies in the xmldocfile() function, which loads an XML file into a tree structure. After we have the document in a tree structure, we loop through that tree, using the process_node() function to process the data.

On the most basic level, we pass the root node (top-level) to the process_node() function, and then we move through the XML document processing any children elements as we find them.

When processing an individual element, we first find out the node type by accessing the current node's type property. If it is XML_ELEMENT_NODE, meaning that it contains the element name (available via the name property) and the element's attributes, you can access the attributes through the attributes() method like so:

```php
<?php
$attr = $node->attributes();
foreach ($attr as $attr_name => $attr_val) {
    print "${attr_name}: ${attr_val}\n<br>\n";
}
?>
```

We check what type of element it is, and print the beginning data as appropriate. We also save the element's name in the $que[last] property if it is an element that will require further processing when we get to the XML_TEXT_NODE for that element. Otherwise, we empty the $que[last] property so that an element won't be processed twice when we handle XML_TEST_NODEs.

If the node's type is XML_TEXT_NODE—meaning it contains the data contained in the previously processed node—we are left to decide whether to output that node's data. If the $que[last] element is not empty, we print the text contained within the element and we add the ending HTML for the element stored in the $end array.

After we have processed the current element, we get a list of that element's children nodes (an array of children nodes to be exact) by calling the children() method. We loop through these nodes and process them with the process_node() function.

If you want to parse raw XML data, you can use the xmldoc() function, which behaves the same way as the xmldocfile() function except that it accepts XML data as the first argument instead of the name of a XML file:

```php
<?php

$doc = xmldoc('<sites>
    <site>
        <title>PHP.net</title>
        <url>http://www.php.net/</url>
        <description>
            The homepage of PHP.
        </description>
        <keywords>
            MySQL, PHP, Documentation, downloads, articles, books
        </keywords>
    </site>
</sites>');

$root = $doc->root();
```

```
// The same process_node() as in the solution
process_node($root);
?>
```

20.10 Building an XML Document

You want to build an XML document with PHP, but using multiple print statements just doesn't seem elegant or efficient.

Technique

Use the DOM-XML functions to help you build an XML document:

```php
<?php

$doc = new_xmldoc('1.0');
$root = $doc->add_root('sites');

$site = $root->new_child('site', '');
$site->new_child('title', 'PHP.net');
$site->new_child('url', 'http://www.php.net');
$site->new_child('description', 'The homepage of PHP');
$site->new_child('keywords',
                 'MySQL, PHP, Documentation, downloads, articles, books');

$fp = @fopen('tst.xml', 'w');
if (!$fp) {
    die('Error couldn't open XML file, tst.xml');
}

fwrite($fp, $doc->dumpmem());

fclose($fp);
?>
```

Description

Here we use a subset of the DOM-XML functions to create the document we parsed in the previous recipe. Using the DOM XML functions makes building XML documents much easier because the functions enable us to view the Web page as a tree structure. Therefore, instead of building the document with multiple, repetitive print statements, we can build the document as we would view it.

This can also be a powerful set of constructs when used in conjunction with text files. We can parse the plain text files into internal data structures, and then use the DOM-XML functions to output them in XML. Consider the following file:

```
Name | Address | Phone | Email
```

With the next script, we parse these entries into the following XML entries:

```
<addressbook>
    <person>
        <name>Name</name>
        <address>Address</address>
        <phone>Phone</phone>
        <email>Email</email>
    </person>
</addressbook>
```

Here is the script:

```php
<?php

$infile  = isset($argv[1]) ? $argv[1] : 'php://stdin';
$outfile = isset($argv[2]) ? $argv[2] : 'php://stdout';

$doc = new_xmldoc('1.0');
if (!$doc) {
    die("Couldn't create new XML document");
}

$root = $doc->add_root('addressbook');
if (!$root) {
    die("Couldn't add root");
}

$infp = @fopen($infile, 'r');
if (!$infp) {
    die("Couldn't open $infile\n");
}

    while ($line = @fgets($infp, 1024)) {
    $data = explode('|', $line);
    $person = $root->new_child('person', '');
    $person->new_child('name', $data[0]);
    $person->new_child('address', $data[1]);
```

```
    $person->new_child('phone', $data[2]);
    $person->new_child('email', $data[3]);
}

@fclose($infp);

$outfp = @fopen($outfile, 'w');
if (!$outfp) {
    die("Couldn't open $outfile\n");
}

@fwrite($outfp, $doc->dumpmem());

@fclose($fp);
?>
```

20.11 Transforming XML with an XSL Template

You want to transform an XML document through an XSL template using PHP.

Technique

Make sure that you have compiled PHP with Sablotron XSL support. Then you can use the xslt_transform() function:

```
<?php

if (!xslt_transform($stylesheet, $xmlfile, "arg:/result" 0, 0, $result)) {
    die(sprintf('Error [%d]: %s',
                xslt_errno(), xslt_error()));
}

print "The transformed document looks like:\n<br>\n";
print $result;
?>
```

Comments

XSL is a language that enables you to describe how structured XML will be displayed. In the synopsis, we take an XML document ($xmlfile) and we transform it through a XSL stylesheet ($stylesheet). The third and fourth arguments to xslt_transform()

are any optional parameters (third argument), and any arguments that you would have to the XSL processor (fourth argument).

The arguments, parameters, and function arguments should be associative arrays in the format `"argument_name" => "argument_value"`. Examine the following, which specifies the document's output to a file instead of a buffer:

```php
<?php

$args = array("/_outputfile" => "test.html");
if (!xslt_transform($stylesheet, $xslfile, "arg:/_outputfile", 0, $args)) {
    die(sprintf('Error [%d]: %s',
                xslt_error(), xslt_errno()));
}

print "Transformation saved in test.html";
?>
```

20.12 Filtering All Output Through an XSL File

You want to filter all XML output through an XSL file and display it to the user.

Technique

Use the Sablotron XSL's output buffering tie-ins to transform your output:

```php
<?php
xslt_output_begintransform('tst.xsl');

$doc = new_xmldoc('1.0');
$root = $doc->add_root('sites');

$site = $root->new_child('site', '');
$site->new_child('title', 'PHP.net');
$site->new_child('url', 'http://www.php.net');
$site->new_child('description', 'The homepage of PHP');
$site->new_child('keywords',
                 'MySQL, PHP, Documentation, downloads, articles, books');

// XML output will be transformed by
// tst.xsl
```

20.12 Filtering All Output Through an XSL File

```
print $doc->dumpmem();

xslt_output_endtransform();
?>
```

Comments

The Sablotron XSL module ties in to PHP's output buffering functions and enables you to transform all output sent to stdout through an XSL stylesheet given by the first argument to the xslt_output_begintransform() function. When you want to finish the output buffering, you can use the xslt_output_endtransform() function, which transforms all the data and outputs it to stdout.

Part V

The Zend API

CHAPTER

21 Zend API

APPENDIXES

A PHP Installation

B Troubleshooting with PHP

C PHP Online Resources

D Migrating to PHP 4

CHAPTER 21
Zend API

Thompson's rule for first-time telescope makers: "It is faster to make a four-inch mirror, then a six-inch mirror, than to make a six-inch mirror."

Programming Pearls Communications of the ACM, Sept. 1985

21.0 Introduction

When Rasmus Lerdorf created PHP, he intended it to be a macro language rather than as a full-fledged programming language. In its original inception, the functions and features were written in C and then simply called from PHP. By version 4, PHP has become a full-fledged programming language, and a good part of fully utilizing PHP is knowing how to work with the Zend API to create your own functions and extensions.

In this chapter, we discuss the Zend API, which is the API that enables you to add functions and extensions in PHP. If you don't know C, you really won't be able to understand this chapter. So, I suggest you learn C, and then reread this chapter. We first cover the basics—getting function arguments, modifying function arguments, adding your function to PHP— and then move into more advanced topics such as managing resources, fetching resource identifiers, creating a Zend module, and adding that module to the build system. The culmination of our work will be to discuss PHP's curl module.

21.1 Getting Arguments

You want to get arguments passed by the user to your custom function.

Technique

Declare zval variables that correspond to the passed arguments, and then put the value of the arguments into these variables by using the zend_get_parameters_ex() function. After this is done, you need only convert the variables to their various types and access the values:

```
PHP_FUNCTION(sample_function)
{
    char *ret = NULL,
         *fmtstr;
    zval **arg1, **arg2, **arg3;
    if (ZEND_NUM_ARGS() != 3 ||
        zend_get_parameters_ex (3, &arg1, &arg2, &arg3) == FAILURE) {
        WRONG_PARAM_COUNT;
    }

    /* arg1 is an int */
    convert_to_long_ex (arg1);
    /* arg2 is a double */
    convert_to_double_ex (arg2);
    /* arg3 is a string */
    convert_to_string_ex (arg3);

    fmtstr = "arg1 is %d, arg2 is %f and arg3 is %s, arg3 has a length of %d";
    /* Not the best allocation for the integer values
     * but sufficient for the needs of this simple program.
     */
    ret = emalloc(strlen(fmtstr) + 10 + 20 + Z_STRLEN_PP(arg3));
    sprintf(ret, fmtstr, Z_LVAL_PP(arg1), Z_DVAL_PP(arg2),
            Z_STRVAL_PP(arg3), Z_STRLEN_PP(arg3));
    RETURN_STRING(ret, 0);
}
```

Comments

The preceding is an example of a sample function that can be called from PHP with the following line. (There must first be a little more work done to register it as a function; see recipe 21.2 for more information on how to do that.)

```
echo sample_function(23, 23.34003, "Hello World");
```

This would return:

```
arg1 is 23, arg2 is 23.34003 and arg3 is Hello World, arg3 has a length of 11
```

Here is a line-by-line explanation:

Line 1—Declare this as a `PHP_FUNCTION()`.

Line 4—Declare arg1, arg2, and arg3 as zval variables. A zval looks like this:

```
typedef _zval_struct zval;

/* Notice that this is a union, meaning only
   one of the entries exists at a single time. */
typedef union _zvalue_value {
    long lval; /* the long value */
    double dval; /* The double value */
    struct {
        char *val; /* The value of the string */
        int len; /* The length of the string */
    } str;
    char chval;
    HashTable *ht; /* If it is an array */
    struct {
        zend_class_entry *ce;
        HashTable *properties;
    } obj; /* Object properties */
} zvalue_value;

/* The actual zval struct itself, aliased by the typedef above */

struct _zval_struct {
    zvalue_value value; /* Value of the argument */
    zend_uchar type; /* Type of the argument */
    zend_uchar is_ref; /* Whether or not the argument is a reference */
    zend_ushort refcount; /* The reference count on the argument */
};
```

Line 5—Make sure that exactly three arguments are passed to our function. `ZEND_NUM_ARGS()` returns the number of arguments passed to the function.

Line 6—Use the `zend_get_parameters_ex()` function to fetch the value of the arguments into the variables set declared as zvals.

Line 7—If this fails, report to the user that there is an incorrect parameter count.

Line 11—Convert `arg1` to a long.

Line 13—Convert `arg2` to a double.

Line 15—Convert `arg3` to a string.

Line 18—Build the format string.

Line 19—Allocate the return value.

Line 20—Build the return value

Line 21—Return the return value.

If you browse the source code of PHP, in many places you might see

```
pval **argument;
```

instead of

```
zval **argument;
```

This is because in PHP 3, all arguments were `pval`s instead of `zval`s. Therefore, to make it easier to port PHP 3 code (the C code, mind you) to PHP 4, `zval`s and `pval`s are made the same thing by a simple `typedef`.

On an unrelated note, if you want to fetch a variable number of arguments, you can do the following:

```
PHP_FUNCTION(somefunc)
{
    zval **arg1, **arg2;
    int argcount = ZEND_NUM_ARGS();

    if (argcount > 2 || argcount < 0 ||
        zend_get_parameters_ex(argcount, &arg1, &arg2) == FAILURE) {
```

```
        WRONG_PARAM_COUNT;
    }

    if (argcount > 0) {
        convert_to_long_ex(arg1);
        /* php_printf prints out to STDOUT */
        php_printf("%d\n", Z_LVAL_PP(arg1));
    }

    if (argcount > 1) {
        convert_to_string_ex(arg2);
        php_printf("%s\n", Z_STRVAL_PP(arg2));
    }

    php_printf("Above are %d printed out arguments", argcount);
}
```

Because zend_get_parameters_ex() fetches only the number of arguments specified by the first argument, it fetches only the variables you want. After you have fetched a variable, remember to check whether that variable as been passed to the function before performing operations on it (this was done by the if (argcount > x) code).

21.2 Modifying Function Arguments

You want to modify arguments that your user passes to you.

Technique

A function that does this is fsockopen(). Declare the function in the function entry table so as to force its arguments to be passed by reference.

The function table entry:

```
unsigned char first_arg_force_ref[] = {BYREF_FORCE, BYREF_NONE};
PHP_FE(ref_args, first_arg_force_ref)
```

The function itself:

```
PHP_FUNCTION(ref_args)
{
    /* arg1 is a number and arg2 is a string */
    zval **arg1, **arg2;
```

```
    if (ZEND_NUM_ARGS() != 2 ||
        zend_get_parameters_ex(2, &arg1, &arg2) == FAILURE) {
        WRONG_PARAM_COUNT;
    }


    zval_copy_ctor(*arg1); /* For strings only */
    ZVAL_STRING(*arg1, empty_string, 0);

    RETURN_TRUE;
}
```

Comments

In this code, we fetch the parameters as we would any normal set of parameters. The parameters will automatically be passed by reference because of the function table entry specifying that. If you refer back to recipe 21.1, you will see that the zval struct has an entry for is_ref, which is whether the argument is passed by reference. You can check whether a certain zval is a reference like this:

```
if (!(*arg1)->is_ref) {
    /* ... */
}
```

We then use the zval_copy_ctor() function, which creates a new variable with the same value of the old one. We then empty the value of arg2, and by doing so, affect the value passed to the function from the PHP script.

If you want to add values to an array passed to you, you should do something like the following (of course, the same concept applies in reference to the function table entry):

The function table entry:

```
PHP_FE(fill_array, first_arg_force_ref)
```

The function itself:

```
PHP_FUNCTION(fill_array)
{
    zval **ar, *tmp;
    int i;
    if (ZEND_NUM_ARGS() != 1 ||
        zend_get_parameters_ex(1, &ar) == FAILURE) {
        WRONG_PARAM_COUNT;
    }
```

Returning a long:

1. Use the `RETURN_LONG()` macro:

   ```
   RETURN_LONG(num);
   ```

2. Assign it directly:

   ```
   ZVAL_LONG(return_value, num);
   ```

Returning a double:

1. Use the `RETURN_DOUBLE()` macro:

   ```
   RETURN_DOUBLE(num);
   ```

2. Assign it directly:

   ```
   ZVAL_DOUBLE(return_value, num);
   ```

Comments

The preceding are the different ways to return a string, a long, and a double. Note that when returning strings, the syntax (not the definition) of the macro is as follows:

```
RETURN_STRING(char *str, int duplicate);
```

The parameter `duplicate` should always be set to 1, except in some extremely rare cases. The second approach to returning a string is the same as the macro way; in fact, the `RETURN_STRING()` macro is basically identical to the code given in the second approach.

The `RETURN_STRINGL()` macro should be used when you want to specify the string length to return. Its syntax (again, not its definition) is the following:

```
RETURN_STRINGL(char *str, int len, int duplicate);
```

If you want to return true or false, use the `RETURN_TRUE` and `RETURN_FALSE` definitions (self explanatory). If you want to return null, use either an empty `return` or the `RETURN_NULL()` macro.

21.4 Returning Arrays and Objects from Functions

You want to return an array or an object from a function.

Technique

To initialize the return value as an array, use the `array_init()` function and add different values to it through the different array-manipulation functions available in the Zend API.

Returning a numerically indexed array:

```
PHP_FUNCTION(somefunc)
{
    int i;

    if (array_init(return_value) == FAILURE) {
        php_error(E_WARNING, "cannot initialize return value");
        RETURN_FALSE;
    }

    for (i = 0; i < 10; i++) {
        add_next_index_long(return_value, i);
    }

    add_next_index_string(return_value, "Hello World", 1);
    add_next_index_string(return_value, "Goodbye World", 1);
}
```

Returning a string indexed (associative) array:

```
PHP_FUNCTION(somefunc)
{
    if (array_init(return_value) == FAILURE) {
        php_error(E_WARNING, "Cannot initialize return value");
        RETURN_FALSE;
    }

    add_assoc_string(return_value, "key1", "keyValue", 1);
    add_assoc_stringl(return_value, "key2", "keyValue", strlen("keyValue"), 1);
    add_assoc_long(return_value, "key3", 14);
    add_assoc_double(return_value, "key4" 3.23243);
}
```

Returning an object from a function:

```
PHP_FUNCTION(somefunc)
{
    if (object_init(return_value) == FAILURE) {
        php_error(E_WARNING, "Cannot initialize return value from somefunc");
        RETURN_FALSE;
    }

    add_property_string(return_value, "key1", "keyValue", 1);
    add_property_double(return_value, "key2", 4.5);
}
```

Comments

Arrays

Whether the array is an associative array or a numerically indexed array, the steps for returning the array are identical (in a theoretical sense). First, you initialize the array with the array_init() function and then you add values to the array. Adding values to the array is where the implementation differs.

When adding elements to the numerically indexed array, we use the add_next_index_* functions, which enable you to add new items to a numerically indexed array. If the element is a string, you can use the add_next_index_string() function or the add_next_index_stringl() function. If the element is a long, use the add_next_index_long() function; and if the element is a double, use the add_next_index_double() function.

To add elements with string keys, use the add_assoc_*() functions, which are similar to their numerical counterparts.

Objects

Returning objects is almost the same as returning arrays, except that you call object_init() on the zval and use add_property_*() functions instead of add_assoc_*() ones.

21.5 Adding a Function to PHP

You've written yourself a nifty little function and now you want to call it from PHP.

Technique

Let's take the function we wrote in recipe 21.1, and discuss the process of adding it.

1. Place the source of your function in the correct file; for `sample_function()`, we place it in basic_functions.c.

2. Find the place at the top of the file to which you added the function where it says something like the following. (Note that if you placed your function in ext/standard, look at the top of the file basic_functions.c.)

```
function_entry MODULENAME_functions[] = {
    PHP_FE(somefunction,        NULL)
    ...
}
```

Add a new line and place the following on that line:

```
PHP_FE(sample_function,        NULL)
```

Now it should look like this:

```
function_entry MODULENAME_functions[] = {
    PHP_FE(somefunction,        NULL)
    PHP_FE(sample_function,     NULL) /* You just added this */
    ...
}
```

3. Go to the header file for that file. The header file is usually named php_MODULENAME.h. You should see a bunch of declarations like this:

```
PHP_FUNCTION(somefunction);
```

Add the following declaration:

```
PHP_FUNCTION(sample_function);
```

4. Recompile and install PHP and voilà—your own PHP function.

Comments

The preceding steps are how to add a new function to PHP. The concepts behind adding a function will be discussed in recipe 21.9, when we discuss creating a new PHP module. Adding a function ties in closely with creating a module.

21.6 Creating Resource Identifiers

You want to create a resource identifier; that is, something such as a file pointer or a database handle.

Technique

There are a couple of steps and conventions, so let me walk you through the process.

1. First, create a variable in the global structure (of your module for thread safety) and name it le_YOURNAME (naming conventions are not required, but that's how everyone else does it):

```
typedef struct {
    int le_YOURNAME;
} php_YOURNAME_globals;
```

2. Create a function that you want to execute when the script finishes its execution:

```
/* Completely fictional function */
static void _php_MODULENAME_close(handle *ha) {
    close_handle(ha);
}
```

3. If you have something you want to do with that resource identifier on either startup or shutdown, place that information in PHP_MINIT_FUNCTION() (a function that is called on module startup):

```
PHP_MINIT_FUNCTION(modulename)
{
    YOURMODLS_FETCH();
  ③YOURMODG(le_YOURNAME) = register_list_destructors(php_MODULENAME_close,
                                                       NULL);

    return SUCCESS;
}
```

4. When the time comes, register that resource:

```
PHP_FUNCTION(open)
{
    zval **filename;
    YOURMODLS_FETCH():

    if (ZEND_NUM_ARGS() != 1 ||
        zend_get_parameters_ex(1, &filename) == FAILURE) {
```

```
convert_to_array_ex(ar);

for (i=0; i < 200; i++) {
    MAKE_STD_ZVAL(tmp);
    ZVAL_LONG(tmp, i);
    zend_hash_index_update(Z_ARRVAL_PP(ar), i, &tmp, sizeof(zval *), NULL);
}
}
```

`MAKE_STD_ZVAL()` allocates a new zval, initializes it to have a reference count of 1, and sets is_ref to 0.

21.3 Returning Strings or Numbers from a Function

You want to return a string or a number from a function.

Technique

Use one of the custom macros, or access the special `return_value` structure to add your value.

Returning a string:

1. Use either the `RETURN_STRING()` or `RETURN_STRINGL()` macro:

   ```
   RETURN_STRING(str, 1);
   ```

   or

   ```
   RETURN_STRINGL(str, len, 1);
   ```

2. Assign it directly to the return value itself:

   ```
   ZVAL_STRING(return_value, str, 1);
   ```

   or

   ```
   ZVAL_STRINGL(return_value, str, len, 1);
   ```

```
        WRONG_PARAM_COUNT;
    }

    convert_to_string_ex(filename);
    Handle *h = openhandle(Z_STRVAL_PP(filename));
    ZEND_REGISTER_RESOURCE(return_value, h, YOURMODG(le_YOURNAME));
}
```

5. You just created a resource.

Comments

A resource indicator is something like the file handle you pass to `fwrite()` or the connection handle that a database returns when you connect to it. In PHP, you can use the preceding steps to create a resource indicator. For information on how to manage this resource indicator, see recipe 21.5.

The `ZEND_REGISTER_RESOURCE` macro will insert your resource into the resource table and then place its corresponding resource identifier in the first argument (in this case, the function's return value).

The `register_list_destructors()` function registers a function (given by the first argument) to be executed when the script finishes execution. This ensures that you don't have resource identifiers lying around when your script closes if your user doesn't manually free the resources.

The `ZEND_REGISTER_RESOURCE()` macro is really a placeholder for the following code:

```
ZVAL_RESOURCE(return_value, zend_list_insert(h, YOURMODG(le_YOURNAME)));.
```

21.7 Fetching Resource Identifiers

You want to fetch a resource identifier and perform an action on it.

Technique

Use the `ZEND_FETCH_RESOURCE()` macro:

```
/* Completely useless function, example only */
PHP_FUNCTION(anyfetch)
{
    zval **listid;
```

```
type_of_resource *handle;
YOURMODLS_FETCH();

if (ZEND_NUM_ARGS() != 1 ||
    zend_get_parameters_ex(1, &listid) == FAILURE) {
    WRONG_PARAM_COUNT;
}
ZEND_FETCH_RESOURCE(handle, type_of_resource *, listid, -1,
                    "type_of_resource pointer", YOURMODG(le_YOURNAME));
RETURN_LONG(anyfetch(handle));
}
```

Comments

The `ZEND_FETCH_RESOURCE()` macro fetches the resource given by the third argument into the variable given by the first argument. It then typecasts that resource to the value given by the second argument with a resource identifier type of the sixth argument. The fourth and fifth arguments are for error-handling purposes. The fourth argument is what to return on error and the fifth argument is the name of the resource to be printed.

21.8 Looping Through Arrays

Your function loops through an array and you want to perform an action on, or do something with, every element in that array.

Technique

For numerically indexed arrays, use the `zend_hash_index_find()` function along with the `zend_hash_num_elements()` function:

```
PHP_FUNCTION(print_array)
{
    zval **ar, **var = NULL;
    HashTable *array;
    char *string_key = NULL;
    ulong num_key;

    if (ZEND_NUM_ARGS() != 1 ||
        zend_get_parameters_ex(1, &ar) == FAILURE) {
```

```
        WRONG_PARAM_COUNT;
    }

    array = HASH_OF(*ar);

    for (zend_hash_internal_pointer_reset(array);
         zend_hash_get_current_data(array, (void **)&var) == SUCCESS;
         zend_hash_move_forward(array)) {
        SEPARATE_ZVAL(var);
        convert_to_string_ex(var);

        switch (zend_hash_get_current_key(array, &string_key, &num_key)) {
            case HASH_KEY_IS_LONG:
                php_printf("Element %d: %s", num_key, Z_STRVAL_PP(var));
                break;
            case HASH_KEY_IS_STRING:
                php_printf("Element %s: %s", string_key, Z_STRVAL_PP(var));
                efree(string_key);
                break;
        }
    }
}
```

Comments

Here we use a combination of the zend_hash_internal_pointer_reset(),
zend_hash_get_current_data(), and zend_hash_move_forward() functions to loop
through the array. We then use the zend_hash_get_current_key() function to fetch
the key relating to the current value being manipulated. If the key is a string, the value
of the key is placed in the string_key variable; otherwise, the contents are placed in
the num_key variable.

The preceding method, although simple, affects the current position of the array
pointer, meaning that after we've looped through the array once, the
zend_hash_internal_pointer_reset() function needs to be called on it for the array
to be processed again. If you do not want to affect the internal array pointer, use the
*_ex() counterparts to these functions:

```
PHP_FUNCTION(print_array)
{
    zval **ar, **var = NULL;
    HashTable *array;
    HashPosition pos;
```

```c
char *string_key = NULL;
ulong num_key;

if (ZEND_NUM_ARGS() != 1 ||
    zend_get_parameters_ex(1, &ar) == FAILURE) {
    WRONG_PARAM_COUNT;
}

array = HASH_OF(*ar);

for (zend_hash_internal_pointer_reset_ex(array, &pos);
     zend_hash_get_current_data_ex(array, (void **)&var, &pos) == SUCCESS;
     zend_hash_move_forward_ex(array, &pos)) {
    SEPARATE_ZVAL(var);
    convert_to_string_ex(var);

    switch (zend_hash_get_current_key(array, &string_key, &num_key, &pos)) {
        case HASH_KEY_IS_LONG:
            php_printf("Element %d: %s", num_key, Z_STRVAL_PP(var));
            break;
        case HASH_KEY_IS_STRING:
            php_printf("Element %s: %s", string_key, Z_STRVAL_PP(var));
            efree(string_key);
            break;
    }
}
}
```

21.9 Creating a PHP Module

We've discussed some different features of PHP modules—now it's time to cover the creation of a custom PHP module.

Technique

In this recipe, we discuss the curl module. For more information about curl, visit `http://curl.haxx.se/`.

The format of my explanation is different than that of the other recipes. Here, I will embed my explanations (in italic text) at critical points, rather than explaining it all in the end.

```
/*
   +----------------------------------------------------------------------+
   | PHP version 4.0                                                      |
   +----------------------------------------------------------------------+
   | Copyright (c) 1997, 1998, 1999, 2000 The PHP Group                   |
   +----------------------------------------------------------------------+
   | This source file is subject to version 2.02 of the PHP license,     |
   | that is bundled with this package in the file LICENSE, and is        |
   | available at through the world-wide-web at                           |
   | http://www.php.net/license/2_02.txt.                                 |
   | If you did not receive a copy of the PHP license and are unable to   |
   | obtain it through the world-wide-web, please send a note to          |
   | license@php.net so we can mail you a copy immediately.               |
   +----------------------------------------------------------------------+
   | Author: Sterling Hughes <sterling@php.net>                           |
   +----------------------------------------------------------------------+
*/
```

I wrote this for PHP, therefore the preceding is the standard copyright. This is not required unless you are contributing your extension back to PHP.

```
#include "php.h"
#include "php_curl.h"
```

Include all the necessary headers and API definitions.

```
#if HAVE_CURL
```

*Test whether curl support has been enabled. This is defined by curl's **config.m4**, which is discussed later.*

```
/* Standard Includes */
#include <stdio.h>
#include <string.h>
#include <sys/stat.h>

#if HAVE_UNISTD_H
#include <unistd.h>
#endif

#ifdef PHP_WIN32
#include <winsock.h>
#include <sys/types.h>
```

```
#define fstat(handle, buff) _fstat(handle, buff)
#define stat _stat
#endif
```

Allow our module to compile on more than just one system, adding support for both UNIX and Windows NT.

```
/* CURL Includes */
#include <curl/curl.h>
#include <curl/easy.h>

/* PHP Includes */
#include "ext/standard/info.h"

ZEND_DECLARE_MODULE_GLOBALS(extname)

static void _php_curl_close(php_curl *);
#define SAVE_CURL_ERROR(__handle, __err) \
    __handle->cerrno = (int)__err;
```

*_php_curl_close() is the list destructor for the curl handle (of type php_curl *). The SAVE_CURL_ERROR() macro saves an error for later retrieval by the curl_errno() function.*

```
#ifdef PHP_WIN32
/* {{{ win32_cleanup()
   Clean-up allocated socket data on win32 systems */
static void win32_cleanup()
{
    WSACleanup();
}
/* }}} */

/* {{{ win32_init()
   Initialize WSA stuff on Win32 systems */
static CURLcode win32_init()
{
    WORD wVersionRequested;
    WSADATA wsaData;
    int err;
    wVersionRequested = MAKEWORD(1, 1);
```

```
        err = WSAStartup(wVersionRequested, &wsaData);

    if (err != 0) return CURLE_FAILED_INIT;

    if (LOBYTE(wsaData.wVersion) != 1 ||
        HIBYTE(wsaData.wVersion) != 1) {
        WSACleanup();
        return CURLE_FAILED_INIT;
    }
    return CURLE_OK;
}
/* }}} */
#else
static CURLcode win32_init(void) { return CURLE_OK; }
#define win32_cleanup()
#endif
```

This is more "Win32-izing." The preceding code is cut and pasted from the source code of curl itself.

```
function_entry curl_functions[] = {
    PHP_FE(curl_init,     NULL)
    PHP_FE(curl_version,  NULL)
    PHP_FE(curl_setopt,   NULL)
    PHP_FE(curl_exec,     NULL)
    PHP_FE(curl_error,    NULL)
    PHP_FE(curl_errno,    NULL)
    PHP_FE(curl_close,    NULL)
    {NULL, NULL, NULL}
};
```

The preceding snippet of code declares all the functions that will be in the bzip2 module. The PHP_FE *macro has the following syntax:*

```
    PHP_FE(functionName,    argument_types)
```

In general, the argument_types *parameter should be* NULL *unless you want to accept references to variables. In that case*

```
    unsigned char first_arg_force_ref[] = {BYREF_FORCE, BYREF_NONE, ..};
    PHP_FE(functionName,    first_arg_force_ref)
```

forces the first argument to be passed by reference, and

```
unsigned char second_arg_force_ref[] = {BYREF_NONE, BYREF_FORCE, ..};
PHP_FE(functionName,    second_arg_force_ref)
```

causes the second argument to be a reference, and so on.

```
zend_module_entry curl_module_entry = {
    "curl",
    curl_functions,
    PHP_MINIT(curl),
    PHP_MSHUTDOWN(curl),
    NULL,
    NULL,
    PHP_MINFO(curl),
    STANDARD_MODULE_PROPERTIES
};
```

The preceding code creates an entry for the module and registers it with zend. The type
zend_module_entry is defined like so:

```
typedef struct _zend_module_entry zend_module_entry

struct _zend_module_entry {
    char *name;
    zend_function_entry *functions;
    int (*module_startup_func)(INIT_FUNC_ARGS);
    int (*module_shutdown_func)(SHUTDOWN_FUNC_ARGS);
    int (*request_startup_func)(INIT_FUNC_ARGS);
    void (*request_shutdown_func)(SHUTDOWN_FUNC_ARGS);
    void (*info_func)(ZEND_MODULE_INFO_FUNC_ARGS);
    int (*global_startup_func)(void);
    int (*global_shutdown_func)(void);
    int globals_id;
    int module_started;
    unsigned char type;
    void *handle;
    unsigned char zend_debug;
    unsigned char zts;
    unsigned int zend_api;
}
```

However, the only entries we need to be concerned about are the entries from char *name to
(void *info_func). The rest of the entries are taken care of by

STANDARD_MODULE_PROPERTIES. For more information about the definition of STANDARD_MODULE_PROPERTIES, see modules.h in the Zend directory.

The first entry in the structure is name, *which is a character string with the name of the module (in this case,* bzip*). The second entry in the structure is the name of the function entry. This is what we defined as a* function_entry *earlier, and it contains all the functions to be exported to PHP.*

The third entry in the zend_module_entry *structure is the module startup function argument, which defines the function that is to be called when this module is first loaded. The fourth entry is the module shutdown function, which is called when the module is unloaded or execution is about to stop.*

The fifth entry in the zend_module_entry *structure is the request startup function, which is called when PHP starts processing a request. The sixth entry is the request shutdown function, which is called at the end of request processing. The final entry is the more information function. This is the name of the* PHP_MINFO() *function that is called by* phpinfo()*, and prints information about the module to the user.*

```
#ifdef COMPILE_DL_CURL
ZEND_GET_MODULE (curl)
#endif
```

Return the special dynamic loading–specific code, if the user has chosen to compile this extension as a dynamic loading extension.

```
PHP_MINFO_FUNCTION(curl)
{
    php_info_print_table_start();
    php_info_print_table_row(2, "CURL support", "enabled");
    php_info_print_table_row(2, "CURL Information", curl_version());
    php_info_print_table_end();
}


PHP_MINIT_FUNCTION(curl)
{
    CURLLS_FETCH();
    CURLG(le_curl) = register_list_destructors(_php_curl_close, NULL);

    /* Constants for curl_setopt() */
    REGISTER_LONG_CONSTANT("CURLOPT_PORT", CURLOPT_PORT, CONST_CS |
                           CONST_PERSISTENT);
    REGISTER_LONG_CONSTANT("CURLOPT_FILE", CURLOPT_FILE, CONST_CS |
                           CONST_PERSISTENT);
```

```
    REGISTER_LONG_CONSTANT("CURLOPT_INFILE", CURLOPT_INFILE, CONST_CS |
                          CONST_PERSISTENT);

    /*
 *  The other 60-70 or so constants have been ommited for
 *  brevity.  If you want to see them you can always check out
 *  the source of curl in php4/ext/curl/curl.c
     */
    if (win32_init() != CURLE_OK) {
        return FAILURE;
    }

    return SUCCESS;
}

PHP_MSHUTDOWN_FUNCTION(curl)
{
    win32_cleanup();
}

/* {{{ proto string curl_version(void)
   Return the CURL version string. */
PHP_FUNCTION (curl_version)
{
    RETURN_STRING(curl_version(), 1);
}
/* }}} */

/* {{{ proto int curl_init([string url])
   Initialize a CURL session */
PHP_FUNCTION(curl_init)
{
    zval **url;
    php_curl *curl_handle = NULL;
    int argc = ZEND_NUM_ARGS();
    CURLLS_FETCH();
```

CURLLS_FETCH() fetches the module globals stored in our global structure. This allows our module to be threadsafe.

```
    if (argc < 0 || argc > 1 ||
        zend_get_parameters_ex(argc, &url) == FAILURE) {
```

```
        WRONG_PARAM_COUNT;
    }

    curl_handle = (php_curl *)emalloc(sizeof(php_curl));
    if (!curl_handle) {
        php_error(E_WARNING, "Couldn't allocate    a CURL Handle");
        RETURN_FALSE;
    }
    memset(curl_handle, 0, sizeof(php_curl));

    curl_handle->cp = curl_easy_init();
    if (!curl_handle->cp) {
        php_error(E_ERROR, "Cannot initialize CURL Handle");
        RETURN_FALSE;
    }

    if (argc > 0) {
        char *urlstr;
        convert_to_string_ex(url);

        urlstr = estrndup(Z_STRVAL_PP(url), Z_STRLEN_PP(url));
        curl_easy_setopt(curl_handle->cp, CURLOPT_URL, urlstr);
```

You should always duplicate strings unless the prototype for the function you are calling is a `const char *`.

```
    }

    curl_easy_setopt(curl_handle->cp, CURLOPT_NOPROGRESS, 1);
    curl_easy_setopt(curl_handle->cp, CURLOPT_VERBOSE,    0);
    curl_easy_setopt(curl_handle->cp, CURLOPT_ERRORBUFFER, curl_handle->error);

    curl_handle->output_file = 0;
    curl_handle->php_stdout  = 1;

    ZEND_REGISTER_RESOURCE(return_value, curl_handle, CURLG(le_curl));
```

Register the resource and return the identifier. The `CURLG()` *macro is for accessing members of our global structure.*

```
}
/* }}} */
```

```
/* {{{ proto bool curl_setopt(int ch, string option, mixed value)
   Set an option for a CURL transfer */
PHP_FUNCTION(curl_setopt)
{
    zval **curl_id,
         **curl_option,
         **curl_value;
    php_curl *curl_handle;
    CURLcode ret;
    int option;
    CURLLS_FETCH();

    if (ZEND_NUM_ARGS() != 3 ||
        zend_get_parameters_ex(3, &curl_id, &curl_option, &curl_value)
        == FAILURE) {
        WRONG_PARAM_COUNT;
    }

    ZEND_FETCH_RESOURCE(curl_handle, php_curl *, curl_id, -1, "CURL    Handle",
                        CURLG(le_curl));
```

Fetch the resource of type `php_curl *` into `curl_handle` with a resource identifier of `curl_id` and a list destructor having the identifier of `CURLG(le_curl)`.

```
    convert_to_long_ex(curl_option);
    option = Z_LVAL_PP(curl_option);

    switch (option) {
        case CURLOPT_INFILESIZE:
        case CURLOPT_VERBOSE:
        case CURLOPT_HEADER:
        case CURLOPT_NOPROGRESS:
        case CURLOPT_NOBODY:
        case CURLOPT_FAILONERROR:
        case CURLOPT_UPLOAD:
        case CURLOPT_POST:
        case CURLOPT_FTPLISTONLY:
        case CURLOPT_FTPAPPEND:
        case CURLOPT_NETRC:
        case CURLOPT_FOLLOWLOCATION:
        case CURLOPT_PUT:
        case CURLOPT_MUTE:
```

```
case CURLOPT_TIMEOUT:
case CURLOPT_LOW_SPEED_LIMIT:
case CURLOPT_SSLVERSION:
case CURLOPT_LOW_SPEED_TIME:
case CURLOPT_RESUME_FROM:
case CURLOPT_TIMEVALUE:
case CURLOPT_TIMECONDITION:
case CURLOPT_TRANSFERTEXT:

    convert_to_long_ex(curl_value);
    ret = curl_easy_setopt(curl_handle->cp, option,
            Z_LVAL_PP(curl_value));
    break;

case CURLOPT_URL:
case CURLOPT_PROXY:
case CURLOPT_USERPWD:
case CURLOPT_PROXYUSERPWD:
case CURLOPT_RANGE:
case CURLOPT_CUSTOMREQUEST:
case CURLOPT_USERAGENT:
case CURLOPT_FTPPORT:
case CURLOPT_COOKIE:
case CURLOPT_SSLCERT:
case CURLOPT_SSLCERTPASSWD:
case CURLOPT_COOKIEFILE:

    {
        char *copystr = NULL;

        convert_to_string_ex(curl_value);
        copystr = estrndup(Z_STRVAL_PP(curl_value),
                        Z_STRLEN_PP(curl_value));

        ret = curl_easy_setopt(curl_handle->cp, option, copystr);
    }
    break;

case CURLOPT_FILE:
case CURLOPT_INFILE:
case CURLOPT_WRITEHEADER:
case CURLOPT_STDERR:
```

```
{
    FILE *fp;

    ZEND_FETCH_RESOURCE(fp, FILE *, curl_value, -1, "File-Handle",
                        php_file_le_fopen());
    ret = curl_easy_setopt(curl_handle->cp, option, fp);
```

In the preceding, we fetch a file pointer resource into fp. The `php_file_le_fopen()` function is an API function that allows PHP extensions to access file pointer (`FILE *`) resources.

```
    if (option & CURLOPT_FILE) {
        curl_handle->output_file = Z_LVAL_PP(curl_value);
        curl_handle->php_stdout  = 0;
    }
}
break;

case CURLOPT_RETURNTRANSFER:

    convert_to_long_ex(curl_value);

    curl_handle->return_transfer = Z_LVAL_PP(curl_value);
    curl_handle->php_stdout       = !Z_LVAL_PP(curl_value);
break;

case CURLOPT_POSTFIELDS:

    if (Z_TYPE_PP(curl_value) == IS_ARRAY ||
        Z_TYPE_PP(curl_value) == IS_OBJECT) {

        zval **current;
        HashTable *u_post = HASH_OF(*curl_value);
        struct HttpPost *first = NULL,
                        *last  = NULL;

        for (zend_hash_internal_pointer_reset(u_post);
            zend_hash_get_current_data(u_post, (void **)&current)
                                    == SUCCESS;
            zend_hash_move_forward(u_post)) {
```

```
        char *string_key = NULL,
             *str      = NULL,
             *val_str    = NULL;
        ulong num_key;

        SEPARATE_ZVAL(current);
        convert_to_string_ex(current);

        if (zend_hash_get_current_key(u_post, &string_key, &num_key)
            == HASH_KEY_IS_LONG) {
            php_error(E_WARNING, "Array passed to %s() must be an
            associative array", get_active_function_name());
            RETURN_FALSE;
        }

        val_str = estrndup(Z_STRVAL_PP(current),
                           Z_STRLEN_PP(current));

       str = emalloc(strlen(string_key) + strlen(val_str) + 1 + 2);
        if (!str) {
            php_error(E_WARNING, "Couldn't allocate a post field
            from %s()", get_active_function_name());
            RETURN_FALSE;
        }
        sprintf(str, "%s=%s", string_key, val_str);

        ret = curl_formparse(str, &first, &last);

        efree(string_key);
        efree(val_str);
    }

    if (ret != CURLE_OK) {
        SAVE_CURL_ERROR(curl_handle, ret);
        RETURN_FALSE;
    }

  ret = curl_easy_setopt(curl_handle->cp, CURLOPT_HTTPPOST, first);
} else {
```

```c
            char *post_str = NULL;

            convert_to_string_ex(curl_value);
            post_str = estrndup(Z_STRVAL_PP(curl_value),
                                Z_STRLEN_PP(curl_value));

            ret = curl_easy_setopt(curl_handle->cp, CURLOPT_POSTFIELDS,
                                   post_str);
            if (ret != CURLE_OK) {
                SAVE_CURL_ERROR(curl_handle, ret);
                RETURN_FALSE;
            }

            ret = curl_easy_setopt(curl_handle->cp, CURLOPT_POSTFIELDSIZE,
                                   Z_STRLEN_PP(curl_value));
            break;

        }
        break;

    case CURLOPT_HTTPHEADER:

        {
            zval **current;
            HashTable *headers = HASH_OF(*curl_value);
            struct curl_slist *header = NULL;

            header = (struct curl_slist *)
            emalloc(sizeof(struct curl_slist));
            if (!header) {
                php_error(E_WARNING,
                "Couldn't allocate    header list from %s()",
                get_active_function_name());
                RETURN_FALSE;
            }
            memset(header, 0, sizeof(struct curl_slist));

            for (zend_hash_internal_pointer_reset(headers);
                 zend_hash_get_current_data(headers, (void **)&current)
                                            == SUCCESS;
                 zend_hash_move_forward(headers)) {
```

```c
                        char *indiv_header = NULL;

                        SEPARATE_ZVAL(current);
                        convert_to_string_ex(current);

                        indiv_header = estrndup(Z_STRVAL_PP(current),
                                                Z_STRLEN_PP(current));
                        header = curl_slist_append(header, indiv_header);
                        if (!header) {
                            php_error(E_WARNING, "Couldn't build header from
                                      %s()", get_active_function_name());
                            RETURN_FALSE;
                        }

                    }

                    ret = curl_easy_setopt(curl_handle->cp, CURLOPT_HTTPHEADER,
                                           header);
                }
                break;
        }

        if (ret != CURLE_OK) {
            SAVE_CURL_ERROR(curl_handle, ret);
            RETURN_FALSE;
        } else {
            RETURN_TRUE;
        }
    }
    /* }}} */

    /* {{{ proto bool curl_exec(int ch)
       Perform a CURL session */
    PHP_FUNCTION(curl_exec)
    {
        zval **curl_id;
        php_curl *curl_handle;
        CURLcode ret;
        FILE *fp;
        char buf[4096];
        int b;
        unsigned long pos = 0;
```

```
CURLLS_FETCH();

if (ZEND_NUM_ARGS() != 1 ||
    zend_get_parameters_ex(1, &curl_id) == FAILURE) {
    WRONG_PARAM_COUNT;
}

ZEND_FETCH_RESOURCE(curl_handle, php_curl *, curl_id, -1, "CURL Handle",
                    CURLG(le_curl));

if ((curl_handle->return_transfer &&
    !curl_handle->output_file) || curl_handle->php_stdout) {

    if ((fp = tmpfile()) == NULL) {
        php_error(E_WARNING, "Cannot initialize temporary file to save
                    output from %s()",
        get_active_function_name());
        RETURN_FALSE;
    }

    curl_easy_setopt(curl_handle->cp, CURLOPT_FILE, fp);

} else if (curl_handle->return_transfer &&
        curl_handle->output_file) {

  ZEND_FETCH_RESOURCE(fp, FILE *, (zval **)NULL, curl_handle->output_file,
                        "File-Handle", php_file_le_fopen());

}

ret = curl_easy_perform(curl_handle->cp);

if ((!curl_handle->return_transfer && !curl_handle->php_stdout) ||
    (ret != CURLE_OK)) {

    if (ret != CURLE_OK) {
        SAVE_CURL_ERROR(curl_handle, ret);
        RETURN_FALSE;
    } else {
        RETURN_TRUE;
    }
```

```
    }

    fseek(fp, 0, SEEK_SET);

    if (curl_handle->php_stdout) {

        while ((b = fread(buf, 1, sizeof(buf), fp)) > 0) {
            php_write(buf, b);
        }

    } else {

        char *ret_data;
        struct stat stat_sb;

        if (fstat(fileno(fp), &stat_sb)) {
            RETURN_FALSE;
        }

        ret_data = emalloc(stat_sb.st_size+1);

        while ((b = fread(buf, 1, sizeof(buf), fp)) > 0) {
            memcpy(ret_data + pos, buf, b);
            pos += b;
        }
        ret_data[stat_sb.st_size - 1] = '\0';

        RETURN_STRINGL(ret_data, stat_sb.st_size, 0);

    }

}
/* }}} */

/* {{{ proto string curl_error(int ch)
   Return a string contain the last error for the current session */
PHP_FUNCTION(curl_error)
{
    zval **curl_id;
    php_curl *curl_handle;
    CURLLS_FETCH();
```

```
    if (ZEND_NUM_ARGS() != 1 ||
        zend_get_parameters_ex(1, &curl_id) == FAILURE) {
        WRONG_PARAM_COUNT;
    }

    ZEND_FETCH_RESOURCE(curl_handle, php_curl *, curl_id, -1, "CURL Handle",
                        CURLG(le_curl));
    RETURN_STRING(curl_handle->error, 1);
}
/* }}} */

/* {{{ proto int curl_errno(int ch)
   Return an integer containing the last error number */
PHP_FUNCTION(curl_errno)
{
    zval **curl_id;
    php_curl *curl_handle;
    CURLLS_FETCH();

    if (ZEND_NUM_ARGS() != 1 ||
        zend_get_parameters_ex(1, &curl_id) == FAILURE) {
        WRONG_PARAM_COUNT;
    }

    ZEND_FETCH_RESOURCE(curl_handle, php_curl *, curl_id, -1, "CURL Handle",
                        CURLG(le_curl));
    RETURN_LONG(curl_handle->cerrno);
}
/* }}} */

/* {{{ proto void curl_close(int ch)
   Close a CURL session */
PHP_FUNCTION (curl_close)
{
    zval **curl_id;
    php_curl *curl_handle;
    CURLLS_FETCH();

    if (ZEND_NUM_ARGS() != 1 ||
        zend_get_parameters_ex(1, &curl_id) == FAILURE) {
        WRONG_PARAM_COUNT;
    }
```

```
        ZEND_FETCH_RESOURCE(curl_handle, php_curl *, curl_id, -1, "CURL Handle",
                            CURLG(le_curl));

        zend_list_delete(Z_LVAL_PP(curl_id));
}
/* }}} */

/* {{{ _php_curl_close()
   List destructor for curl handles */
static void _php_curl_close(php_curl *curl_handle)
{
    curl_easy_cleanup(curl_handle->cp);
    efree(curl_handle);
}
/* }}} */

#endif


FILE:   php_bzip.h
/*
   +----------------------------------------------------------------------+
   | PHP version 4.0                                                       |
   +----------------------------------------------------------------------+
   | Copyright (c) 1997, 1998, 1999, 2000 The PHP Group                    |
   +----------------------------------------------------------------------+
   | This source file is subject to version 2.02 of the PHP license,      |
   | that is bundled with this package in the file LICENSE, and is         |
   | available at through the world-wide-web at                           |
   | http://www.php.net/license/2_02.txt.                                 |
   | If you did not receive a copy of the PHP license and are unable to    |
   | obtain it through the world-wide-web, please send a note to           |
   | license@php.net so we can mail you a copy immediately.                |
   +----------------------------------------------------------------------+
   | Author: Sterling Hughes <sterling@php.net>                           |
   +----------------------------------------------------------------------+
*/

#ifndef _PHP_CURL_H
#define _PHP_CURL_H
```

Make sure that this file is not included twice.

```
#ifdef COMPILE_DL_CURL
#undef HAVE_CURL
#define HAVE_CURL 1
#endif

#if HAVE_CURL

#include <curl/curl.h>

extern zend_module_entry curl_module_entry;
#define curl_module_ptr &curl_module_entry

#define CURLOPT_RETURNTRANSFER 19913

PHP_MINIT_FUNCTION(curl);
PHP_MSHUTDOWN_FUNCTION(curl);
PHP_MINFO_FUNCTION(curl);
PHP_FUNCTION(curl_version);
PHP_FUNCTION(curl_init);
PHP_FUNCTION(curl_setopt);
PHP_FUNCTION(curl_exec);
PHP_FUNCTION(curl_error);
PHP_FUNCTION(curl_errno);
PHP_FUNCTION(curl_close);

typedef struct {
    int return_transfer;
    int output_file;
    int php_stdout;
    int cerrno;
    char error[CURL_ERROR_SIZE+1];
    CURL *cp;
} php_curl;
```

A php_curl structure (a php_curl type, to be exact) is the structure we store in Zend's resource list (actually, it's a pointer to a php_curl structure).

```
typedef struct {
    int le_curl;
} php_curl_globals;

#ifdef ZTS
#define CURLG(v) (curl_globals->v)
```

```
#define CURLLS_FETCH() php_curl_globals *curl_globals =
ts_resource(curl_globals_id)
#else
#define CURLG(v) (curl_globals.v)
#define CURLLS_FETCH()
#endif
```

The preceding is the thread safety code; it defines the access of this module's global variables (this is used to access le_curl).

```
#else
#define curl_module_ptr NULL
#endif /* HAVE_CURL */
#define phpext_curl_ptr curl_module_ptr
#endif  /* _PHP_CURL_H */
```

Comments

The preceding is the full source of the curl module, minus the configuration file (config.m4) and the makefile (Makefile.in), which are discussed in full during the next recipe.

Although the source is quite massive, try to break it into smaller pieces and you'll see that the essential elements are quite simple. You have a function entry, a module entry, and then all the surrounding functions and code for your module. If you know the Zend API, you can simply create your basic module.

In PHP 4, you can use the ext_skel tool to generate an extension skeleton, meaning that it has all the essentials: macros and definitions for thread safety, a function entry, a fully filled-out module entry, and other important definitions.

To use ext_skel (only on *nix-based systems), go to the ext directory of your PHP distribution and run ext_skel:

```
% ./ext_skel --extname=yourmod
```

ext_skel will create the necessary directories and files, with the necessary elements.

When you run the ext_skel script, it will generate extra "help" comments, explaining the different parts of the module. If you want to have ext_skel omit this extra stuff, add the --no-help option.

```
% ./ext_skel –extname=yourmod --no-help
```

21.10 Adding Your File to the PHP Installation

You want to add your module to the PHP build system so that you can compile _PHP, `--with-yourmodulename`.

Technique

Add your file to its own folder in php4/ext/ and create files config.m4 and Makefile.in that look something like this (these are for the curl module earlier):

```
FILE:   config.m4
dnl config.m4 for extension CURL

PHP_ARG_WITH(curl, for CURL support,
[  --with-curl[=DIR]        Include CURL support])

if test "$PHP_CURL" != "no"; then
  if test -r $PHP_CURL/include/curl/easy.h; then
    CURL_DIR=$PHP_CURL
  else
    AC_MSG_CHECKING(for CURL in default path)
    for i in /usr/local /usr; do
      if test -r $i/include/curl/easy.h; then
        CURL_DIR=$i
        AC_MSG_RESULT(found in $i)
      fi
    done
  fi

  if test -z "$CURL_DIR"; then
    AC_MSG_RESULT(not found)
    AC_MSG_ERROR(Please reinstall the libcurl distribution -
    easy.h should be in <curl-dir>/include/curl/)
  fi

  AC_ADD_INCLUDE($CURL_DIR/include)

  PHP_SUBST(CURL_SHARED_LIBADD)
  AC_ADD_LIBRARY_WITH_PATH(curl, $CURL_DIR/lib, CURL_SHARED_LIBADD)

  AC_DEFINE(HAVE_CURL,1,[ ])

  PHP_EXTENSION(curl, $ext_shared)
```

```
fi

FILE:  Makefile.in

LTLIBRARY_NAME      = libcurl.la
LTLIBRARY_SOURCES = curl.c
LTLIBRARY_SHARED_NAME    = curl.la
LTLIBRARY_SHARED_LIBADD = $(CURL_SHARED_LIBADD)

include $(top_srcdir)/build/dynlib.mk
```

Comments

I can't really cover the syntax of shell-scripting languages and makefiles in this small recipe, but I can explain the basic idea of the preceding code.

The basic idea of the config.m4 file is to verify that the necessary files are installed and add the directories for these files to the $PATH. So, when you enter

```
#include <curl/curl.h>
#include <curl/easy.h>
```

the compiler will look in the nonstandard directory for curl/curl.h and curl/easy.h as well as the standard directories.

Makefile.in is a basic makefile. It tells PHP what the final result will be and where the sources of the module will be located (in this case, curl.c).

APPENDIX A

PHP Installation

PHP installation is really an easier process than many people make it out to be. The key to a proper PHP installation is simply to follow the instructions, step-by-step. However, sometimes there are problems that are not covered in the bundled documentation or the online documentation, and that is what this appendix is for. This appendix is not a substitute for the online documentation, but rather a supplement to it.

This appendix addresses some common problems and questions that I've noticed users of PHP from the `php-install@lists.php.net` mailing list are having.

PHP always displays header information saying that my Web site uses PHP. How do I change that?

You can stop that header information from being displayed by setting the `expose_php` php.ini entry to `"Off"`.

I run PHP for my shell scripts. How do I get PHP to stop printing the content-type header every time my script executes?

Comment out the `default_mimetype` and `default_charset` php.ini entries, and you shouldn't see any unnecessary headers being printed. Alternatively, run PHP with `--q` (quiet) option.

Where can I get the latest PHP distribution?

You can get the latest PHP distribution from `http://www.php.net/`; look under the Downloads section.

Appendixes

How do I install PHP with Zeus Web server?

You have two options: You can install PHP in CGI mode and then use it with Zeus as you would do with Perl or any other language, or you can install PHP as an ISAPI module. You should read the README.Zeus file in the top-level directory of the PHP 4 distribution.

Why can't I work with BCMath as I can with PHP 3?

PHP can no longer be bundled with the BCMath library because of licensing issues. Therefore, you must download the BCMath package separately and then configure PHP with `--enable-bcmath`. An example of this is given in the next section.

How do I install PHP 4 with Apache/MySQL/GD/BCMath and SSL support?

Although configure processes might vary, here is a sample configure I use and that should work pretty well for you:

```
#Grab the sources from the following URLs
OpenSSL: ftp://ftp.openssl.org/source/openssl-0.9.5.tar.gz
ModSSL: ftp://ftp.modssl.org/source/mod_ssl-2.6.4-1.3.12.tar.gz
Apache: http://www.apache.org/dist/apache_1.3.12.tar.gz
MySQL: http://www.mysql.org/Downloads/MySQL-3.22/mysql-3.22.32.tar.gz
PHP4:  http://www.php.net/do_download.php?download_file=
php-4.0.0.tar.gz&source_site=www.php.net
GD 1.8.2: ftp://ftp.boutell.com/pub/boutell/gd/gd-1.8.2.tar.gz
BCMath: http://www.php.net/extra/number4.tar.gz

# Decompress the sources:
% tar xvzf openssl-0.9.5.tar.gz
% tar xvzf mod_ssl-2.6.2-1.3.12.tar.gz
% tar xvzf apache_1.3.12.tar.gz
% tar xvzf php-4.0.0
% tar xvzf mysql-3.22.32.tar.gz
% tar xvzf gd1.8.2.tar.gz

# Compile the sources:
# GD support
% cd gd1.8.2
% make

#MySQL Support
% cd ../mysql-3.22.32
% ./configure
% make
```

```
% make install
% scripts/mysql_install_db
% safe_mysqld &
% mysqladmin -u root password 'yourpasswordhere'

#OpenSSL Support
% cd ../openssl-0.9.5
% sh config \
>     -fPIC
% make

#ModSSL Support
% cd ../mod_ssl-2.6.2-1.3.12
% ./configure \
>       --with-apache=../apache_1.3.12

#Initial Apache Build
% cd ../apache_1.3.12
% SSL_BASE=../openssl-0.9.5 \
% ./configure \
>         --prefix=/usr/local/apache \
>         --enable-module=most \
>         --enable-shared=max \
>         --enable-module=ssl \
>         --enable-shared=ssl

% make
% make certificate
```

At this point, if you don't already have a file called /usr/local/apache/conf/httpd.conf, you should do the following:

```
% mv conf/httpd.conf /usr/local/apache/conf/httpd.conf
```

That way you'll have a fresh httpd.conf file with all the Apache modules listed and loadable. Otherwise, you will need to merge your existing custom httpd.conf information into the new one.

```
% make install

# Ahhh, at last the PHP4 installation
% cd ../php-4.0.0
% mv /usr/local/number4.tar.gz .
```

Appendixes

```
% tar xvzf number4.tar.gz
% ./configure \
>       --with-apxs=/usr/local/apache/bin/apxs \
>       --with-config-file-path=/usr/local/apache/conf \
>       --enable-versioning \
>       --with-mysql \
>       --with-ftp \
>       --with-gd=/usr/local/gd1.3 \
>       --enable-bcmath=yes \
>       --disable-debug \
>       --enable-memory-limit=yes \
>       --enable-track-vars
% make
% make install
```

How do I send the PHP build script to different nonstandard directories to look for specific libraries and header files?

Just specify the path after the `--with-` argument. So if you wanted the configure script to look in `/root/dist/` for the header files to the swf module, you could do the following:

```
./configure --with-swf=/root/dist/
```

How do I build shared PHP extensions?

Almost every PHP extension can be built as a shared library. To do so, specify `shared` after the `--with-` or `--enable-` argument and before any optional library paths. Some examples are

```
./configure --with-mysql=shared --with-swf=shared,/root/dist
```

How do I make PHP look in a nonstandard directory for header files and libraries?

You can achieve this by setting the `CFLAGS` and `LDFLAGS` environment variables before installing PHP:

```
CFLAGS=-I/path/to/include
LDFLAGS=-L/path/to/library
```

Then all you have to do is configure!

Where can I find the libraries I need for building different PHP options?

Here's a list of links to the Web sites with the different options:

LDAP (UNIX): `ftp://ftp.openldap.org/pub/openldap/openldap-stable.tgz`

LDAP (UNIX/Windows): Netscape Directory (LDAP) SDK 1.1--there is also a free LDAP server at `ftp://ftp.critical-angle.com/pub/cai/slapd/`

Berkeley DB2 (UNIX/Windows): `http://www.sleepycat.com/`

SNMP (UNIX): `http://www.ece.ucdavis.edu/ucd-snmp/` (Note: PHP uses the native SNMP interface in Windows)

GD (UNIX/Windows): `http://www.boutell.com/gd/#buildgd`

mSQL (UNIX): `http://www.hughes.com.au/`

MySQL (UNIX): `http://www.mysql.com/`

InterBase: `http://www.interbase.com/`

Hyperwave: `http://www.hyperwave.com/`

filePro: `http://www.fileproplus.com/`

FTP: Nothing required

EXIF: Nothing required

WDDX: Nothing required

IMAP (Windows/UNIX): `ftp://ftp.cac.washington.edu/imap/old/imap-4.5.tar.Z`

FreeType (libttf): `http://www.freetype.org/`

ZLib (UNIX/Win32): `http://www.cdrom.com/pub/infozip/zlib/`

expat XML parser (UNIX/Win32): `http://www.jclark.com/xml/expat.html`

PDFlib: `http://www.pdflib.com`

ClibPDF: `http://www.fastio.com`

DOM XML: `ftp://ftp.gnome.org/pub/GNOME/stable/sources/libxml/`

mcrypt: `ftp://argeas.cs-net.gr/pub/unix/mcrypt/`

mhash: `http://sasweb.de/mhash/`

t1lib: `http://www.neuroinformatik.ruhr-uni-bochum.de/ini/PEOPLE/rmz/t1lib/t1lib.html`

dmalloc: `http://www.dmalloc.com/`

Appendixes

aspell: `http://download.sourceforge.net/aspell/aspell-.29.1.tar.gz`

Readline: `ftp://prep.ai.mit.edu/pub/gnu/readline/`

SWF (*nix systems only): `http://reality.sgi.com/graphica/flash`

GNU gettext: `ftp://ftp.gnu.org/gnu/gettext/`

Recode: `ftp://ftp.gnu.org/gnu/recode/`

MCAL: `http://mcal.chek.com/`

FDF: `http://partners.adobe.com/asn/developer/acrosdk/forms.html`

Informix: `http://www.informix.com/`

Oracle: `http://www.oracle.com/`

CyberCash: `http://www.cybercash.com/`

I compiled PHP and MySQL with `mod_perl` and now I'm getting an error. What happened?

Most likely, you compiled PHP with the bundled MySQL sources. If you do that, everything will blow up in your face. Instead, install PHP with your own MySQL libraries, so the following configure line:

```
./configure --with-mysql --with-apxs
```

becomes

```
./configure --with-mysql=/usr/local/mysql --with-apxs
```

when `mod_perl` is installed.

Why aren't my old DLLs and DSOs working with PHP 4?

When you use PHP 4, you have to use PHP 4 DLLs, not PHP 3 DLLs. The same thing applies for the DSOs. If you're on a Windows system and you need the functionality from one of PHP's DLLs, check out `http://download.swwwing.com/`.

It's not my fault, it's PHP's fault. Where do I report this?

Make sure that it's really PHP's fault. Bogus bug reports waste the time of the people who develop PHP. First, report your problem to `php-install@lists.php.net` and if no one helps you and it seems like a bug, go to the Bugs database at

```
http://bugs.php.net/
```

How do I install PHP on a Windows system?

php.net does have some nice installation links, such as one to a PHP Installer, which is a friendly interface to install PHP on Windows systems. Should you need more resources than php.net provides, try php4win.de which offers a comprehensive set of information for installing PHP on Windows systems.

This appendix hasn't answered my question. I'll never get PHP installed, right?

Wrong. If you need more help installing PHP on your system, you can post your question to the PHP mailing list and usually get a response back within an hour or two. For help with PHP installation, send your questions to php-install@lists.php.net.

APPENDIX B
Troubleshooting with PHP

Errors are inevitable in any large program. However, the trick is to understand the messages that you are given so that you can locate the bug and fix it. That is what this appendix is all about. First, I discuss the common errors given by either the Zend engine or by the different PHP modules, and then I discuss some of the classic ways to cut down on errors in your code. Please keep in mind that although the information in this appendix will help you gain valuable time when debugging your program, there is no substitute for proper planning.

Common Errors and What They Mean

PHP has many, many different error messages, ranging from a general error such as `"Call to undefined function"` to a specific error such as `"MySQL Connection Failed."` Although no one can cover all the possible error messages, I can cover the most commonly seen error messages.

`0 is not a * Result index`

This means that your query to an * (* represents the database type) database failed and the result resource returned by the query function is not valid. To eliminate this error, do some error checking in your script:

Appendixes

```php
<?php
$sth = @mysql_query($stmt, $dbh)
  or die("Cannot execute Query");
?>
```

By prepending the @ sign to the function call, we suppress PHP's error messages for that function call. The next interesting section of this code snippet is the "or die..." part. Here we check whether the function returns 0; if so, we stop the script execution and print out our own error message.

`Call to undefined function: *`

This means that you have requested a function that is neither a built-in function nor a user-defined function. This is commonly done when you prepend a $ to the function like so:

```php
<?php
$echo("hello");
?>
```

This would fail because you accidentally put the $ sign before the function, so it looks for the $echo variable which is not in the script. Because it doesn't find the $echo variable, $echo("hello") ends up being equivalent to ("Hello").

Another common error in PHP 3 was to call a function before it was declared. But now that Zend has support for run-time binding of function names, allowing you to declare a function after it is called in the script, this problem is nonexistent.

Finally, you'll get this message if you try to call a function from an extension that has not been compiled into your version of PHP.

`PHP Timed out!`

Large, memory-intensive scripts tend to take a while to run. Therefore, after a certain amount of time, PHP will stop executing and return this error message. There are two ways to solve this: One way is to make your script more efficient, or perhaps break your script up into smaller scripts that achieve the same purpose. The second way is to increase the maximum execution time either in your php.ini file or by using the set_time_limit() function:

```php
<?php
set_time_limit(70);
?>
```

This example would make the script time out after 70 seconds.

You can also turn off the time limit by passing `0` as the argument to `set_time_limit()`.

Premature End of script headers

This error can be a major pain. The most that I can tell you about this error is that one of two things occurred: The first and most likely occurrence is that you didn't correctly install PHP. For more information on how to install PHP, refer to Appendix A, "PHP Installation." The second occurrence is if PHP is installed as a CGI rather than a module, the path at the top of your script is probably not correct. Remember that you need the `-q` after the PHP script location and the `#!` declaration must be the first line of the script.

Headers already sent

This error occurs when you have already sent the body of your Web page and then you send additional headers via `setcookie` or the `header` function. In general, you must send your headers and set cookies before any other output is sent. If, for some reason, you need to send output before you enable certain headers, set the output buffering option in your PHP script to `true`. However, please note that after you enable output buffering, you will notice a slight performance lag.

Techniques to Cut Down on Errors and Bugs

When you are programming, there are a few techniques that will help you to cut down on errors in general.

- Plan

  Before you start any large project, you should always plan the different steps of that project. Going into the project, you should at least know what technology is needed and have a rough sketch of the events that are going to happen. It also helps to diagram the different uses of your program and the errors that could occur in order so that your program has fewer bugs in the long run.

- Reverse testing

  Reverse testing is the idea of putting the value first—rather than the variable—when testing for equality. Consider the following:

```php
<?php
if ($some_variable = 5) {
```

Appendixes

```
    print "5 matches \$some_variable";
} else {
    print "5 no match, me cry!";
}
?>
```

As you can see, there is a bug in the `if` conditional. Instead of testing for equality, we assign the value of 5 to some variable. However, if you run this script, PHP will not report that anything has gone awry. Therefore, to generate error messages, you must reverse the sequence of the test:

```
<?
if ( 5 = $some_variable) {
    print "5 matches \$some_variable";
} else {
    print "5 no match, me cry!";
}
?>
```

This snippet would generate a warning. You would then correct the error that caused the warning and the final, correct version of the snippet would look like this:

```
<?
if ( 5 == $some_variable ) {
    print "5 matches \$some_variable";
} else {
    print "5 no match, me cry!";
}
?>
```

- `error_reporting`

  When testing your script, set `error_reporting` to `E_ALL` so that all errors are reported to you, and you know everything that is going on with your script. You can set `error_reporting` to `E_ALL` either by the `error_reporting()` function

  ```
  error_reporting(E_ALL);
  ```

  or by setting it your php.ini file.

Techniques to Cut Down on Errors and Bugs

- Breakpoints

  When you are debugging your scripts, it is often useful to set breakpoints at which you dump all relevant information going into and coming out of the different parts of your script. Examine the following:

  ```php
  <?php
  $var1 = 10;

  print "the value of var1 is $var1 before somefunc()"; // Breakpoint
  somefunc($var1);
  print "now the value of var1 is $var1"; // Breakpoint

  function somefunc (&$var) {
      $var = 20;
  }
  ?>
  ```

  Notice how we print out the value of 5 before somefunc() and then after somefunc(). This lets us know whether somefunc() is doing its job. Setting breakpoints like this one can often help you narrow down where a problem is located.

Appendix C
PHP Online Resources

Books are great, but no book can cover it all. New PHP functions are constantly being created. The following online resources are the ones that I find to be the most informative and well developed in covering everything about PHP. However, there are more—many more—online resources, and I cannot cover them all in this appendix. So, with that said, happy surfing!

The Official PHP Web Site

http://www.php.net/

This is perhaps the most useful of the sites listed in this appendix, simply because this is the site that contains up-to-date versions of not only the official documentation, but also the latest releases of PHP, including the PHP source and PHP binaries. If that is not enough, this site also contains an up-to-date listing of the major sites that use PHP, and a listing of all the books written on PHP. Not only does this site contain a plethora of resources, it also contains links to the other PHP sites, the latest news about all things PHP, and links to projects using PHP (such as Phorum and PHPLIB).

Appendixes

The Zend Web Site

http://www.zend.com

The Zend engine is the engine that powers PHP. The Zend Web site is the site of the company that puts out the Zend engine, as well as many other tools. For example, at this site you can also download the Zend Optimizer, which gives your PHP scripts a 40-100% increase in speed on average.

In addition to great software (even if it isn't all freeware), this site also contains an active online message board (powered by Phorum), and many articles and tutorials about everything involving PHP (I write for them). One sample article by Andi Gutmans (co-creator of the Zend engine), which takes you under the hood of the Zend engine and describes all the exciting new features. Another sample article is an article by Till Gerken on how to create and manipulate images with PHP.

PHPBuilder

http://www.phpbuilder.com

The documentation on PHP is an awesome reference, but some of the more abstract concepts of PHP can't be covered by a simple function reference; they need to be explained by experts who have been there and done that. PHPBuilder offers an impressive set of tutorials ranging in level from beginner to advanced. I find gems there all the time, such as "Building your website with cached dynamic modules" (JP) and "HTML_Graphs" by Tim Purdue. This site also includes links to a code repository and an active message board system.

PHPWizard.net

http://www.phpwizard.net

This site contains an excellent repository of daily tips and tricks. In addition to the daily tips, this Web site contains high-quality programs such as an online quiz system and an online chat program. PHPWizard.net also contains a set of highly useful functions and classes (such as a sendmail class and others).

APPENDIX **D**

Migrating to PHP 4

PHP 4 is nearly 100% compatible with PHP 3, but there are a few, minimal incompatibilities.

Static Variable and Default Argument Initializers Accept Only Scalar Values

That means the values of these initializers must be known at compilation time; that is, they cannot be an expression.

Valid in PHP 3

```php
<?php
$variable = "GLOBALS";
function print_array ($varname = $variable)
{
    global $$varname;

    reset ($$varname);
    while (list ($na, $val) = each ($$varname))
        print "$na: $val";
}
?>
```

Valid in PHP 4

```php
<?php
function print_array ($varname = "GLOBALS")
{
    global $$varname;

    reset ($$varname);
    while (list ($na, $val) = each ($$varname))
        print "$na, $val\n<br>\n";
}
?>
```

The Scopes of break and continue Are Local to That of an Included File, or an eval'd String

Included files and eval'd strings now have a different scope than the main code. Therefore, the break and continue statements will not affect the main code.

Valid in PHP 3

```php
<?php
$names = array ("Jackie", "Greg", "Grant", "Julie", "Peter");

while (list (, $name) = each ($names))
{
    eval('if (!strcmp ($name, "Grant")) break;');
    print "$name\n";
}
?>
```

Valid in PHP 4

```php
<?php
$names = array("Jackie", "Greg", "Grant", "Julie", "Peter");

while (list (, $name) = each ($names))
{
    $should_break =
        eval ('if (!strcmp ($name, "Grant")) return 0;
               else return 1;');
```

```
    if ($should_break) break;

    print "$name\n";
}
?>
```

A `return` **Statement from a** `required` **File Does Not Work**

When you required a file in PHP 3, you could have require return a value by placing a return statement in the global scope of the required file. If you want to have this functionality with PHP 4, you should use the include statement.

Valid in PHP 3
```
<?php
$ret = require 'somefile.php';
?>
```

Valid in PHP 4
```
<?php
$ret = include 'somefile.php';
?>
```

Unset Is Now a Statement, Not a Function

That means unset() is declared in the parser itself, rather than as an entry in PHP's function tables.

Valid in PHP 3
```
<?php
$var = "Hello";
$ret = unset($var);
?>
```

Appendixes

Valid in PHP 4

```php
<?php
$var = "Hello";
unset($var);
?>
```

"{$" Is Not Supported in Strings

The "{$" combination is not allowed in strings. To place the "{$" combination in strings, you must escape it like this: "\{$".

Valid in PHP 3

```php
<?php
$foo = "Windows";
print str_replace ("{$foo}", "Linux", "This {Windows} rules.");
?>
```

Valid in PHP 4

```php
<?php
$foo = "Windows";
print str_replace ("\{$foo}", "Linux", "This {Windows} rules.");
?>
```

The PHP Class Repository

http://phpclasses.upperdesign.com

Before I start implementing a new program, I often visit this Web site in search of classes that will make my life easier. I am rarely, if ever, disappointed. In fact, rather than rewrite the classes myself, I rely on classes from the PHP Class Repository for a few recipes in this book.

Weberdev

http://www.weberdev.com

Weberdev, founded by Boaz Yahav, was started as a repository for code snippets that illustrate certain points. For example, if you are wondering how to connect to an Informix database, this site has an example for that. However, Weberdev has since evolved into a site that offers many different features, such as a program that will hook up employers with developers. Weberdev also has all related techie news on the front page. I suggest that you visit this site and search the archives if you ever wonder how some task could be achieved.

DevShed

http://www.devshed.com/

DevShed is an excellent resource for all things open source including Perl, Python, Jserv, Zope, and, of course, PHP. It contains a nice repository of introductory PHP tutorials and an active message board. It also has the latest PHP news posted on its site. Although DevShed's PHP section is not as comprehensive as Zend's or PHPBuilder's, beginning and intermediate PHP programmers are sure to find something they like.

Index

Symbols

^ character, 103-104
{} characters, 105
?: conditional, 15-16
$ (dollar) sign, 102
$GLOBAL array, 96-98
$HTTP GET VARS array, 98-99
$HTTP POST VARS array, 98-99
 :: notation, 199
[] operator, 18-19
| (pipe delimiter) character, 107
? (question mark) character, 106-107
$this object, 191-193
$this variable, 196-197
0 is not a * Result index, 445-446

A

abbreviations, matching, 125-126
accept connect() function, 298
accessing
    custom Java methods and classes, 290-294
    data using built-in arrays, 98-99
    files, 127
    frames, 243
    predefined Java methods and classes, 290
    variables from within classes, 191-193
    variables outside functions, 180
adding entries to LDAP servers, 329-331
adding values to arrays, 404
addslashes() function, 23
anonymous functions, dynamically
  creating, 185-186
applets, 127
arbitrary precision numbers
    rounding, 38-40
    working with, 36-38
arcs, drawing, 354
arguments
    functions and, 179
    getting, 400-403
    modifying, 403-405
    passing by reference, 182-183
array diff() function, 83-84
array init() function, 407-408

array intersect() function, 85-86
array merge recursive() function, 75
array merge() function, 75
array pad() function, 75
array push() function, 76
array rand() function, 152
array reverse() function, 20-21, 89
array slice() function, 80-81
array splice() function, 73-74
array unique() function, 72-73
array values() function, 20
array walk() function, 76-77
array() construct, 16-17, 70, 184
arrays
    adding values to, 404
    appending one to another, 75-76
    changing size of, 73-75
    computing union, intersection, or
        difference of, 85-86
    executing queries and getting results in,
        332-333
    extracting unique elements from lists,
        72-73
    fetching SNMP type into, 327
    finding elements in, 83-84
    finding elements that match criteria,
        82-83
    finding elements that pass test, 82
    generating <select> lists from, 363-365
    iterating over by reference, 78
    loading all files in directory into, 164-165
    loading dates into, 53-54
    looping through, 412-414
    overview of, 69-70
    parsing XML documents into, 375-377
    performing action on elements of, 76-77
    Perl-based features for, 90
    printing lists with commas, 71-72
    processing multiple elements of, 80-81
    randomizing, 84
    returning current element from, 79
    returning from functions, 407-408
    reversing, 89
    sorting, 88
    sorting by user-defined comparison, 87
    specifying, 70
arrays, 91. See also built-in arrays
ASCII, converting to HTML, 362

ASCII characters and values, working
    with, 17-19
ASP, 287-289
associative array mapping, 125-126
associative arrays, recognizing two names
    for same file, 162-163
atan2() function, 47
attachments to e-mail, sending, 315-316

B

backticks, 284
base convert() function, 40-42
basename() function, 164
BCMath, 438-439
bcmath functions, 36-38
bcround() function, 38-40
Benchmark_Iterate class, 67
Benchmark_Timer class, 66-67
benchmarks, performing, 63-67
biased random numbers, generating,
    52-53
binary attachments to e-mail, sending,
    316-320
binary data, 135
bind() function, 306
bindec() function, 41
blocking, sockets and, 307
Boolean value, 118-119
boundary, using, 315-316
break statement, 82
breakpoints, setting, 94-95, 449
buffering issues, 299
bugs, decreasing. See errors, decreasing
build script, sending to directories, 440
building
    DOM-XML functions and, 391-393
    shared extensions, 440
built-in arrays
    $GLOBAL, 96-98
    $HTTP GET VARS, 98-99
    $HTTP POST VARS, 98-99
    overview of, 91
built-in "track" variables, 99
button.php code, 358-359

C

C
  directories and, 159
  pointers in, 182
  Zend API and, 399
cache, flushing, 136-137
Call to undefined function: *, 446
calling functions
  from PHP, 408-409
  indirectly, 186
CGI scripts, PHP and, 368
change name() method, 193
character classes
  matching, 104
  predefined, 120
character, matching more than one
  occurrence of, 105
checkdate() function, 54-56
checking validity of dates, 54-56
chop() function, 23
chr() function, 17
circles, drawing, 355
class declaration, 190
classes, 104. *See also* character classes
  accessing variables from within, 191-193
  Benchmark_Iterate, 67
  Benchmark_Timer, 66-67
  constructors, creating, 195-196
  constructors, returning different objects
    from, 196-197
  creating, 190-191
  destructors, creating, 197-198
  Find File (PEAR), 164-169
  functions, using in without initializing
    objects, 199
  HTML Email, 322
  indirectly accessing methods of parent
    type, 199-201
  inheritance, 193-194
  instances, 191
  making variables or functions public and
    private, 194-195
  methods, 190
  MIME, 320
  Numbers Roman, 42-43
  overview of, 189

returning error objects on failure,
  201-203
Unique Random, 49-51
variables, 190
clearstatcache() function, 136-137
clients
  UNIX domain servers, connecting with,
    305
  UNIX domain sockets, connecting with,
    303
closedir() function, 166-167
codes
  opening files, 134
  specifying lock operations, 139
color palette, 348
COM objects, 287-289
comma, use of, 17
comma-separated value (CSV) data,
  parsing, 25
commas
  placing in number, 45-46
  printing lists with, 71-72
compiling PHP and MySQL, 442
config.txt source code, 170
configuration files, reading and creating,
  156-157
connecting to databases, 255-257. *See
  also* database-independent API
constants
  defining own, 95-96
  error type, 94-95
  file type, 92-93
  OS and VERSION, 93-94
  overview of, 91
constructors
  creating, 195-196
  returning different objects from, 196-197
constructs
  array(), 16-17
  list(), 16-17
content-type declaration, changing,
  316-320
continuation characters, reading lines
  with, 142-143
convert cyr string() function, 31

converting

ASCII to HTML, 362

ASCII values, 17, 19

between binary and decimal numbers, 41

between degrees and radians, 46

between octal and hexadecimal numbers, 40

case of strings, 21-22

Cyrillic character sets, 31

e-mail messages to readable format, 314

numbers, 33-34

numbers between bases, 40

cookies

default value for, 212

description of, 205

parameters, setting, 213-214

sending, 238-239

copy() function, 162

copying, 109

files in directories, 162

one part of image to another, 351

count() function, 151

counting, strings and, 12

create function() function, 77, 185-186

creating resource identifiers, 410-411

credit card number, validating, 43-45

crypt() function, 30

CSV (comma-separated value) data, parsing, 25

curl extension

HTTP file, uploading, 237-238

HTTP POST operation, performing, 235

SSL transaction, performing, 234

Web site, 233

curl module, 414-433

cURL transfers, debugging, 241-242

current() function, 79

Cyrillic character sets, converting, 31

D

data transfer timeout, controlling, 308-309

data, accessing using built-in arrays, 98-99

database-independent API

advantages of, 257

creating, 256-257

feature set, 268

InterBase module, creating, 274-277

mSQL module, creating, 263-265

MSSQL module, creating, 268-270

ODBC module, creating, 270-272

Oracle module, creating, 265-268

PostgreSQL module, creating, 273-274

set of functions, creating, 258-259

Sybase module, creating, 277-279

wrapper functions, implementing, 260-263

databases, connecting to, 255-257

datagram sockets, 299-301

date() function, 54, 58-60

dates

checking validity of, 54-56

determining intervals between, 56-57

finding for different locales, 57

loading into array, 53-54

parsing from strings, 61-62

DB, 51

db connect() function, 265

db fetchall assoc() function, 259

db fetchall() function, 259

db simulate execute() function, 259

db simulate prepare() function, 259

DB/standard.php, creating, 258-259

debugging, 445-447. *See also* **error messages.**

See also **errors, decreasing**

cURL transfers, 241-242

decbin() function, 41

declaration of classes, 190

declaring functions dynamically, 184

decreasing errors. *See* **errors, decreasing**

decrypting strings, 29-30

default value, passing to function, 178-179

define() function, 95-96

defining constants, 95-96

deg2rad() function, 46

deleting

entries from LDAP servers, 331

files from directories, 161

session variables, 215

deserialization, 228-229
destructive functions, 183
destructors, creating, 197-198
detecting duplicate words, 123-124
DevShed Web site, 453
dir() function, 166-167
direct comparison operator, 36
directories
 filenames matching patterns, getting,
  165-166
 files,
  copying or moving, 162
  deleting, 161
  loading into arrays, 164-165
  processing in, 166-167
  recognizing two names for, 162-163
  splitting into component parts, 164
 overview of, 159-160
 removing, 167-169
 search engines, 169-175
 timestamps, getting and changing, 160
directory servers, 329
dirname() function, 164
diskfreespace() function, 139-140
displaying
 header information, 437
 textfiles to users, 140
DLLs, 442
dollar ($) sign, 102
DOM (Document Object Module)-based
 processors, 389
DOM-XML functions
 building documents with, 391-393
 parsing documents with, 387-390
drawing
 arcs, 354
 circles, 355
 ellipses, 355
 lines, 353
 polygons, 353-354
 rectangles, 352
dynamic buttons, creating, 356-359
dynamically creating anonymous
 functions, 185-186

E

each(), 17
ellipses, drawing, 355
e-mail
 attachments, sending, 315-316
 binary attachments, sending, 316-320
 checking whether IMAP stream is active,
  313
 converting message format, 314
 HTML, sending, 320-322
 opening IMAP mailbox, 312
 overview of, 311
 parsing mail headers, 323
 sending, 314-315
 size of message, getting, 322-323
e-mail addresses, validating, 122-123
embedded scripting language, 367
empty() function, 122
encapsulation, 189
encoding session variables, 217-218
encrypting strings, 29-30
ereg() function, 13, 102
eregi() function, 108, 120-123
error constants, 95
error handling and XML, 371-372
error messages
 0 is not a * Result index, 445-446
 Call to undefined function:*, 446
 Headers already sent, 447
 overview of, 445
 PHP Timed out!, 446
 Premature End of script headers, 447
error objects, returning on failure,
 201-203
error reporting() function, 94-95, 123,
 448
errors, decreasing
 breakpoints, setting, 449
 error reporting, 448
 planning and, 447
 reverse testing, 447-448
escape sequences, matching, 103
escapeshellcmd() function, 121-122, 285
escaping characters in strings, 23-25
exec() function, 284
Expat, 374

explode() function, 61, 117-118, 145-146
ext skel tool, 433
extends statement, 193-194
Extensible Markup Language. *See* XML
extensions, adding. *See* Zend API
external ent ref() function, 383
external reference entity handlers, setting
  up, 379-383
extracting
  HTML tags, 361-362
  range of lines, 118-119
  URLs, 243-244

F

fetching
  resource identifiers, 411-412
  URLs, 231-232
  Web pages, 231
fetching arbitrary number of parameters,
  187
fgetcsv() function, 25-26
fgets() function, 128
fgetss() function, 362
FILE constant, 92-93
file exists() function, 129-130
file() function, 133-135, 140, 151
file*time() function, 160
filenames, pattern matching, 165-166
fileperms() function, 130-131
files
  accessing, 127
  adding to PHP installation, 434-435
  copying into memory, 132-133
  copying or moving in directories, 162
  deleting from directories, 161
  displaying to user, 140
  extracting random line from, 152
  flushing cache, 136-137
  free space on drives and, 139-140
  loading all in directory into arrays,
    164-165
  locking, 137-139
  opening, 133-135
  permissions, checking, 130-131

  picking random line from, 152
  processing
    all in directory, 166-167
    binary type, 135
    every word in, 143-144
    fixed-length text fields, 146
    in reverse, 145
    variable-length text fields, 145-146
  randomizing lines in, 153-155
  reading
    backward by line, 145
    and creating configuration type,
      156-157
    fixed-length records, 148
    lines with continuation characters,
      142-143
    particular lines in, 149-150
    and printing, 127-128
  recognizing two names for in directories,
    162-163
  removing last lines from, 150-151
  splitting into component parts, 164
  standard streams and, 141-142
  tabulating lines in, 151
  temporary, creating, 131-132
  testing for existence of, 129-130
  updating random-access type, 147
filesize() function, 132-133
filesystem functions, 232
filtering output through XSL files,
  394-395
finalize.php source code, 172-173
Find File class (PEAR), 164-169
finding
  dates for different locales, 57
  element in one array, 83-84
  elements in arrays that match criteria,
    82-83
  elements in arrays that pass test, 82
  fresh links, 244-246
  nth occurrence of match, 115-117
  parts of strings, 11-15
  soundex key of strings, 27-28
  stale links, 244, 246
  times for different locales, 57
flock() function, 137-139
flushing cache, 136-137

fopen() function, 133-134, 231-232
for loop, 18-19, 35-36
foreach loop, 80, 82-83
format codes, unpack() function, 14-15
formatting
    log files, 248
    timestamps, 58-61
formatting codes
    date() function, 59
    strftime() function, 60-61
fpassthru() function, 140
frames, accessing, 243
fread() function, 132-135, 147
free space on drives, 139-140
freeing LDAP result sets, 333-334
fsockopen() function, 287, 295-296,
    300-301, 403-405
ftell() function, 150-151
ftp sites, library resources, 441-442
FTP sites, mycrypt library, 30
ftruncate() function, 150-151
func get args() function, 187
function declaration, 177
function-oriented approach
    advantages of, 257
    overview of, 256-257
    set of functions, creating, 258-259
functions
    accept connect(), 298
    addslashes(), 23
    advantages of, 178
    array diff(), 83-84
    array init(), 407-408
    array intersect(), 85-86
    array merge recursive(), 75
    array merge(), 75
    array pad(), 75
    array push(), 76
    array rand(), 152
    array reverse(), 20-21, 89
    array slice(), 80-81
    array splice(), 73-74
    array unique(), 72-73
    array values(), 20
    array walk(), 76-77
    as nondestructive, 109
    atan2(), 47

base convert(), 40-42
basename(), 164
bcmath, 36-38
bcround(), 38-40
bind(), 306
bindec(), 41
calling from PHP, 408-409
checkdate(), 54-56
chop(), 23
chr(), 17
clearstatcache(), 136-137
closedir(), 166-167
convert cyr string(), 31
copy(), 162
count(), 151
create function(), 77, 185-186
crypt(), 30
current(), 79
date(), 54, 58-60
db connect(), 265
db fetchall assoc(), 259
db fetchall(), 259
db simulate execute(), 259
db simulate prepare(), 259
decbin(), 41
define(), 95-96
deg2rad, 46
destructive type, 183
dir(), 166-167
dirname(), 164
diskfreespace(), 139-140
empty(), 122
ereg(), 13, 102
eregi(), 108, 120-123
error reporting(), 94-95, 123, 448
escapeshellcmd(), 121-122, 285
exec(), 284
explode(), 61, 117-118, 145-146
external ent ref(), 383
fgetcsv(), 25-26
fgets(), 128
fgetss(), 362
file exists(), 129-130
file(), 133-135, 140, 151
file*time(), 160
fileperms(), 130-131
filesize(), 132-133

filesystem, 232
flock(), 137-139
fopen(), 133-134, 231-232
fpassthru(), 140
fread(), 132-133, 135, 147
fsockopen(), 287, 295-296, 300-301, 403-405
ftell(), 150-151
ftruncate(), 150-151
func get args(), 187
fwrite(), 135, 147
getdate(), 53, 58
GetImageSize(), 342-343
getmicrotime(), 64
getmypid(), 28
getsockname(), 305-306
gettype(), 35
glob(), 165-166
gmdate(), 57
hexdec(), 40
htmlentities(), 362
htmlspecialchars(), 24
ImageArc(), 354-355
ImageChar(), 344
ImageCharUp(), 344
ImageColorAllocate(), 340
ImageColorAt(), 347-348
ImageColorsForIndex(), 347-348
ImageColorsTotal(), 349
ImageColorTransparent(), 350
ImageCopy(), 351
ImageCopyResized(), 351
ImageCreate(), 340
ImageCreateFrom*, 341-342
ImageFilledPolygon(), 353-354
ImageFilledRectangle(), 352
ImageFillToBorder(), 355
ImageGif(), 341
ImageInterlace(), 356
ImageLoadFont(), 345
ImagePolygon(), 353-354
ImagePsEncodeFont(), 346
ImagePsFreeFont(), 346
ImagePsLoadFont(), 345
ImagePsText(), 346
ImageRectangle(), 352

ImageString(), 347
ImageStringUp(), 347
ImageTTFText(), 359-360
imap 8bit(), 314
imap fetchstructure(), 322-323
imap header(), 323
imap open(), 312
imap ping(), 313
implode(), 71-72, 140
is double(), 34-35
is int(), 34-35
is numeric(), 34
ldap add(), 329-330
ldap bind(), 330
ldap close(), 330
ldap delete(), 331
ldap free result(), 333-334
ldap get entries(), 332-333
ldap list(), 332-333
ldap mod add(), 330
ldap search(), 334-335
ldap unbind(), 330
localtime(), 54
log(), 41
log10(), 41
lost data(), 384
ltrim(), 23
mail(), 314-315
making public and private, 194-195
md5(), 28-30
microtime(), 28, 63-64
mktime(), 56-58, 61
msql connect(), 265
mt rand(), 48
mt srand(), 49
mysql connect(), 255
natsort(), 88
nl2br(), 362
number format(), 45-46
object init(), 408
OCILogon(), 255
octdec(), 40
open listen sock(), 298
opendir(), 166-167
ord(), 17
parse str(), 26-27

parse url(), 26-27
passthru(), 285
pclose(), 286
pi handler(), 383
popen(), 286
preg grep(), 82-83
preg match all(), 115-117
preg quote(), 24
preg split(), 19-21, 117
quotemeta(), 23
rad2deg, 46
readdir(), 166-167
readfile(), 140, 232, 248
readv(), 307-308
recvfrom(), 301-302
register list destructors(), 411
register shutdown function(), 197-198
regular expressions and, 102
rtrim(), 23
select(), 299-300
serialization type, 206
serialize(), 51, 226-227
session decode(), 217-218
session destroy(), 215
session encode(), 217-218
session name(), 212
session register(), 206-207
session set cookie params(), 213-214
session set save handler(), 208-211
session start(), 206
session unregister(), 214
set nonblock(), 306
set of needed, creating, 258-259
set time limit(), 297-298, 446
shuffle(), 84, 153-155
similar text(), 28
sleep(), 67-68
snmgset(), 326-327
snmpset(), 326
snmpwalk(), 327
socket get status(), 309
socket set blocking(), 306-307
socket set timeout(), 308
soundex(), 27-28
sprintf(), 17, 38-39
status type, 136-137

strcasecmp(), 22
strftttime(), 58-61
strip tags(), 361-362
strpos(), 12
strrev(), 21
strtolower(), 21
strtotime(), 62
strtoupper(), 21
substr replace(), 11-12
substr(), 11-12, 148
tempnam(), 131-132
tmpfile(), 26
touch(), 160
trigonometry, 47
types of, 177
ucfirst(), 21
ucwords(), 21-22
uniqid(), 28
universaltime(), 57
unlink(), 132, 161
unpack(), 13-15, 18-19, 146-148
unserialize(), 226-227
unset(), 64-66
urldecode(), 24
urlencode(), 24
using in classes without initializing
   objects, 199
usleep(), 67-68
usort(), 87, 335-336
validate credit card(), 45
wddx deserialize(), 228-229
wrapper type, 256, 260-263
writev(), 307-308
xml con(), 383
xml error string(), 371-372
xml get error code(), 371
xml parse into struct(), 375-377, 384-385
xml parser free(), 386
xml parser get option(), 386-387
xml parser set option(), 386-387
xml set external ref handler(), 379-383
xmldoc(), 390
xmldocfile(), 389-390
xslt transform(), 393-394
zend get parameters ex(), 400-403
zend hash index find(), 412-414

zend hash num elements(), 412-414
zval copy ctor(), 404

functions, 177. *See also* **user-defined
functions**

functions, 399. *See also* **Zend API**

fwrite() function, 135, 147

G

GD module
adding text to images, 343-347
arcs, drawing, 354
circles, drawing, 355
copying one part of image to another,
351
creating images with, 340-341
dynamic buttons, creating, 356-359
ellipses, drawing, 355
getting color of part of images, 347-348
getting size of images, 342-343
getting total number of colors in images,
349
interlacing images, 356
lines, drawing, 353
making GIF or PNG transparent, 350
opening preexisting images, 341-342
overview of, 339
polygons, drawing, 353-354
rectangles, drawing, 352
resizing copied images, 351
TrueType fonts, using, 359-360
generating JavaScript, 365-366
getdate() function, 53, 58
GetImageSize() function, 342-343
getmicrotime() function, 64
getmypid() function, 28
getsockname() function, 305-306
getting new links, 246-247
gettype() function, 35
GIFs
GD module and, 339
making transparent, 350
glob() function, 165-166
global declaration, 180
global variables, 96-98, 207

gmdate() function, 57
GMT (Greenwich mean time), 57

H

headers
cURL transaction, excluding or including
from, 239-240
displaying, 437
printing, 437
Headers already sent, 447
hexdec() function, 40
HTML
converting ASCII to, 362
HTML tags, extracting or removing,
361-362
HTML tags, stripping, 361-362
HTML templates, creating, 367-368
JavaScript, generating, 365-366
<select> list, creating, 363-365
HTML compared to XML, 371
HTML Email class, 322
HTML e-mail, sending, 320-322
HTML processor class (PEAR), 362
HTML tags
extracting or removing, 361-362
stripping, 361-362
HTML templates, creating, 367-368
htmlentities() function, 362
htmlspecialchars() function, 24
HTTP file, uploading, 236-238
HTTP POST operation, performing, 235
HTTP POST request, performing, 234
HTTP redirects, 232

I

if statement, 118-119
ImageArc() function, 354-355
ImageChar() function, 344
ImageCharUp() function, 344
ImageColorAllocate() function, 340
ImageColorAt() function, 347-348

ImageColorsForIndex() function, 347-348

ImageColorsTotal() function, 349

ImageColorTransparent() function, 350

ImageCopy() function, 351

ImageCopyResized() function, 351

ImageCreate() function, 340

ImageCreateFrom* functions, 341-342

ImageFilledPolygon() function, 353-354

ImageFilledRectangle() function, 352

ImageFillToBorder() function, 355

ImageGif() function, 341

ImageInterlace() function, 356

ImageLoadFont() function, 345

ImagePolygon() function, 353-354

ImagePsEncodeFont() function, 346

ImagePsFreeFont() function, 346

ImagePsLoadFont() function, 345

ImagePsText() function, 346

ImageRectangle() function, 352

images
   adding text to, 343-347
   copying one part of to another, 351
   creating with GD module, 340-341
   drawing
      arcs, 354
      circles, 355
      ellipses, 355
      lines, 353
      polygons, 353-354
      rectangles, 352
   dynamic buttons, creating, 356-359
   getting
      color of part of, 347-348
      size of, 342-343
      total number of colors in, 349
   interlacing, 356
   making GIF or PNG transparent, 350
   opening preexisting, 341-342
   resizing copied, 351
   TrueType fonts, using, 359-360

ImageString() function, 347

ImageStringUp() function, 347

ImageTTFText() function, 359-360

IMAP (Internet Message Access Protocol)
   checking whether stream is active, 313
   converting message format, 314
   description of, 311
   getting size of message, 322-323
   opening mailbox, 312
   parsing mail headers, 323
   sending attachments, 315-316
   sending binary attachments, 316-320
   sending e-mail, 314-315
   sending HTML e-mail, 320-322
   Web site, 311

imap 8bit() function, 314

IMAP client library, 311

imap fetchstructure() function, 322-323

imap header() function, 323

imap open() function, 312

imap ping() function, 313

implode() function, 71-72, 140

include statement, 367

incompatibilities. *See* migrating from PHP 3 to PHP 4

inheritance, 193-194

installation, adding files to, 434-435

installing PHP
   Apache/MySQL/GD/BCMath, and SSL support, 438-439
   BCMath and, 438-439
   build script, 440
   building shared extensions, 440
   compiling with MySQL, 442
   displaying header information, 437
   DLLs, DSOs, and, 442
   library resources, 441-442
   obtaining latest distribution, 437
   overview of, 437
   printing headers, 437
   reporting bugs, 442
   setting to look in nonstandard directories, 440
   Zeus Web server and, 438

instances, 191

interaction with user, 339

InterBase
   module, creating, 274-277
   overview of, 274

interlacing images, 356
Internet Message Access Protocol. *See*
 IMAP (Internet Message Access
 Protocol)
interprocess communication (IPC)
  capturing output of other programs, 284
  COM objects, 287-289
  Java methods and classes, accessing
   custom, 290-294
  Java methods and classes, accessing
   predefined, 290
  opening pipe to other programs, 286
  opening sockets, 287
  overview of, 283
  printing output of other programs, 285
intersection of arrays, finding, 85
interval between dates, determining,
 56-57
IP addresses, handling multiple, 305-306
IPC. *See* interprocess communication
 (IPC)
is double() function, 34-35
is error method, 201, 203
is int() function, 34-35
is numeric() function, 34
ISO Cyrillic character set, 31
iterating over arrays by reference, 78

J-L

Java
  methods and classes, accessing custom,
   290-294
  methods and classes, accessing
   predefined, 290
JavaScript, generating, 365-366
Javascript Rollover class (PEAR), 365-366

language, loosely typed, 33
LDAP (Light Directory Access Protocol)
  adding entries to servers, 329-331
  deleting entries from servers, 331
  executing queries, 332-333
  freeing result sets, 333-334
    overview of, 329
    sorting search results, 335-336
    tree search, performing, 334-335
ldap add() function, 329-330
ldap bind() function, 330
ldap close() function, 330
ldap delete() function, 331
ldap free result() function, 333-334
ldap get entries() function, 332-333
ldap list() function, 332-333
ldap mod add() function, 330
ldap search() function, 334-335
ldap unbind() function, 330
Lerdorf, Rasmus, 399
letters, matching, 120-121
library resources, 441-442
Light Directory Access Protocol. *See*
 LDAP (Light Directory Access
 Protocol)
LINE constant, 92-93
lines in files, tabulating, 151
lines, drawing, 353
links
  finding fresh, 244-246
  finding stale, 244-246
  getting new, 246-247
list() construct, 16-17, 184
lists, 72. *See also* arrays
LoadConfig.php source code, 175
loading
  dates into arrays, 53-54
  files in directory into arrays, 164-165
local variables, 207
localtime() function, 54
locking files, 137-139
log files, formatting, 248
log files, parsing, 248-251
log() function, 41
log10() function, 41
logarithms, 41
looping through arrays, 412-414
loosely typed language, 33
lost data() function, 384
ltrim() function, 23
Luhn-10 algorithm, 43-45

M

mail headers, parsing, 323
mail() function, 314-315
mailing list for PHP, 437, 443
maintaining state
    cookie parameters, setting, 213-214
    definition of, 205
    serialization, 226-227
    serialization functions, 206
    session management, 205-206
    session name, setting, 212
    session variable,
        creating, 206-207
        deleting, 215
        encoding, 217-218
        removing or unregistering, 214
        saving in database, 208-211
        using objects as, 215-217
    shopping cart script, 218-226
    WDDX deserialization, 228-229
    WDDX serialization, 228
mapping XML tags, 377-378
maptree() method, 164-169
matching
    ?, using, 106-107
    abbreviations, 125-126
    character classes, 104
    escape sequences, 103
    letters, 120-121
    more than one occurrence of character,
        105
    over multiple lines, 114-115
    strings, 102-103
matching portions of strings, 13
md5() function, 28-30
memory, copying files into, 132-133
<meta> tags, extracting information from,
    107-108
methods
    change name(), 193
    classes and, 190
    indirectly accessing from parent classes,
        199-201
    is error, 201-203
    maptree(), 164-169
    print name(), 193

microtime() function, 28, 63-64
migrating from PHP 3 to PHP 4
    {$ combination, 458
    break and continue statements, scope of,
        456
    return statement, 457
    static variable and default argument
        initializers, 455
    unset(), 457
MIME class, 320
mirroring Web pages, 248
mktime() function, 56-58, 61
module, creating, 414-433
moving files between directories, 162
mSQL
    module, creating, 263-265
    overview of, 263
msql connect() function, 265
MSSQL module, creating, 268-270
mt rand() function, 48
mt srand() function, 49
mycrypt library FTP site, 30
MySQL
    compiling PHP with, 442
    connecting to, 255-256
    implementing wrapper functions for,
        260-263
    installing PHP with, 438-439
    mSQL compared to, 263
    overview of, 260
mysql connect() function, 255

N

Nagle algorithm, 299
natsort() function, 88
negating character classes, 104
Net Curl module (PEAR), 232
    cookies, sending, 238-239
    cURL transfers, debugging, 241-242
    header from cURL transfer, excluding or
        including, 239-240
    HTTP file, uploading, 236-237
    HTTP POST operation, performing,
        235

HTTP POST request, performing, 234

proxy servers, connecting through, 240-241

SSL transaction, performing, 233

new statement, 191, 195-196

nl2br() function, 362

nondestructive function, 109

nonstandard directories, setting PHP to look in, 440

NULL value as default, 179

number format() function, 45-46

numbers

arbitrary precision numbers, 38-40

arbitrary-precision type, 36-38

calculating trig functions, 47

checking whether variable is valid type, 34-35

converting between bases, 40

converting between binary and decimal, 41

converting between octal and hexadecimal type, 40

generating biased random type, 52-53

generating different random type, 49-51

generating random, 48

logarithms, 41

overview of, 33-34

placing comma in, 45-46

returning from functions, 405-406

Roman, 42-43

series of, working with, 35-36

trigonometry in degrees not radians, 46

validating credit card type, 43-45

Numbers Roman class, 42-43

O

object init() function, 408

object-oriented approach, 256

object-oriented design and programming, 189

objects, 191

returning from functions, 407-408

using as session variables, 215-217

using functions in classes without initializing, 199

OC18 extension compared to Oracle extension, 268

OCILogon() function, 255

octdec() function, 40

octopus.php source code, 171-172

ODBC

module, creating, 270-272

overview of, 270

one-way encryption, 30

online resources. *See* **Web sites**

open listen sock() function, 298

opendir() function, 166-167

opening

files, 133-135

IMAP mailbox, 312

pipes to programs, 284-286

preexisting images, 341-342

sockets, 287

operators

direct comparison, 36

[], 18-19

options, setting and getting with XML, 386-387

Oracle, module, creating, 265-268

Oracle extension compared to OC18 extension, 268

ord() function, 17

output of other programs

capturing, 284

printing, 285

overriding, 193

P

parameters, fetching arbitrary number of, 187

parent class, 199-201

parse str() function, 26-27

parse url() function, 26-27

parsing

comma-separated data, 25-26

dates and times from strings, 61-62

DOM-XML functions and, 387-390

large, complex files, 117-118

log files, 248-251

mail headers, 323
newsgroup messages, 119
URLs, 26-27
XML documents, 372-374
XML documents into arrays, 375-377
passing
arguments by reference, 182-183
default value to function, 178-179
passthru() function, 285
password authentication, accessing pages requiring, 232
pattern matching. *See* **regular expressions**
pclose() function, 286
PCRE. *See* **Perl Compatible Regular Expressions Library (PCRE)**
PEAR, 233. *See also* **Net Curl module (PEAR)**
Find File class, 164-169
HTML processor class, 362
Javascript Rollover class, 365-366
Net Curl module, 232
Web site, 233
PEAR, 233. 233
performing benchmarks, 63-67
Perl
array manipulation features based on, 90
chomp() function, 23
code for collecting data, 91
DBI, 255-256
files, reading and printing, 128
incompatibilities between PCRE library and regular expressions, 112-114
map() function, 77
merging arrays in, 76
regular expressions, 101
regular expressions, using in PHP, 110
Perl Compatible Regular Expressions Library (PCRE), 110-114
permissions, checking on files, 130-131
PHP
BCMath and, 438-439
build script, 440
building shared extensions, 440
compiling with MySQL, 442
displaying header information, 437
DLLs, DSOs, and, 442

embedded scripting language, 367
features of, 255
installing, 437
installing with Apache/MySQL/GD/BCMath and SSL support, 438-439
installing with Zeus Web server, 438
library resources, 441-442
mailing list, 437, 443
obtaining latest distribution, 437
printing headers, 437
reporting bugs, 442
setting to look in nonstandard directories, 440
PHP Class Repository Web site, 453
PHP OS constant, 93-94
PHP Timed out!, 446
PHP VERSION constant, 93-94
PHP Web site, 31, 39, 451
PHP, 455. *See also* **migrating from PHP 3 to PHP 4**
PHPBuilder Web site, 452
PHPWizard.net Web site, 452
pi handler() function, 383
pipe delimiter (|) character, 107
pipe, opening to program, 284-286
planning, decreasing bugs and errors and, 447
PNG, making transparent, 350
polling sockets, 300
polygons, drawing, 353-354
popen() function, 286
POSIX standard, 19
PostgreSQL
module, creating, 273-274
overview of, 273
predefined character classes, 120
preg grep() function, 82-83
preg match all() function, 115-117
preg quote() function, 24
preg split() function, 19-21, 117
Premature End of script headers, 447
print name() method, 193
printing
files, 127-128
headers, 437

lists with commas, 71-72

output of other programs, 285

private, declaring functions and variables, 194-195

process creation, 283

processing

binary files, 135

every word in files, 143-144

files in reverse, 145

fixed-length text fields, 146

strings one character at a time, 18-19

variable-length text fields, 145-146

program executions, halting, 67-68

programs

capturing output of, 284

opening pipe to, 286

printing output of, 285

proxy servers, connecting through, 240-241

Python, files, reading and printing, 128

Q-R

question mark (?) character, 106-107

quotemeta() function, 23

rad2deg() function, 46

random element, 152

random numbers

generating, 48

generating biased, 52-53

generating different, 49-51

random-access files, updating, 147-148

randomizing lines in files, 153-155

randomizing arrays, 84

readdir() function, 166-167

readfile() function, 140, 232, 248

reading

configuration files, 156-157

files, 127-128

files backward by line, 145

fixed-length records, 14-15, 148

from standard streams, 141-142

lines with continuation characters, 142-143

particular lines in files, 149-150

string to first occurrence of character, 12

to sockets, 298-300

vectors, 307-308

reading fixed-length records, 13

reading records separated by strings, 117-118

readv() function, 307-308

recognizing two names for same file in directories, 162-163

rectangles, drawing, 352

recvfrom() function, 301-302

references, iterating over arrays by, 78

register list destructors() function, 411

register shutdown function() function, 197-198

regular expressions

character classes, 104

configuration files and, 156-157

copying and substituting at same time, 109

detecting duplicate words, 123-124

extracting information from <meta> tags, 107-108

extracting range of lines, 118-119

finding nth occurrence of match, 115-117

matching

abbreviations, 125-126

escape sequences, 103

letters, 120-121

over multiple lines, 114-115

strings, 102-103

using ?, 106-107

more than one occurrence of character, 105

overview of, 101

Perl-compatible, using, 110-114

pipe delimiter (|), 107

reading records separated by strings, 117-118

testing for validity, 123

UNIX and, 111-112

validating e-mail address, 122-123

validating Web data, 121-122

writing, 108-109

removing
directories, 167-169
HTML tags, 361-362
last lines from files, 150-151
session variables, 214
reporting bugs, 442
resizing copied images, 351
resource identifiers
creating, 410
fetching, 411-412
resource identifiers, creating, 411
retaining variable's value between
function calls, 183
return statement, 181
RETURN STRING() macro, 406
return value structure, 405-406
returning
different objects from constructors,
196-197
doubles, 406
error objects on failure, 201, 203
longs, 406
more than one value from functions, 184
strings, 405
values from functions, 181
reverse testing, 447-448
reversing words or characters in strings,
20-21
reversing arrays, 89
Roman numerals, working with, 42-43
root, 329
rounding arbitrary precision numbers,
38-40
rtrim() function, 23

S

Sablotron XSL module, 394-395
saving session variables in database,
208-211
saving memory and XML, 386
SAX-based processors, 389
search engines
overview of, 169
source code, 170-175

searching XML, 384-385
seeding random number generator, 48
select() function, 299-300
<select> lists, creating, 363-365
sending
attachments to e-mail, 315-316
binary attachments to e-mail, 316-320
e-mail, 314-315
HTML e-mail, 320-322
sending cookies, 238-239
serialization, 226-228
serialization functions, 206
serialization, 228
serialize() function, 51, 226-227
series of numbers, working with, 35-36
servers
formatting log files, 248
multiple IP addresses, handling, 305-306
nonblocking sockets, 306-307
parsing log files, 248-251
UNIX domain sockets, connecting with,
303-304
session decode() function, 217-218
session destroy() function, 215
session encode() function, 217-218
Session id, 211
session management
cookie parameters, setting, 213-214
overview of, 205-206
session name, setting, 212
session variable
creating, 206-207
deleting, 215
encoding, 217-218
removing or unregistering, 214
saving in database, 208-211
using objects as, 215-217
shopping cart script, 218-226
session name() function, 212
session register() function, 206-207
session set cookie params() function,
213-214
session set save handler() function,
208-211
session start() function, 206
session unregister() function, 214

session variable
deleting, 215
encoding, 217-218
removing or unregistering, 214
using objects as, 215-217
set nonblock() function, 306
set time limit() function, 297-298, 446
shopping cart script, 218-226
shuffle() function, 84, 153-155
similar text() function, 28
Simple Network Management Protocol.
See **SNMP (Simple Network Management Protocol)**
size of e-mail message, getting, 322-323
size of arrays, changing, 73-75
sleep() function, 67-68
SNMP (Simple Network Management Protocol)
fetching objects into arrays, 327
objects, getting, 326-327
objects, setting up, 326
overview of, 325-326
snmpget() function, 326-327
snmpset() function, 326
snmpwalk() function, 327
Snoopy class, 243-246
socket get status() function, 309
socket set blocking() function, 306-307
socket set timeout() function, 308
sockets
binding, 306
getting information on, 309
module, 296
multiple IP addresses, handling, 305-306
nonblocking, 306-307
nonblocking sockets, 306-307
opening, 287
overview of, 295
reading and writing to, 298-300
remote machines, connecting to, 295-296
sockets on remote machine, connecting to, 295-296
TCP servers, creating, 297-298
timing out, 308-309
UDP clients, creating, 300-301
UDP servers, creating, 301-302

UNIX domain sockets, connecting with, 303-304
vectors, reading and writing, 307-308
sorting
arrays, 88
arrays by user-defined comparison, 87
results of LDAP searches, 335-336
soundex key of strings, finding, 27-28
soundex() function, 27-28
splitting files into component parts, 164
sprintf() function, 17, 38-39
SQL Server, overview of, 268
SSL transaction, performing, 233-234
standard streams, reading from or writing to, 141-142
stateless environment, 205
stateless, definition of, 127
static statement, 183
status functions, 136-137
STDIN, STDOUT, and STDERR, 141-142
stopping program executions, 67-68
strcasecmp() function, 22
stream sockets, 299-301
strftime() function, 58-61
strings
ASCII characters, 17
converting, 21-22
converting Cyrillic character sets, 31
counting and, 12
creating unique identifiers, 28
encrypting and decrypting, 29-30
escaping characters in, 23-25
establishing default value for variable, 15-16
finding parts of, 11-15
finding soundex key of, 27-28
matching, 102-103
overview of, 11
parsing comma-separated data, 25-26
parsing dates and times from, 61-62
parsing URLs, 26-27
processing one character at a time, 18-19
reading records separated by, 117-118
returning from functions, 405-406
reversing words or characters, 20-21

trimming blanks from, 23
variable exchange, 16-17
strip tags() function, 361-362
stripping HTML tags, 361-362
strpos() function, 12
strrev() function, 21
strtolower() function, 21
strtotime() function, 62
strtoupper() function, 21
substituting, 109
substr replace() function, 11-12
substr() function, 11-12, 148
Suraski, Zeev, 256
switch..case loop, 263
Sybase
  module, creating, 277-279
  overview of, 277
symmetric difference of arrays,
  calculating, 86
syntactical sugar, 16

T

tabulating lines in files, 151
tar.gz files Web site, 291
TCP connection, sockets on remote
  machine, 295-296
TCP servers, creating, 297-298
tempnam() function, 131-132
temporary files, creating, 131-132
ternary operator, 15-16
testing
  for existence of files, 129-130
  for valid regular expressions, 123
textfiles, displaying to users, 140
times
  finding for different locales, 57
  parsing from strings, 61-62
timestamps
  formatting, 58-61
  getting and changing, 160
timing out sockets, 308-309
tmpfile() function, 26
touch() function, 160

transforming XML with XSL templates,
  393-394
transparency of images, 350
tree search, performing on LDAP
  servers, 334-335
trigonometry
  calculating more functions, 47
  functions, 47
  working in degrees not radians, 46
trimming blanks from strings, 23
TripleDES encryption, 29
troubleshooting installation. *See*
  installing PHP
troubleshooting. *See* error messages
TrueType fonts, using, 359-360

U

ucfirst() function, 21
ucwords() function, 21-22
UDP clients, creating, 300-301
UDP servers, creating, 301-302
underscore (_), 194
uniform resource locators. *See* URLs
union of arrays, calculating, 85
uniqid{} function, 28
unique identifiers, creating, 28
Unique Random class, 49-51
universaltime() function, 57
UNIX
  deleting files, 161
  times associated with files, 160
UNIX domain sockets, connecting with,
  303-304
UNIX, converting script using PHP,
  111-112
unlink() function, 132, 161
unpack() function, 13-15, 18-19, 146-148
unregistering session variables, 214
unserialize() function, 226-227
unset() function, 64-66
updating random-access files, 147
urldecode() function, 24
urlencode() function, 24

URLs
extracting, 243-244
fetching, 231-232
parsing, 26-27
user-defined functions
accessing variables outside of, 180
calling indirectly, 186
declaring dynamically, 184
dynamically creating anonymous type, 185-186
fetching arbitrary number of parameters, 187
overview of, 177-178
passing arguments by reference, 182-183
passing default value to, 178-179
retaining variable's value between function calls, 183
returning more than one value from functions, 184
returning values from, 181
users
displaying textfiles to, 140
interaction with, 339
usleep() function, 67-68
usort() function, 87, 335-336
UUCP (UNIX-to-UNIX copy), 314

V

validate credit card() function, 45
validating
e-mail addresses, 122-123
Web data, 121-122
validating credit card number, 43-45
values
adding to arrays, 404
NULL as default, 179
returning from functions, 181
returning more than one from functions, 184
variables
$this, 196-197
accessing from within classes, 191-193
accessing outside functions, 180
checking whether valid numbers, 34-35
classes and, 190
creating references to, 78
establishing default value for, 15-16
global, 96-98
making public and private, 194-195
memory address of, 182
retaining value of between function calls, 183
swapping value of, 16-17
types of, 207
vectors, reading and writing, 307-308
voyager.php source code, 173-175

W

WDDX deserialization, 228-229
wddx deserialize() function, 228-229
WDDX serialization, 228
Web applications programming
file access and, 127
Web Distributed Data eXchange (WDDX), 228
Web interaction
accessing frames, 243
cookies, sending, 238-239
cURL transfers, debugging, 241-242
extracting URLs, 243-244
fetching URLs, 231-232
fetching Web pages, 231
formatting server log files, 248
header from cURL transfer, excluding or including, 239-240
HTTP file, uploading, 236-238
HTTP POST operation, performing, 235
HTTP POST request, performing, 234
links, 244-247
mirroring Web pages, 248
overview of, 231
parsing server log files, 248-251
proxy servers, connecting through, 240-241
SSL transaction, performing, 233-234

Web pages
fetching, 231
mirroring, 248
Web sites
curl extension, 233
curl module, 414
Dev Shed, 453
DLLs, 442
IMAP information, 311
InterBase, 274
library resources, 441-442
mSQL, 263
MySQL, 260
natsort() function, 89
Oracle, 265
PEAR, 233
PHP, 31, 39, 451
PHP Class Repository, 453
PHPBuilder, 452
PHPWizard.net, 452
POSIX standard, 19
PostgreSQL, 273
SNMP information, 326
Snoopy class, 244
tar.gz files, 291
WDDX, 228
WDDX standard, 228
Web techniques, 339
Weberdev, 453
Zend, 452
Weberdev Web site, 453
Webtechniques Web site, 339
while loop, 82
Windows Cyrillic character set, 31
words in files, processing every, 143-144
world, 329
wrapper, 178
wrapper functions
description of, 256
implementing, 260-263
writev() function, 307-308
writing
to sockets, 298-300
to standard streams, 141-142
vectors, 307-308
writing regular expressions, 108-109

X-Z

XML
building using DOM-XML functions, 391-393
error handling, 371-372
filtering output through XSL files, 394-395
mapping tags, 377-378
overview of, 369-371
parsing documents, 372-374
parsing documents into arrays, 375-377
parsing using DOM-XML functions, 387-390
saving memory, 386
searching, 384-385
setting and getting options, 386-387
setting up external reference entity handlers, 379-383
transforming with XSL templates, 393-394
xml con() function, 383
xml error string() function, 371-372
xml get error code() function, 371
xml parse into struct() function, 375-377, 384-385
xml parser free() function, 386
xml parser get option() function, 386-387
xml parser set option() function, 386-387
xml set external ref handler() function, 379-383
xmldoc() function, 390
xmldocfile() function, 389-390
XSL files, 394-395
XSL templates, 393-394
xslt transform() function, 393-394

Zend API
adding files to PHP installation, 434-435
calling functions from PHP, 408-409
getting arguments, 400-403
looping through arrays, 412-414
modifying function arguments, 403-405
overview of, 399
PHP module, creating, 414-433
resource identifiers, creating, 410-411
resource identifiers, fetching, 411-412

    returning arrays or objects from
        functions, 407-408
    returning strings or numbers from
        functions, 405-406
**ZEND FETCH RESOURCE() macro,
  411-412**
**zend get parameters ex() function,
  400-403**
zend hash index find() function, 412-414
**zend hash num elements() function,
  412-414**
zend module entry structure, 419
**ZEND REGISTER RESOURCE macro,
  411**
Zend Web site, 452
**Zeus Web server, installing PHP with,
  438**
zval copy ctor() function, 404

SAMS DEVELOPER'S LIBRARY

Cookbook   Handbook   Dictionary

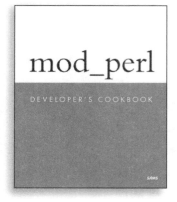

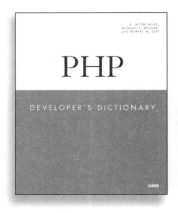

mod_perl
DEVELOPER'S COOKBOOK

Geoffrey Young

ISBN: 0-672-32240-4
$39.99 US/$59.95 CAN

Python
DEVELOPER'S HANDBOOK

André Lessa

ISBN: 0-672-31994-2
$44.99 US/$67.95 CAN

PHP
DEVELOPER'S DICTIONARY

Allen Wyke,
Michael J. Walker,
and Robert M. Cox

ISBN: 0-672-32029-0
$39.99 US/$59.95 CAN

OTHER DEVELOPER'S LIBRARY TITLES

Perl
DEVELOPER'S DICTIONARY

Clinton Pierce

ISBN: 0-672-32067-3
$39.99 US/$59.95 CAN

mod_perl
DEVELOPER'S HANDBOOK

Barrie Slaymaker
and James Smith

ISBN: 0-672-32132-7
$39.99 US/$59.95 CAN
(Available Spring 2002)

JavaScript
DEVELOPER'S DICTIONARY

Alexander Vincent

ISBN: 0-672-32201-3
$39.99 US/$59.95 CAN
(Available Spring 2002)

PostgreSQL
DEVELOPER'S HANDBOOK

Ewald Geschwinde and
Hans–Jürgen Schönig

ISBN: 0-672-32260-9
$44.99 US/$67.95 CAN

ALL PRICES ARE SUBJECT TO CHANGE

www.samspublishing.com